First Steps To Botany: Intended As Popular Illustrations Of The Science, Leading To Its Study As A Branch Of General Education

James Lawson Drummond

FIRST STEPS

TO

BOTANY.

Oh, Nature! all-sufficient! over all!
Enrich me with the knowledge of thy works!
Snatch me to Heaven; thy rolling wonders there,
World beyond world, in infinite extent,
Profusely scatter'd o'er the blue immense,
Show me; their motions, periods, and their laws,
Give me to scan; through the disclosing deep
Light my blind way; the mineral *strata* there;
Thrust, blooming, thence the vegetable world;
O'er that the rising system, more complex,
Of animals; and higher still, the mind,
The varied scene of quick-compounding thought,
And where the mixing passions endless shift;
These ever open to my ravish'd eye;
A search, the flight of time can ne'er exhaust!
But if to that unequal; if the blood,
In sluggish streams about my heart, forbid
That *best* ambition; under closing shades,
Inglorious, lay me by the lowly brook,
And whisper to my dreams. From thee begin,
Dwell all on thee, with thee conclude my song:
And let me never, never stray from thee!

FIRST STEPS TO BOTANY,

INTENDED AS

Popular Illustrations

OF THE SCIENCE,

LEADING TO ITS STUDY AS A BRANCH OF

GENERAL EDUCATION.

BY JAMES L. DRUMMOND, M.D.

PROFESSOR OF ANATOMY AND PHYSIOLOGY IN THE BELFAST
ACADEMICAL INSTITUTION.

THIRD EDITION.

LINNÆUS

LONDON:

PRINTED FOR

LONGMAN, REES, ORME, BROWN, AND GREEN,

PATERNOSTER-ROW.

1831.

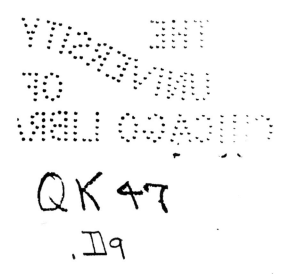
LONDON :
Printed by A. & R. Spottiswoode,
New-Street-Square.

TO

THE PRESIDENT AND VICE-PRESIDENTS,

THE JOINT BOARDS OF MANAGERS AND VISITORS,

THE BOARD OF FACULTY,

AND THE BOARD OF MASTERS,

OF THE

BELFAST ACADEMICAL INSTITUTION,

THIS LITTLE WORK

IS INSCRIBED,

BY

THE AUTHOR.

PREFACE.

THE plan adopted in the present work has been, to unite to the technicalities of Botany a considerable share of interesting or entertaining information on many parts of the vegetable kingdom, in the hope that a work so constituted as to be of a popular, and, at the same time, of a strictly scientific description, may be found useful. The present form of publication has been adopted as being most convenient, and the author has preferred wood to copper-plate engravings, considering it an advantage that the figure referred to should be in the text, and immediately under the reader's eye. The figures have been derived from various sources: a considerable number of them were drawn by Mr. Sowerby, whose name is a sufficient passport; a few were drawn by the author himself; but the greater number by the very ingenious artist (Mr. G. W. Bonner), who engraved the whole of the cuts.

It has been recommended to add to this edition a sketch of the system of Jussieu; but, whatever may be the merits of that natural arrangement, any account of it which could be introduced here would necessarily either be too short to afford sufficient information, or too long to be compatible with the general nature and object of the work. On these grounds the suggestion alluded to, of some kind and able friends, has not been acted on.

BELFAST,
May 27. 1826.

FIRST STEPS TO BOTANY.

CHAPTER I.

OF THE ROOT (RADIX).

1. RADIX *fusiformis*, a *fusiform*, or spindle-shaped root. (*Fusus*, a spindle, *Lat.*) This root is thick above, and grows gradually smaller as it descends; it is almost always perpendicular, and is generally simple, though sometimes branched. Good examples of it occur in some common culinary vegetables, as the carrot, parsnip, and radish; and in order to fix your attention, I shall dwell a little on the history of these plants.

I have first, however, to observe, that whatever be the form of the root at large, the *true* roots, the parts which absorb nourishment, consist of the small hair-like fibres which shoot out from the larger part or body; these branchlets are named radicles (*radiculæ*), fibres, or rootlets, and are annually renewed; the old ones become exhausted and die, and new radicles are necessary to support the life of the plant. In the vegetables of this climate, each new set of these is produced in early spring; and hence the best time for transplant-

B

ing is in winter, because then the radicles are either dead or torpid, and may be torn off with impunity to the plant. In hot countries they are formed during the rainy season, a period in which, as Willdenow observes, the vegetable world seems as in a kind of slumber.

Fig. 1.

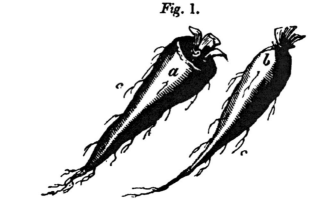

Fusiform roots; *a, b,* body or *caudex* of the root.
c, radicles, or true roots.

Some botanists would call (*a*) a *conical,* and (*b*) a *fusiform* root, the former resembling a cone, and the latter more exactly the spindle formerly used with the distaff; the distinction is perhaps of little use.

The changes effected by culture on many vegetables, are very surprising, and with some of them you are most probably well acquainted. Perhaps, however, you are not aware that the garden carrot is produced from the common wild carrot (often called bird's nest), so frequent about ditches and highways. Nothing, indeed, can differ more widely than the roots of the two; that of the wild plant being small, tough, and woody, while that of the garden carrot is large, fleshy, and succulent.

The term *carrot* is thought to be derived from *cara*, a name given by the old Roman writers to a plant with large esculent roots, which the soldiers of Julius Cæsar, sometimes, when distressed for provisions, made into bread. The plant which they thus used, however, is stated by Dioscorides, and Paulus Ægineta, to have been a sort of parsnip.*

The root of the *wild* carrot can scarcely be considered as an article of food, though we learn from Lightfoot that it is frequently eaten by the Scotch Highlanders, who consider it wholesome and nutritious.† The roots of the garden carrot possess both these properties in a high degree. To all domestic cattle they are very grateful, and it is said, that for a time, they will support the strength of carriage-horses nearly as well as oats.‡ At the Cape of Good Hope, indeed, the Dutch planters cultivate large fields of carrots for feeding their sheep and horses : and they consider a bunch or two of them as equivalent to an ordinary feed of corn in England. " In many places," says Percival, " their horses get nothing else during the day but a few bunches of this vegetable." §

The root of the *parsnip* has *also* been rendered esculent by culture, for in the wild state it is small

* Vide Parr's London Med. Dict.
† Flora Scotica, vol. ii. p. 1095.   ‡ Vide Withering.
§ Percival's Account of the Cape of Good Hope, p. 145.

and rigid. *Pastinaca*, its Latin name, is derived from *pascor*, to feed, because it was used as nutriment; and from the Latin term originates our word parsnip. According to Bryant, the roots of this vegetable "seem to claim the preference to all other esculent roots of English growth, they being very agreeable to most palates, easy of digestion, and affording excellent nourishment."[*] This high character, however, seems now to be lost; for parsnips are comparatively little esteemed, while the reputation of the carrot and turnip remains undiminished. To many persons, indeed, the sweet mawkish taste of the parsnip, resembling a frosted potato, is extremely disagreeable. It was formerly used in the north of Ireland for making a kind of beer, being brewed instead of malt, with hops, and fermented with yest.[†] It has also been occasionally made into bread; on which circumstance Gerard makes the following laconic observation: " There is a good and pleasant foode or bread made of the rootes of parsneps, as my friend master *Plat* hath set foorth, in his booke of Experimenes, which I have made no triall of, nor meane to do."[‡] Salmon, however, in his Herbal, published in 1710, above a century after Gerard, attributes to the bread of parsnips, which was made of the boiled roots baked with wheaten flour, all the virtues of the plant, which he considered as of no trifling de-

---

[*] Flora Diætetica, p. 40.   [†] Bryant. Fl. Diætetica.
[‡] Herbal, p. 871.

scription, since he asserts that "boiled, baked, or roasted parsnips, eaten as common food, sweeten the blood and juices above all other roots in the world; restore in consumptions, and make the eater of them grow fat and fleshy." In some parts of France these roots are cultivated in great abundance, and form a principal part of the food of the populace during winter.* They are esteemed an excellent diet for horses and cattle.†

The third common plant mentioned as an example of the *fusiform root* is the radish. It was originally brought from China, and its use as a salad is too well known to require comment. Common parsley, also, has a root of this description; and one variety of it, much cultivated in Holland, has roots as large as carrots, and is brought to market like the latter tied up in bundles. Parsley came originally from Sardinia.

The fusiform root often forks into two or more divisions, as may not unfrequently be seen in the plants just noticed, but in some other species it is of more regular occurrence. The *mandrake* (Atropa *Mandragora*) is a memorable example, since from so simple a circumstance arose a most absurd super-

* Young mentions that about Morlaix, " and in general through the bishopric of Pol de Leon, the culture of parsnips is of very great consequence to the people. Almost half the country subsists on them in winter, boiled in soup, &c. and their horses are in general fed with them." — *Tour in France.*

† " They are reckoned the best of all foods for a horse, and much exceeding oats; bullocks fatten quicker and better on them than on any other food." — *Ibid.*

stition, which at one period was widely prevalent.
The mandrake is common in many of the hotter
climates of Europe, and its fusiform root is often
forked, so as to present a distant similitude to the
lower half of the human figure; and, if the plant
be pulled when the fruit is ripe, one of the berries
may be supposed to represent the head, and then
the whole figure will be tolerably complete. Im-
postors, taking advantage of the credulity of mankind, carved the roots of briony and other plants
into the human form, and pretended that they were
mandrakes, and the most incredible virtues were
attributed to them in removing infirmities, and in
preserving from misfortunes. There would have
been little sale, however, for such factitious amulets
had the imposition stopped here. The *mandrake*
was not an uncommon plant, and a root of it could
at any time have been procured; but it was indus-
triously reported, and as credulously believed, that
to pull it up would be followed by the instantaneous
death of the perpetrator; that it shrieked, or
groaned, when separated from the ground; and
that whoever was unfortunate enough to hear the
shriek, died shortly after, or became afflicted with
madness. Shakspeare, in the fourth act of Romeo
and Juliet, speaks of the shrieks of mandrakes

> Torn out of the earth,
> That living mortals hearing them, run mad;

and in the second part of Henry the Sixth, Suffolk
says, —

Would curses *kill* as doth the *mandrake's groan,*
I would invent as bitter searching terms,
As curst, as harsh, and horrible to hear.

When, however, the root was once dislodged from
its place of growth, the danger ceased, and it became the good genius of its possessor. The mode
(or at least the reported mode) of uprooting it, was
to fasten the tail of a dog by cords to the bottom
of the stem, and then the animal was whipped,
until by his struggles the plant was dragged from
the earth, while the persons who directed this operation had their ears filled with pitch, lest they
should hear the fatal shriek or groan. The dog
of course fell dead at the time, or soon after.

The prices obtained for the factitious mandrakes
were very great. A mountebank, whom Matthio-
lus had cured of some disease at Rome, showed
him a great many, and informed him that he sometimes for a single specimen received twenty-five,
or even thirty pieces of gold. The way in which
they imitated the hair of the head and the beard
was not a little singular. They formed, first, the
recent root of the cane, marsh-mallow, briony, or
some other plant, into human shape, and where
they wanted to produce the appearance of hair,
they made little holes, and into these fixed grains
of millet-seed. The figure was then buried in
sand until these grains germinated; it was then
dug up, and the fine radicles and shoots were
trimmed so as to imitate hair.*

* Matth. Dioscorid. p. 536.

B 4

The word mandrake is said to be derived from the German *man dragen,* resembling man.*

Sometimes, in digging up plants, we shall find that the main body of the root, instead of running onward to a point, appears as if the greater part of it had been cut off. The part (*a*), *Fig.* 2., for example, instead of running, as we should *à priori* expect, to (*b*), terminates at (*c*), as if by some accident all the space from (*c*) to (*b*) had been removed.

Fig. 2.

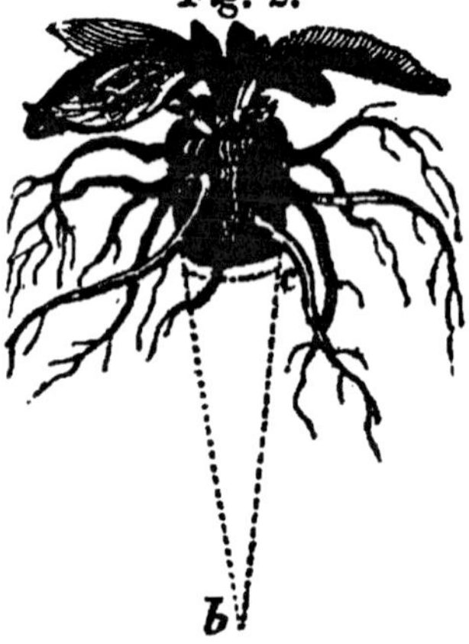

This, however, is not the effect of accident, but is natural to many plants, and forms what is called a premorse root. — Therefore

2. RADIX *præmorsa,* a *premorse* root, which means bitten off, as though the lower part of the root had been bitten away by a person's teeth. It is also called an abrupt, or a stumped, or an end-bitten root; but certainly *premorse* is much preferable to any of these terms. Among plants having a root of this kind may be mentioned the primrose, and cowslip, the greater plantain, the valerian, various hawkweeds, and the Scabiosa *succisa,* or devil's bit. We are not always, however,

---

* Parr's Lond. Med. Dict. — The Chinese call the *ginseng* the *man-herb,* because its fusiform root forks.—*Vide Hamilton's East Indies.*

to expect that when any of these plants are dug up, the root will be found uniformly premorse. This is only the case when the plant is above a year old, for during the first year it is fusiform; after that it becomes woody, dies, and rots, the upper part excepted, and this causes the eroded or bitten-off appearance; while new lateral branches shooting out from the portion left, compensate the want of the old main root.*

The Scabiosa *succisa* has its English name from a superstitious notion that the devil bit it off; for, as Gerard remarks, " it is commonly called Morsus diaboli, or Divel's bite, of the root (as it seemeth,)"—" For the superstitious people hold opinion, that the divell for the envie that he beareth to mankind bit it off, bicause it wood be otherwise good for many uses."   Threlkeld says that it is a great sudorific, and that " the name Devil's bit made that scribbler *Colepepper* drol upon the ignorant *Fryars*, who say the root was once longer, until the devil bit away the rest of it for spite, for he needed it not to make him sweat, who is always tormented with fear of the day of judgment."†
The plant is at present destitute of any beneficial qualities; for, as Sir James E. Smith wittily observes, " the malice of the devil has unhappily been so successful, that no virtues can now be found in the remainder of the root or herb."‡

* Vide Willdenow, 261. note.   † Irish Herbal.
‡ Intr. to Bot. ed. 4th. p. 83.

3. RADIX *ramosa.* The *ramose* or branched root
is more frequent than any other. It is divided
into numerous ramifications, like the branches of
a tree, and all trees have roots of this kind. The
structure of the ramose root differs in scarcely any
respect from that of the trunk and branches; and
indeed the branches, stem, and root of a tree may
be considered as essentially the same, since any apparent difference seems to arise merely from their
being placed in different circumstances. Branches
may, for the sake of illustration, be considered as
roots growing in the air; and roots as branches
growing in the earth. Trees of various kinds have
been inverted, their branches that formerly bore
leaves have been changed into roots by being
buried in the soil; and the roots, elevated into the
atmosphere, have become covered with foliage.
For this experiment the willow answers particularly well; and as a farther illustration of the principle, I may mention a method of propagating
various fruit-trees practised in China and Bengal.

Suppose this figure to represent a fruit-bearing

Fig. 3.

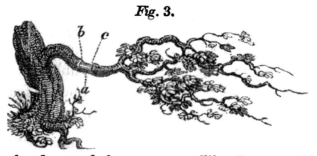

branch of one of these trees. The first step is to

remove a circle of the bark of about an inch in length, the space, for instance, from (*b*) to (*c*), this being done the interspace (*a*) will, of course, be naked; the next step, therefore, is to surround this naked circle with a ball of earth, which is to be retained with a slip of matting, and then a vessel of water is suspended over it, with a small orifice just sufficient to let as much water slowly drop as will keep the earth moist.   This operation is to be done in spring; in autumn the branch is to be sawn off, and then it will be found that a number of *roots* have sprung from the upper circumference (*c*) and have shot into the ball; the branch is then to be planted in the ground, and in the following year it will be a small tree, bearing fruit.* In the roots of some trees we find a particularly strong tendency to assume the functions of branches when exposed to the atmosphere; hence we learn

---

* The above is the method used by the Chinese for obtaining dwarf specimens of fruit-bearing trees, of which they are remarkably fond.   In Lord Macartney's Embassy to China, the following account is given :—" The hall of audience furnished also another object of curiosity, striking at least to strangers. On several tables were placed in frames, filled with earth, dwarf pines, oaks, and orange-trees, bearing fruit.   None of them exceeded, in height, two feet.   Some of those dwarfs bore all the marks of decay from age : and upon the surface of the soil were interspersed small heaps of stones, which in proportion to the adjoining dwarfs, might be termed rocks. These were honeycombed and moss-grown, as if untouched for ages, which served to maintain the illusion, and to give an antique appearance to the whole.   This kind of stunted vegetation seemed to be much relished by the curious in China; and specimens of it were to be found in every considerable dwelling." —*Staunton's Embassy*, vol. i. p. 428.

that in the cocoa-tree (Theobroma *Cacao*), "*flowers* spring out from the ligneous roots wherever the earth leaves them uncovered."* When trees also are blown down, and survive, their roots which are exposed to the air become covered with foliage.†

4. RADIX *fibrosa*, a *fibrous* root.

This is found in most annual plants, and in most grasses. It consists entirely of fibres or threads, the ultimate divisions of which are named fibrillæ or fibrils. The fibres are frequently much branched; and in grasses which grow in loose sand are generally clothed thickly with down. Sometimes they are filiform or like threads, and in the palms and succulent plants of hot climates, they resemble cords, spreading far and wide under the surface of the soil, and have been named funiliform, or cord-like roots.

Fig. 4.

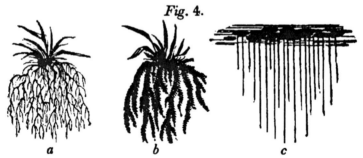

a   *b*   *c*

a, Fibrous root of a grass.
b,   Ditto   downy, from growing in loose sand.
c, Filiform root of duckweed.

---

* Humboldt's Pers. Nar. vol. iv. p. 234.

† " On the morning of the 28th, I saw a tamarisk of an enormous size planted on the bank of the Nile: it had been

5. RADIX *tuberosa*, a *tuberous* or knobbed root.

It consists of fleshy knobs or tubers, connected to each other by intervening threads or fibres, as in the potato and Jerusalem artichoke, *Fig. 5. (a).* The term, however, is of more extensive latitude, and is applied to plants which have only one tuber, and there are several varieties of the tuberous root which have their appropriate names. Sometimes the knobs are connected by intervening cords in form of a necklace or chain, and hence the term moniliform root (*monile*, a necklace, *Lat.*), as in dropwort and king's spear, *Fig. 5. (b);* or the tubers are in contact with each other, as in some species of grass, *Fig. 5. (c).*

Fig. 5.

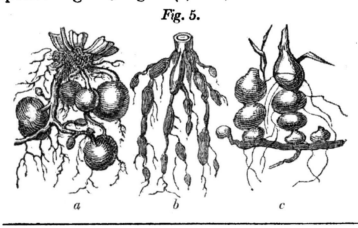

a   *b*   *c*

loosened at the roots by progressive inundations, and at last overthrown; the greater number of its roots had ranged themselves upright, and produced leaves; the old branches on which the tree had fallen were fixed in the earth, and served as a footstool, so that the enormous trunk, which remained suspended horizontally, by a confusion in the system of circulation, vegetated in every direction, and gave it such a grotesque appearance, that the Turks had not failed to make a miracle of this vegetable monster." — *Denon's Trav.*

Sometimes a great many *small* tubers or bulbs grow in *clusters*, or scattered on the radical fibres, forming a granulated root (RADIX *granulata*), as in *Fig.* 6. which is the root of the white saxifrage (Saxifraga *granulata*).

Fig. 6.

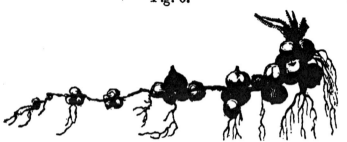

The didymous, or twin root (RADIX *didyma*), is when two tubers grow together, as in many of the orchis tribe, *Fig.* 7. (*a*); and in many species of the same family the tubers split into finger-like divisions, forming the palmated root (RADIX *palmata*), *Fig.* 7. (*b*)

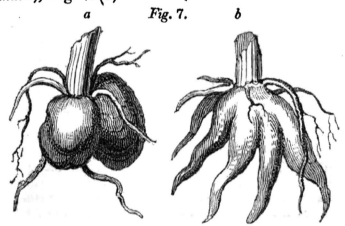

a   *Fig.* 7.   *b*

6. RADIX *bulbosa*, the *bulbous root*, which we shall now consider, appertains to many plants, and

assumes several varieties in shape and structure. It is usually described as being solid, or tunicated, or scaly. We have an example of the *solid* bulb in *crocus, Fig.* 8. (*a*), and in this plant we find a small bulb standing immediately over a larger, forming a BULBUS *duplicatus,* or duplicated bulb, or in other words, a RADIX *duplicata,* duplicated root.

In some plants, that part which is between the stem and the root, and which bears the name of intermediate stem, swells into a bulbous form, and is not unfrequently described as a real bulb; the turnip is an instance; but it is a gross mistake to consider the turnip as a bulb, though it is not unfrequently cited and figured as such.

We often find, on cutting a bulbous root across, that it is not solid, but composed of many concentric layers, or coats; this forms the tunicated bulb, as in the onion, *Fig.* 8. (*b*)

In other instances the bulb is composed of many scales or *squamæ,* forming the scaly bulb (BULBUS *squamosus*), of which the lily affords a familiar example, *Fig.* 8. (*c*)

Fig. 8.

a   b   c

Sometimes a number of small bulbs are enclosed in one common covering, as in the roots of common garlic. This is named a compound bulb (BULBUS *compositus*), and sometimes a nestling root (RADIX *nidularis*); but the former appellation seems more proper.

Having adverted to these different kinds of bulbous roots, I must observe that the bulb is not really the part which performs the true office of a root. We have already seen that the radiculæ, or fibrous ramifications, are the essential organs for conveying nutriment to the plant. Now, we do not find bulbs sending out such fibres; but the *base* of the bulb is a solid stratum or plate, and from *it* many threads shoot down into the soil; and these are to be regarded as the real roots. This plate is represented at *Fig.* 9. (*a*).

Fig. 9.

Bulbs, indeed, are altogether analogous to the buds of trees, and in some plants they are, like the latter, produced upon the stems or branches, as in several of the lily tribe, the bulbiferous coral-wort (Dentaria *bulbifera*), the magical onion, garlic, &c.

In general, bulbs which bear flowers, die after that operation is over; but the plant is often continued, exclusively of its propagation by seeds, by the formation of *new* bulbs, which shoot out from the base or sides of the original bulb, and grow into new plants, after the latter has perished. See *Fig.* 9.(*b*). We may particularly observe this mode of propagation in the *tubers* of the orchis tribe, which are usually two in number, and which, by the by, Linnæus names bulbs. Of these tubers, one belongs to the plant of the *present* year; the other to that of *next* year; which again shoots out a tuber at *its* side for the *third* year, and so on. In this way such plants change their situation; the flower of every successive year becoming further removed from the place of the original one.

With respect to the economical uses of bulbous roots, many of them are profitable as food or medicines. In Africa, the bulbs of several species of Ixia are used as articles of diet; and in some places, those of the *Star of Bethlehem*, especially of the broad-leaved species, are much consumed by the lower classes. The roots of the tulip are converted to a similar purpose in some parts of Italy; but perhaps no people derive so much advantage from bulbous roots as the Kamtschatkans do from the *Kamtschatka lily* (Lilium *Camschatcense*), called *saranne* in their language. At the period of its flowering, the whole ground is covered with its blossoms. The roots are dried in the sun, and preserved for use; and when baked they are ground into flour, of which the best bread of these people is made. They are used also as we do potatoes.*

You have not, perhaps, before heard of the eco-

* Pennant's Arctic Zoology.

nomical uses of the bulbs now mentioned; let me, therefore, beg your attention a little to some with which you are well acquainted. I allude to the onion, leek, and garlic.

The name of the onion in Latin was *cepa,* which was taken from *caput* the head, on account of the shape of the bulb. The English word onion is said to be derived from the Latin *unio,* which means the number *one,* because this plant sends off no offsets or bulbs from the original, for no one ever saw two onions at one stalk. This vegetable is cultivated over most of the known world, but its original country is unknown. It is most probable that Egypt was its native place; we know, at least, that it was used there as food more than two thousand years before the birth of Christ, as it was one of the things the want of which the Israelites deplored after their departure from that kingdom. We find in the eleventh chapter of Numbers these words : — " And the children of Israel also wept again, and said, Who shall give us flesh to eat? We remember the fish which we did eat in Egypt freely; the cucumbers, and the melons, and the leeks, and the onions, and the garlic."

Now in this country the loss of the latter articles would not be considered as a very grievous privation; but the onion we are accustomed to is very different from that of Egypt, which, by the uncontradicted testimony of travellers, is delicious.

" Whoever," Hasselquist says, " has tasted onions in Egypt, must allow that none can be had better in any part in the universe; here they are sweet, in other countries they are nauseous and strong; here they are soft, whereas in the north and other parts they are hard, and the coats so compact that they are hard of digestion. Hence they cannot in any place be eaten with less prejudice and more satisfaction than in Egypt. They eat them roasted, cut into four pieces, with some bits of roasted meat, which the Turks in Egypt call *kebab;* and with this dish they are so delighted, that I have heard them wish they might enjoy it in Paradise."

Brown notices their mildness, and says they are of the purest white*; and we are told by Sonnini †, that they are sold in the streets and markets, both raw and dressed, for a mere trifle, and that they form almost the only sustenance of the poor. It is, however, a just remark of the same author, that, notwithstanding their great mildness, still they are onions, and the excessive use of them must increase the disposition which the Egyptians have to disorders in the eyes.

Perhaps the garlic mentioned in Scripture is not the species we are familiarly acquainted with, as it does not appear to be a native of Egypt, nor is it cultivated there, though it is imported in large quantities from Syria, under the name of " Seeds

* Brown's Travels in Africa, p. 136.
† Sonnini's Travels in Egypt, pp. 282, 283.

of Damascus."* The *leek* is in high estimation in Egypt, and often, with a little bread, forms the favourite dinner of the lower classes. As the latter plant forms the national emblem of Wales, it might be supposed that the inhabitants of that country are much addicted to its use. It owes its estimatian among them, however, to a very different circumstance. On the first of March, in the year 640, the Welsh, under the command of their king Cadwallo, obtained a complete victory over the Saxons: the battle happened near a place where leeks were cultivated, and the Welsh soldiers put each a bit of leek in his cap. Fluellen says, in the fourth act of Henry the Fifth, " If your Majesties is remember'd of it, the Welshmen did goot service in a garden where leeks did grow, wearing leeks in their Monmouth caps; which your Majesty knows to this hour is an honourable padge of the service: and I do believe your Majesty takes no scorn to wear the leek upon St. Tavy's day." †

The onion is a favourite, it appears, even amidst the delicious productions of India. " Our *best vegetable*," Maria Graham says, " is the onion, for which Bombay is famous throughout the east." ‡ The Brahmins, however, and many other Hindoos,

* Sonnini's Travels in Egypt, p. 283.

† The plant used by the Welsh on the above occasion was most probably a different species from the leek, the latter being a native of Switzerland, and, according to the Hortus Kewensis, not introduced into England till about the year 1562.

‡ Journal of a Residence in India, p. 24.

reject it, according to Forbes, from their bill of fare. *

The intolerable smell which onions, and more particularly garlic, communicate to the breath, is an insurmountable obstacle to their use among the better classes of society in this country. Eating some parsley leaves is said, most effectually, to cover their scent; but scarcely any thing will conceal it. In Cochin China, cardamom seeds are used for this purpose. In *currie*, which is the standing dish of that country, onions and garlic are introduced with a very unsparing hand; and to sweeten the breath from their taint these seeds are chewed. " Every lady," says Barrow, " carries about with her box of cardamoms, which she presents to her friends or strangers in the same manner as the snuff-box is presented in Europe." † It would be much wiser, however, could they do as Bottom advises: " And, most dear actors, eat no onions, nor garlic, for we are to utter sweet breath." These roots are in very general use throughout Spain; and among the poor, whose food is chiefly or entirely vegetable, they are valuable, as affording a salutary stimulus to the stomach. The poor fishermen in China, who reside constantly upon the water, form rafts of bamboo, interwoven with reeds and grass, which they cover with earth; and

* Oriental Memoirs, vol. ii. p. 51.
† Travels in Cochin China, p. 188.

on these, which are towed after their boats, they
cultivate their onions and garlic.

Roots are sometimes named from the direction
they take.   The fusiform root, we have seen, penetrates in general perpendicularly into the earth;
and hence, by some authors, the term *fusiform*
is dropped, and that of *perpendicular* is used in
its place: but this must be erroneous, for many
plants have roots strictly perpendicular as to direction which are not spindle-shaped; and some
spindle-shaped roots run horizontally.   Willden-
now's definition of the perpendicular root is, that
it is " *equally thick*, and goes perpendicularly into
the ground, as in the shepherd's purse;" but this
is a distinction too finely drawn.

Some plants have roots, which, instead of striking *down* into the soil, run in a horizontal direction
near its surface, and hence the

7. RADIX *horizontalis*, or *horizontal* root, as in
iris, common polypody, wood anemone, &c.   The
superficial situation and horizontal direction of the
roots of some trees render them easily blown down.
" It is not," Mary Woolstonecraft observes, " surprising that the *pine* should be often undermined;
it shoots its fibres in such a horizontal direction,
merely on the surface of the earth, requiring only
enough to cover those that cling to the crags." *
The superficial situation of the roots of many
American trees is assigned as one reason why the

* Letters from Norway, p. 154.

Americans have a dislike to woods and forest scenery. " To them," says an intelligent traveller, " the sight of a wheat-field, or a cabbage-garden, would convey pleasure far greater than that of the most romantic woodland views. They have an unconquerable aversion to trees, and whenever a settlement is made, they cut away all before them without mercy: not one is spared; all share the same fate, and are involved in the general havoc. It appears strange, that in a country where the rays of the sun act with such prodigious power, some few trees near the habitations should not be spared, whose foliage might afford a cooling shade during the parching heat of summer; and I have oftentimes expressed my astonishment that none were ever left for that purpose. In answer, I have generally been told, that they could not be left standing near a house without danger. The trees, it seems, in the American forests, have but a very slender hold in the ground, considering their immense height, so that when two or three fully grown are deprived of shelter, in consequence of the others which stood around them being cut down, they are very apt to be levelled by the first storm that chances to blow. This, however, would not be the case with trees of a small growth, which might safely be spared, and which would soon afford an agreeable shade, if the Americans thought proper to leave them standing: but the fact of the matter is, that, from the face of the country being

entirely overspread with trees, the eyes of the
people become satiated with the sight of them.
The ground cannot be tilled, nor can the inhabitants support themselves till they are removed;
they are looked upon as a nuisance; and the man
that can cut down the largest number, and have
the fields about his house most clear of them, is
looked upon as the most industrious citizen, and
the one that is making the greatest improvement
in the country.   The same author mentions his
having heard of Americans, who, on landing on
the north-west coast of Ireland, evinced the greatest
surprise and pleasure at the beauty of the country,
" so clear of trees." *

The latter part of the above quotation is calculated to refute the assertion, that the American
trees are easily blown down; but I apprehend this
to be really the fact, and perhaps it may account
for the great preference given in America to the
Lombardy poplar, which is planted not only along
the roads, but in the towns, and is supposed to
enhance the value of every place where it is grown.†

* Weld's Travels in North America, vol. i. p. 39.
† " Great numbers of these poplars, which serve for not one
useful purpose, have been planted in America. They border
all the streets in Philadelphia, and all the roads about the
town." — Liancourt's Travels, vol. i. p. 47.
The Lombardy poplar is much cultivated in the Crimea
also. " As soon (says Pallas) as the trees begin to thrive, they
are sometimes cleared of all their shoots; when they speedily
form the most beautiful pyramidal heads, and attain to an
astonishing height; but, notwithstanding their solitary and
frequently exposed situation, they have never been observed

Travellers, too, who were certainly not thinking on our present subject, have been struck with surprise at the facility with which they have observed large trees to be uprooted with the wind. " It is surprising," says Liancourt, " that the largest trees seldom strike their roots deeper than about four or five inches into the ground; this was, at least, the case with all those which had been overturned with the winds, and lay near the road."*

This superficial situation of the root may, perhaps, arise entirely from the trees growing originally in great numbers together, and affording mutual protection; and I think we may observe that wherever trees stand alone, or are thinly planted, their roots very seldom protrude above the ground; but in thick woods we find them running in numbers upon the surface. The American trees, therefore, if planted in situations where, as they grow up, they would have to depend on their own roots, singly, for support, instead of being upheld by their neighbours, may perhaps acquire as much firmness as the trees of Europe. It is at least a common, and I think a rational opinion, that trees acquire greater stability of root in proportion as they are accustomed to contend with the elements.

---

to be shivered by lightning, broken by violent storms, or *torn out of the soil.* Their *long and vigorous roots* run by the side of ditches to a great distance, with *extensive ramifications,* and sometimes make their way into wells." — *Pallas's Travels,* vol. ii. p. 442.

* Liancourt's Travels in North America, vol. i. p. 48.

Mark yonder oaks! superior to the power
Of all the warring winds of heaven they rise,
And from the stormy promontory tower,
And toss their giant arms amid the skies,
While each assailing blast increase of strength supplies.

Some, indeed, only grow in situations where they are unavoidably exposed to every storm that blows. Such is a species of fir, which Lord Byron mentions as being peculiar to the Alps, and thriving only in very rocky parts, where it might be supposed there could not be soil sufficient for its nourishment. Yet trees of this kind acquire a giant size, and

——— grow
Loftiest on loftiest and least sheltered rocks,
Rooted in barrenness, where naught below
Of soil supports them 'gainst the Alpine shocks
Of eddying storms; yet springs the trunk, and mocks
The hovering tempest, till its height and frame
Are worthy of the mountains from whose blocks
Of bleak, gray granite, into life it came.

When a horizontal root pushes up stems, at intervals, through the ground, as at *Fig*. 10., it is named a *repent* or creeping root (RADIX *repens*), as in mint, couch-grass, &c.

Fig. 10.

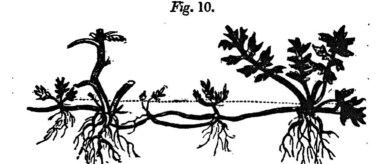

This root is very tenacious of life, as any portion of it will grow; and hence weeds furnished with it are very troublesome to the gardener and husbandman. One of the most familiar examples is the couch or squitch grass (Triticum *repens*), which is the pest of gardens, and grows in almost every climate. Its root has a sweetish taste, and in seasons of scarcity has been made into bread. At Naples, and in some parts of France, it is collected for feeding horses.*

The repent root is in some instances highly useful; for some plants provided with it inhabit naturally the loose sand of the sea-coast, and by their spreading and interlacing roots prevent the sands from travelling with the winds, and encroaching on the arable land. Among the most beneficial in this respect, are the *sea-lime-grass*, the *sea-reed*, and the *sea-seg* or sedge. The very existence of Holland depends on these and some other plants, which bind its dikes so firmly together, as to enable them to resist the action of the sea. Some other plants, not of the family of grasses, serve a similar purpose; as the creeping *rest-harrow* (Ononis *repens*), and the *single-seeded* broom, which grow in the loose sands of the shore of Spain, and which latter plant, according to Osbeck, "turns the most

* " Upon the banks of the Garonne I met women loaded with the roots of this plant, going to sell it at market; and they informed me it was bought to feed horses with." — *Young's Travels in France.*

barren place into a fine odoriferous garden, by its
flowers, which last a long while." *   The beautiful
sea-eryngo is one of the repent-rooted plants which
inhabit the barren sands, and draw their nourishment from a source in which we might naturally
suppose nothing but sterility could exist.

> —— Th' Eryngo here
> Sits as a queen among the scanty tribes
> Of vegetable race.   Around her neck
> A gorgeous ruff of leaves, with arrowy points,
> Averts all harsh intrusion.   On her brow
> She binds a crown of amethystine hue,
> Bristling with spicula, thick interwove
> With clustering florets, whose light anthers dance
> In the fresh breeze, like tiny topaz gems.
> Here the sweet rose would die.   But she imbibes
> From arid sands, and salt-sea dew-drops, strength ;
> The native of the beach, by nature formed
> To dwell among the ruder elements. †

Roots, also, by retaining the earth and mud,
change marshes into dry and habitable land. Hasselquist mentions a small reed which grows in the
Nile, and to which, though useless in ordinary life,
" the very soil of Egypt is owing; for the matted
roots have stopped the earth which floated in the
waters, and formed out of the sea a country that is
habitable."‡

Roots are distinguished by their duration, as
well as their direction, substance, or form.   They
are said to be *annual,* when both root and herb
perish within the year ; *biennial,* when they live till

* Osbeck's Voyages, vol. i. p. 42.
† Clontarf, a Poem, by the Rev. W. H. Drummond, D.D.
‡ Hasselquist's Voyage, p. 97.

the second year, or longer, then flower and *perish* ; and *perennial*, when they live and flower many years. Some plants, which in their native warm countries are perennial, as the *mignonette* and *nasturtium*, become annual with us ; and some, as the ray-grass (Lolium *perenne*), which with us are perennial, become annual when transplanted to more southern regions.*

The roots hitherto mentioned are fixed in the earth ; but there are plants in which they are not attached to any solid body, but float in the water — there are some which grow only upon *other* plants — and some are almost *independent of* a root.

The *Lemna*, or duck-meat, which is found in almost every ditch, offers a ready example of the first. Its roots, which are filiform or thread-like, hang down from the surface of the water, quite unattached to any thing solid ; and if you collect some good specimens in summer, when they have acquired the length of six or seven inches, and put them into a glass vessel of pure water, you will remark that these roots will present a very beautiful appearance, waving like threads of silver in the fluid. On minutely inspecting the extremity of each of these roots, you will perceive that it is

---

* " Many plants, perennial in northern, are annual in southern regions. The heat and drought of the latter cause the roots to die away." — *Link, in Botanical Tracts, London*, 1805, p. 47.

thickened; and by using a magnifier, you may be able to ascertain, from your own observation, that this thickening is caused by a sheath which encloses the point of the root. A similar calyptra or veil is found in the roots of ferns, palms, and some other plants; and Sprengel, with some appearance of truth, supposes it to be an organ of absorption.

There is another small plant which grows in water, often floating on the surface, and frequently mixed along with the duck-weed, which at one period of its growth has floating roots, that at another are fixed in the earth and mud at the bottom. This plant is the water star-grass (Callitriche *aquatica*). Until flowering it floats on the surface, and is nourished by the suspended roots; but it would appear, that before the seeds can be ripened, it is requisite that these roots should be exposed to a more substantial source of nourishment, and therefore, the flowering being over, the whole plant sinks to the bottom, strikes root, and ripens its seeds. These, germinating in course, produce a young progeny of plants which rise to the surface, float there till after flowering, then, like their parent, sink to the bottom, and produce new progenies in their turn.*

* " It is generally supposed to be annual, floating by means of its thick-set broad upper leaves," till flowering; " then each flower sinks by the elongation of the top of the stem, where new ones are produced; and finally, the whole herb subsides to the bottom, takes root there, ripens, and sows its seeds. The young plants soon rise to the surface, and appear

A number of cryptogamic plants swim about at random in the waters, among which the most interesting, perhaps, in our present state of knowledge, is the sargasso, or gulf-weed of voyagers (Fucus *natans*), which is found in the Gulf of Florida, and some other parts of the ocean, floating in masses or fields many miles in length. No distinct root is found in this plant, and there is no doubt that it vegetates and lives long in this natant state, though originally perhaps attached to some solid substance, and not as now, a weed,

—— flung from the rock, on Ocean's foam to sail
Where'er the surge may sweep, the tempest's breath prevail.

In like manner, the roots of land plants sometimes become detached from the banks of lakes and rivers, but falling into the water, continue to vegetate on the surface, forming floating islands. Pennant describes an island of this kind in Loch Dochart; and in lakes in Prussia, Lithuania, &c. they are found presenting the appearance of large meadows, sometimes clothed with trees.* The great American rivers, in the time of high floods, often carry down masses of their banks, covered with majestic trees and numerous climbers; and these, meeting with other masses similarly swept

to be nourished from the water by slender simple roots from each joint of the slender branching stem, which do not reach the ground till the plant subsides as above mentioned."— *English Botany*, p. 722
* Mirbel.

off, form islands or rafts, which float along with the stream, and sometimes carry destruction to the unwary or nocturnal voyager. " Woe (says Humboldt) to the canoes that during the night strike against these rafts of wood interwoven with lianas ! Covered with *aquatic plants*, they resemble here (Oroonoko), as in the Mississippi, floating meadows, the *chinampas* of the Mexican lakes."* This celebrated traveller mentions, that when the Indians wish to surprise their enemies, they tie several canoes together, and cover them with grass and branches to simulate these islands.† The Spanish smugglers at Angostura practise a similar artifice to elude the vigilance of the custom-house officers.

The water house-leek (Pistia *Stratiotes*), common in American lakes and rivers, often produces a similar phenomenon. It grows in eddy water near the shore, and gradually spreads into the river, forming green plains several miles long, and sometimes a quarter of a mile broad. Its roots are long and fibrous, running into the mud ; and the plant bears a general resemblance to a garden lettuce.

---

* Pers. Nar. vol. v. p. 36.

† By a stratagem of this kind, Vasco de Gama was once attempted to be deceived. " As he was near the shore of Anchediva, he beheld the appearance of a floating isle, covered with trees, advance towards him. But his prudence was not to be deceived thus. A bold pirate, named Timoja, by linking together eight vessels full of men, and covered with green boughs, thought to board him by surprise. But Gama's cannon made seven of them fly; the eighth, loaded with fruits and provisions, he took." — *Notes to Mickle's Lusiad.*

After rains, when the rivers are suddenly raised, large tracts of these floating plains get detached, and are driven about upon the water. Bartram observes, that " these floating islands present a very entertaining prospect: for although we behold an assemblage of the primary productions of nature only, yet the imagination seems to remain in suspense and doubt; as, in order to enliven the delusion, and form a most picturesque appearance, we see not only flowery plants, clumps of shrubs, old weather-beaten trees, hoary and barbed with the long moss waving from their snags, but we also see them completely inhabited and alive with crocodiles, serpents, frogs, otters, crows, herons, curlews, jackdaws, &c. There seems, in short, nothing wanted but the appearance of a wigwam and a canoe to complete the scene." *

I have said that some plants live almost independent of a root: they grow on the driest walls and rocks, the tops of houses, and other situations where no source of nourishment is presented to their radicles, and consequently they absorb their nourishment and moisture from the air, by their leaves;—and as the structure of the latter is adapted for absorbing but not exhaling fluids, their substance is fleshy and full of juice, contrary to what, at a first view, we might have expected. The house-leek and sedums are examples of these among British plants; and in warmer regions the

* Bartram's Travels through Carolina, &c., p. 87.

numerous species of Cactus, Mesembryanthemum, and some other genera, are found flourishing best where there is most aridity and heat, as among burning sands, on fragments of lava, and on the barest rocks and walls, exposed to the hottest sun: the *Stapelia* is hence named the *vegetable camel.* Some species of Epidendrum will grow and flower for years, hung from the ceiling of a room, without ever being supplied with one drop of water. These, and some others, have been called " air plants."

The last description of root which I intend to notice, is the *parasitic,* or that root which, in place of being fixed in the ground, is inserted into the bark of trees and other plants, and lives upon their juices. In some tropical regions these are very numerous, and frequently a single tree is seen to present a wonderful diversity of foliage, from the foreign species that encumber it; but in Britain we can only (Cryptogamics, such as mosses, lichens, &c. excepted) enumerate three true parasitics; these are the *Misseltoe,* and two species of *dodder* (Cuscuta). To the first, many superstitious ideas and ceremonies were attached by the Druids, of which Pliny has given an interesting description. With respect to the *Cuscuta* or *dodder,* it is, as Gerard says, " a strange herbe, altogether without leaves or roote, like unto threads very much snarled, or wrapped together, confusedly winding itselfe about bushes and hedges, and sundrie

kindes of herbes."* When the seed of this plant
opens, it shoots out a little body or thread, which
climbs in a spiral direction from right to left round
any neighbouring plant: as soon as this happens,
the shoot produces, from its inner surface, a number of small warts, which adhere closely to the
foster-plant, and from these other shoots are
pushed out, which insinuate themselves into the
tenderest parts of the stalk and branches; and
thus the dodder is nourished at the expense of the
plant it encumbers, while the latter in consequence
becomes exhausted, and in the end perishes.†
Threlkeld says of the dodder, that it is " a non-
pareil having no leaves, but red threads; and after
it has fastened its claspers or small tendrils upon
a plant, as line, thyme, nettle, madder, or such
like, it quits the root, and like a coshering para-
site lives upon another's trencher, and like an
ungrateful guest, first starves and then kills its
entertainer: for which reason irreligious clowns
curse it by the name of *Hell-weed*, and Devil's
guts, in Sussex."

* Gerard's Herbal, p. 462.　　† Vide Withering.

c 6

CHAPTER II.

OF THE STEM.

THE word CAUDEX means the stem or trunk of a tree, and is derived from the verb *cædo,* to cut down, because, being out of the ground, it comes easily within reach of the axe. But we have seen that the difference in situation alone is the cause of a difference in appearance, between the roots of a tree and its stem and branches ; and, therefore, laying aside the derivation of the word, the term *caudex* might also be applied with considerable propriety to the parts *beneath* the ground. It would be convenient, however, to prefix some qualifying epithet which would at once mark a distinction. Linnæus did this by naming one the *ascending,* the other the *descending* stem: the CAUDEX *ascendens,* or ascending stem, rising into the air and putting out branches and leaves ; the CAUDEX *descendens,* or descending stem, striking into the earth in form of roots.

At the place where these meet, we sometimes find a part that cannot be said strictly to belong to either. I have already instanced this in the turnip, and stated that it was named the intermediate stem (CAUDEX *intermedius*). Often it is undistinguishable, there being no apparent line of demarcation between the stem and root. This part is by many writers named the *rhizoma* or rootstock, by some the neck, by some the collar, and it has various other appellations; though on the whole, perhaps, that of *intermediate stem* is the best. In some trees, what may with truth, I think, be considered as such, exhibits an appearance not a little curious. A tree will rise from the ground strengthened by a number of great ribs that project upwards and coalesce with the main trunk, adding much to its thickness at the base, and supporting it, as it were, by buttresses or pilasters, the ribs sometimes projecting three feet or more, forming interspaces deep enough to conceal several men.

The white cedar of America (Cupressus *disticha*), in which this occurs, is well described by Bartram. " It stands," he says, " in the first order of North American trees. Its majestic stature is surprising; and on approaching it, we are struck with a kind of awe, at beholding the stateliness of the trunk, lifting its cumbrous top towards the skies, and casting a wide shade upon the ground, as a dark intervening cloud, which, for a time, excludes the rays of the sun. The delicacy of its colour, and texture of its leaves, exceed every thing in vegetation. It generally grows in the water, or in low flat lands, near the banks of great rivers and lakes, that are covered, great part of the year, with two or three feet depth of water:

and that part of the trunk which is subject to be under water, *and four or five feet higher up,* is greatly enlarged by *prodigious buttresses,* or pilasters, which in full grown trees project out on every side, to such a distance, that several men might easily hide themselves in the hollows between. Each pilaster terminates underground, in a very large, strong, serpentine root, which strikes off, and branches every way, just under the surface of the earth." From the top of the buttresses the tree, " as it were, *takes another beginning,* forming a grand straight column eighty or ninety feet high, when it divides every way around into an extensive flat horizontal top, like an umbrella, where the eagles have their secure nests, and cranes and storks their temporary resting places; and what adds to the magnificence of their appearance is the streamers of long moss that hang from the lofty limbs and float in the winds. This is their majestic appearance when standing alone in large rice plantations, or thinly planted on the banks of great rivers."*

Forster describes a similar construction in the fig-trees of the island of Tanna, one of the New Hebrides†; and it appears that sometimes these ribs separate from the main trunk and form cylindrical roots of considerable thickness. Humboldt notices this circumstance in the South American fig-trees, which are of such enormous size as to

* Travels, p. 88. et seq.
† Forster's Account of Cook's Voyage, vol. ii. p. 334.

measure sometimes about twenty-two feet in diameter at the base. The trunk is augmented by
ligneous ribs as far as twenty feet from the ground,
and these "sometimes separate from the trunk at
a height of eight feet, and are transformed into
cylindrical roots two feet thick. The tree looks as
if it were supported by buttresses. This scaffold-
ing, however, does not penetrate very deep into
the earth."*

Forster notices a still more remarkable circumstance in the fig-trees of New Caledonia. "The
inhabitants," he says, " were commonly seated at
the foot of these trees, which had this remarkable
quality, that they shot long roots from the upper
part of the stem, perfectly round, as if they had
been made by a turner, into the ground ten, fifteen,
and twenty feet from the tree, and formed a most
exact straight line, being extremely elastic, and as
tense as a bow-string prepared for action."†

I shall conclude this part of our subject by mentioning two more instances of the intermediate
stem from Stedman and Dampier. The former
gives a figure of a tree found in Surinam, called
the Matakee tree, whose roots, he says " spread
above ground in such a manner that they will conceal a score of men from each other;" and he
farther mentions that a man on horseback can ride
through the interstices; and that a table large

* Humboldt's Pers. Nar. vol. iv. p. 93.
† Forster's Cook's Voyages, vol. ii. p. 392.

enough to dine twelve persons may be substituted from one single piece.*

Dampier, in the first volume of his Voyages, describes the *red mangrove* as growing by the sea-side, or by rivers and creeks, and always " *out of many roots* about the bigness of a man's leg, some bigger, some less, which, at about *six, eight,* or *ten feet* above the ground, join into one trunk or body, that seems to be supported by so many *arti-ficial stakes.* Where this sort of tree grows, it is impossible to march by reason of these stalks, which grow so mixed one among another, that I have, when forced to go through them, gone half a mile, and never set my foot on the ground, stepping from *root to root*."

Linnæus used the word TRUNCUS (trunk) as a generical term for all stems; and under it he arranged the seven following species :—

1. CAULIS, the Stalk.
2. CULMUS, the Culm, or Straw.
3. SCAPUS, the Scape.
4. PEDUNCULUS, the Peduncle.
5. PETIOLUS, the Petiole.
6. FRONS, the Frond.
7. STIPES, the Stipe.

The peduncle or flower-stalk, however, and the petiole or leaf-stalk, are to be considered as only parts of the stem; the term *frond* is limited to the palms, and to the ferns, mosses, and other

* Stedman's Surinam, vol. ii. p. 188.

cryptogamic plants; and that of *stipe* is confined to ferns and fungi.

. Before considering the different species of stem, it will be proper to advert to the distinction of plants into trees, shrubs, under-shrubs, and herbs.

The term tree requires no definition; it is designated in Botany by its Latin name *arbor*, a tree, *arbores*, trees. The stem of certain plants, which, though not trees, yet resemble them in habit, is named a tree-like stem (CAULIS *arboreus*); or, if it be first herbaceous, and become woody by age, it is called an arborescent stem (CAULIS *arborescens*); and the similarity which some shrubs and herbs bear to trees supplies not unfrequently a very characteristic name for them. Hence, we have Erica *arborea*, tree-heath; Lavatera *arborea*, sea-tree-mallow; Dianthus *arboreus*, tree-pink, &c.

. It might be thought easy to lay down such a definition as would clearly distinguish a tree and shrub from each other; and yet this is perhaps impossible. At one period Linnæus thought that *buds* were produced by trees, but not by shrubs, and that by this circumstance they might be discriminated, but he did not long retain this opinion; and indeed the truth is, that some shrubs do produce *buds*, and that trees in hot countries do *not*. The definition of the shrub, as given in Martyn's Language of Botany, is perhaps as expressive as any we have. It is this: " In its general acceptation, it is a vegetable with several permanent woody stems, dividing from the bottom, more slender, and low than in trees." The Latin *frutex*, a shrub; *frutices*, shrubs, form its botanical appellations.

Next is the *Suffrutex*, or under-shrub; and one unacquainted with botanical nomenclature would suppose that there could be little difficulty in conceiving the meaning of this term. It means, he would say, " a shrub of small size," — " a shrub lower than shrubs usually are;" but he would be mistaken, for the term has no reference to magnitude.

There is a very pretty plant, which in spring and part of the summer adorns, with corymbs of purplish, white, and flesh-coloured flowers, the cliffs of Gibraltar, and is named Gibraltar Candytuft (Iberis *Gibraltarica*). Before the winter months come on, its flowers, leaves, and even its stems, have disappeared; — they have dried up and are gone. But, on examination, it will be found that the root remains; that it is *woody*; that the bottoms of the stems also remain; and that *they too are woody*. The stems that have vanished were *not*, however, of ligneous texture; — they were *herbaceous*, and, like annual plants, perished when their flowering was over. But the woody root and stumps are perennial, and on the return of spring they throw out *new* herbaceous flowering stems, which again die before winter; and this process goes on year after year for an indefinite period. — Now this is an example of an *under-shrub*, which, as is well expressed in a late work, is a plant, "the lower part only of whose stems is woody; but whose upper part, being of an herbaceous nature, dies every year."*

By the term *herb*, Linnæus meant all the part of a vegetable above the root. In *common* language it serves to express all plants, with the exception of trees and shrubs; but it is better, with Linnæus, to consider the whole vegetable world as consisting of the following seven great families:—

1. FUNGI.
2. ALGÆ, including sea-weeds, lichens, &c.
3. MUSCI, mosses.
4. FILICES, ferns.
5. GRAMINA, grasses.
6. PALMÆ, palms.
7. PLANTÆ, all vegetables not comprehended in any of the preceding families.

The first species of trunk we shall attend to is the CAULIS, stem or stalk, which is derived from the Greek καυλος (kaulos), the trunk of a tree, but in Latin it meant the stalk of an herb only. From it our words cauliflower and colewort are derived.

WITH RESPECT TO CONSISTENCE,

Stems may be woody; succulent or fleshy; medullary or empty.

1. CAULIS *ligneus* or *solidus*.

---

* Elements of the Philosophy of Plants, by Decandolle and Sprengel, p. 52.

Trees and shrubs, in general, have a woody or solid texture, as have also the root and bottoms of the stems of under-shrubs; and it often appears partially in herbaceous vegetables. The root, for instance, of the cabbage is woody, the rest herbaceous.

In the great multiplicity of trees which clothe the earth, there is, as might be expected, much variety in the degree of solidity of their texture. Some, from their extreme hardness, are almost useless for economical purposes; such is the *iron-wood* of Jamaica, which resists, and soon blunts, the best instruments; while others are so soft that they serve for corking bottles. The wood of the *alligator apple-tree*, for instance, is so soft, even when dried, that the country people in the island mentioned use it for stopping their jugs and calabashes, and call it universally by the name of cork-wood.* The outer part of the stem, on the other hand, of the prickly-pole palm (Cocos *Guineensis*), resembles whalebone.† Labillardière was much astonished at seeing among the large trees of the island of Cocos a species of areca palm shooting up to the height of eighteen toises, though only three inches in diameter. It was difficult to conceive how a tree, so apparently weak, could withstand the action even of a moderate breeze; but his surprise ceased on finding that, for a time, it

* Brown's Jamaica, p. 256.
† Ibid. p. 343.

resisted the most forcible strokes of the axe; yet the wood was not above four tenths of an inch thick, the centre of the palm being filled with pith.*

The woody stem also varies greatly in size; and the instances of trees attaining, in the lapse of ages, to an enormous magnitude, are frequent on record. Pliny mentions a plane-tree in Lycia which had mouldered into a cave eighty feet in circumference; and Caligula is said to have had a tree of the same kind, in whose hollow fifteen persons could sit at dinner. Without trusting implicitly to these and similar accounts, we have daily examples of trees reaching to a size truly astonishing. I have said that the fig-trees in South America sometimes exceed twenty-two feet in diameter; but this is surpassed by the African Calabash-tree (Adansonia digitata), whose diameter is sometimes more than twenty-five, or even thirty feet. But the celebrated chestnut of Mount Ætna, if the reports concerning it were true, would be the most remarkable and interesting of any tree on record. At an inch above the ground Swinburne found it to measure 196 feet in circumference. It consists of five great divisions, which resemble separate trees; but below the ground they are said to be all united into one great trunk. The inside of these divisions is destitute of bark; an explanation of which has been attempted in various ways. The writer of the article Ætna in the Edinburgh Cyclopedia thinks

* Labillardière's Voyage, vol. i. p. 284.

we may easily arrive at its solution, " if we only consider that in the circular space formed by these large branches, there are erected a hut and oven, for the accommodation of those who collect its fruits; and that its inhabitants, with the most thoughtless ingratitude, sometimes supply themselves with fuel from the tree which protects them."

Examples of the stem of the chestnut, oak, and several other kinds of trees, acquiring a circumference of from twenty to fifty feet, have been so frequently noticed in magazines and various other popular publications, as to render it superfluous to enumerate any farther instances on the present occasion. I cannot, however, pass over the following beautiful lines, which were attached to a great oak forty feet in girth, and supposed to be above one thousand years old : —

Majestic tree! whose wrinkled form hath stood,
Age after age, the patriarch of the wood;
Thou, who hast seen a thousand springs unfold
Their ravelled buds and dip their flowers in gold,
Ten thousand times yon moon relight her horn,
And that bright star of evening gild the morn;
Gigantic oak! thy hoary head sublime
Erewhile must perish in the wreck of Time:
Should round thy head innocuous lightnings shoot,
And no fierce whirlwind shake thy stedfast root;
Yet shalt thou fall! thy leafy tresses fade,
And those bare scattered antlers strew the glade.
Arm after arm shall leave the mouldering bust,
And thy firm fibres crumble into dust;
The Muse alone shall consecrate thy name,
And by her powerful art prolong thy fame;
Green shall thy leaves expand, thy branches play,
And bloom for ever in th' immortal lay.

From these mighty trunks, we have every intermediate size in the *ligneous stem*, down to the diminutive arctic bramble (Rubus *arcticus*), an entire tree of which may be placed in a six ounce phial *; and the still more diminutive dwarf alpine willow (Salix *herbacea*), of which "half a dozen trees, with all their branches, leaves, flowers, and roots, might be compressed between two of the pages of a lady's pocket book without coming into contact with each other." †

Fig. 11.

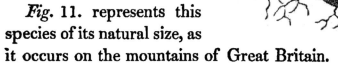

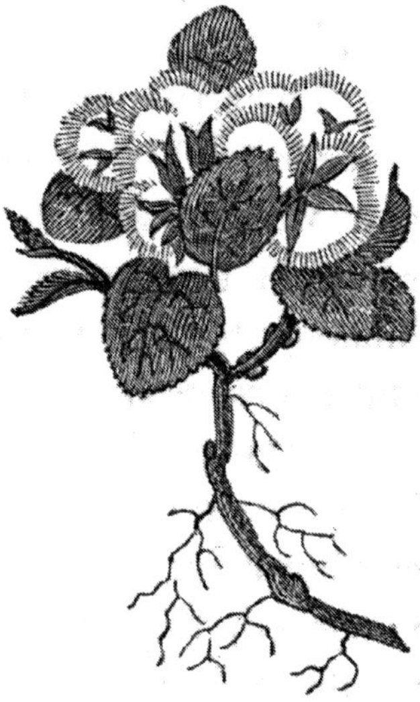

Fig. 11. represents this species of its natural size, as it occurs on the mountains of Great Britain.

2. CAULIS *succulentus*, a *succulent* stem. This belongs to a considerable number of vegetables, as to those of the genera Cactus, Stapelia, Aloe, &c. The term does not mean simply that the stem abounds in juices; it implies, also, that it is of a *fleshy* texture like the eatable part of a pear or apple; and in consequence it is also named CAULIS

* " The plant is so diminutive that an entire tree, with all its branches, leaves, and fruit, was placed within a phial holding about six ounces of alcohol." — *Clarke's Travels*; vol. v. p. 459.

† Clarke's Travels. — The Salix herbacea is the only *tree* in Spitzbergen. — *Arct. Zool.*

carnosus, a fleshy stem.   Some plants of this description, however, become woody by age, of which the *prickly pear* (Cactus *Opuntia*) is an instance. Its joints, which are vulgarly named leaves, are from one to two inches thick, and so juicy and soft, that they are used in Minorca (being first split down the middle) as a cataplasm to boils and abscesses.   Yet by age the plant becomes so hardy and woody, that it will for centuries resist the action of the weather; and Humboldt says, the inhabitants of Cumana prefer it for making oars and door-posts.

A few pages back, some of these succulent plants have been described as growing in the most sterile and burnt-up situations; and it may here be farther remarked, that in tropical climates, the succulent plants perform the same office in the great economy of nature, as the mosses, lichens, and other cryptogamic species, in colder latitudes.   In the latter, the barest rocks become clothed with lichens; these, in decaying, afford footing for mosses; and these, dying in their turn, produce a portion of soil in which more perfect plants can strike root; and thus, by degrees, situations the most barren become clothed with verdure and flowers.   In the sterile and burnt-up wastes of tropical regions, the succulent plants are the only species which at first can exist; but, on decaying, they leave the spot to which they were attached so changed as to form a fertile bed, on which vegetables of a different nature may grow and flourish. These produce a still farther change; and thus trees may at length be produced in places which at first were only barren sands or rocks.*

3. CAULIS *medullosus,* a *medullary,* or pithy stem.

The *medulla,* or *pith,* is that light, spongy, and compressible white substance found in the centre of the rush, the elder, &c. It is found in most plants when young, but in old plants, especially trees, it is often entirely wanting. The term *medullary* can only be applied to those species whose stems *abound* in pith, as the common elder (Sambucus *nigra*), the common rush (Juncus *effusus*), and the round-headed rush (Juncus *conglomeratus*), all which are very familiar and ready examples. The stem of the rush, indeed, does not properly come under the head of *caulis,* as it belongs to that species of stem called the culm, or straw (*culmus*); but this distinction we shall waive for the present.

The elder is indigenous and common. The thick part of the stem is nearly woody throughout, but the branches, especially the younger, abound in pith. From this circumstance it has gotten the

* " In general, it is not by mosses and lichens that vegetation in the countries near the tropics begins. In the Canary Islands, as well as in Guinea, and on the rocky coasts of Peru, the first vegetables that prepare the mould for others, are the succulent plants; the leaves of which, provided with an infinite number of orifices and cutaneous vessels, deprive the ambient air of the water it holds in solution." — *Humboldt's Pers. Nar.* vol. i. p. 259.

D

name of bore-tree; at least if Threlkeld be right; who says it is so called by " the *Northern-men*, because of its large pith, which is easily driven out, and makes it like a bored pipe."

There can scarcely be conceived any thing lighter than the pith of elder, and hence it is used for making the pith-balls of the electrical apparatus: but the wood of this plant is very different.   In the Cocos *Guineensis*, I mentioned that the centre was full of pith, but that the surrounding wood was like whalebone; and it is perhaps a general provision of nature, that such stems as are medullary are protected by a wood particularly strong and elastic.   This certainly is the case with the *elder*, its wood being so tough that it serves for the tops of fishing-rods; butchers prefer it for making skewers, and fishermen for their netting-needles; and it is so compact that it takes a good polish, and is sometimes used as a substitute for box.

The pith of the narrow-leaved cycas (Cycas *revoluta*), of the small date-palm tree (Phœnix *farinifera*), and of some others belonging to the family of *palms*, is of much importance, as it consists of a nutritious fecula of which the sago of commerce is made.   The word sago means *meal*, in the dialect of Amboyna; and of this meal, a single trunk of one species of palm * will sometimes produce six hundred pounds weight.

Minor purposes are occasionally served by the

* Sagus *Rumphii.*

pith of various plants; that, for instance, of the sago-tree is used for corks, and that of the gigantic Furcroea, according to Prince Maximilian, serves as a substitute for the same material to the collector of insects. The late Mr. White, the amiable and able author of the Natural History and Antiquities of Selborne, has thrown much light on an humble, but important branch of rural economy, to which the pith of the common rush is applied. I allude to the formation of rush-lights; with respect to which, I shall state from Mr. White's letter the following calculations: — " A pound of common grease may be procured for fourpence, and about six pounds of grease will dip a pound of rushes; and one pound of rushes may be bought for one shilling: so that a pound of rushes, medicated and ready for use, will cost three shillings." — " A good rush which measured in length two feet four inches and a half, being minuted, burnt only three minutes short of an hour: and a rush still of greater length has been known to burn one hour and a quarter." — " In a pound of dry rushes, avoirdupois, which I caused to be weighed and numbered, we found upwards of one thousand six hundred individuals. Now, suppose each of these to burn, one with another, only half an hour; then a poor man will purchase eight hundred hours of light, a time exceeding thirty-three entire days, for three shillings. According to this account, each rush before dipping costs one thirty-third of a farthing,

and one eleventh afterwards.   Thus a poor family
will enjoy five hours and a half of comfortable light
for a farthing."— " Little farmers use rushes much
in the short days, both morning and evening, in
the dairy and kitchen; but the very poor, who are
always the worst economists, and therefore must
continue very poor, buy an halfpenny candle every
evening, which, in their blowing open rooms, does
not burn much more than two hours.   Thus they
have only two hours light for their money instead
of eleven." *

It must now be observed, that, although no appellation could be more appropriate for such stems
as the above, than that of medullary stem (CAULIS
medullosus), yet the latter is never mentioned in the
description of any plant.   CAULIS *inanis* is the term
used.   Now, the word *inanis* means empty, absolutely void, and it may seem absurd to apply such
an epithet to a stem which, like that of the sago-
tree, contains within it six hundred pounds of
nutritive farina, or even to that of a rush which is
occupied in every part with its spongy pith.   Such,
however, is the case, and *caulis inanis* never means
an *empty*, but always a *pithy* stem.†

When a stem is to be designated that is *truly
empty*, or hollow, the term fistulosus (from *fistula*,
a pipe, *Lat.*), or tubulosus (from *tubus*, a tube, *Lat.*),
is used; and hence,

* Letter 26.
† A pithy stem is sometimes called *caulis farctus*, a
crammed, or stuffed stem (*farctus*, from *farcio*, to stuff).

4. CAULIS *fistulosus*, or C. *tubulosus*, a hollow or tubular stem.

This is not uncommon in herbaceous plants, especially in the *umbelliferæ*, as hemlock, fennel, angelica, &c. which, when full grown, are hollow, through strengthened at regular intervals by transverse partitions. Many of these, though perfectly tubular when old, are substantial and juicy when young; and in some instances it forms a part of the art of the gardener to prevent a change from this solid state taking place. This is familiar to every person with respect to celery, which, when too old or mismanaged, becomes hollow, or, as is commonly expressed, *piped.*

The trumpet-tree (Cecropia *peltata*) of the West Indies, is a remarkable example of this kind of stem. It grows to the height of forty feet, and both trunk and branches are hollow, and have many transverse membranous septa or partitions, to which there are on the surface a corresponding number of rings marking their situation. The branches, when cleared of these partitions, are used as wind instruments, and hence the name "trumpet-tree." These trumpets are often heard many miles off, awaking the echoes among the mountains of Jamaica.*

A STEM MAY BE SIMPLE OR BRANCHED.

5. CAULIS *simplex*, a simple stem, as in *lily*, and *crown imperial.*

* Vide Brown's Jamaica, p. 111.

D 3

6. CAULIS *ramosus*, a branched stem, as in most plants.

7. CAULIS *ramosissimus*, very much branched, as in the *apple*, and many other trees, &c.

8. CAULIS *subramosus*, a slightly branched stem.

WITH RESPECT TO CLOTHING.

9. CAULIS *foliatus*, or *foliosus*, a leafy stem.

Many plants might be enumerated which are destitute of *leaves*, but most of these are clothed, more or less, with spines, &c., and consequently are not strictly naked. The stem of such plants, therefore, would be designated,

10. CAULIS *aphyllus*, a stem without leaves; but in those species which have their surface neither clothed with leaves, spines, scales, nor any other covering, it is a

11. CAULIS *nudus*, or naked stem.

There is a small plant common on most of our muddy sea-shores, and salt marshes, which affords a good example of both these terms. I allude to the Salicornia *herbacea*, which in English is called *jointed glass-wort*, because the soda prepared from its ashes was formerly used in manufacturing glass. It is named also *sea-grass*, *salt-wort*, and *marsh-samphire*. " The English," says Threlkeld, " use the pickled shoots like *sampire*, to stir up an appetite, and call it *marsh-sampire*. I ate some of it so prepared in an Englishman's house in this city, (Dublin,) and who would threap me down that it was *sampire*, and so named in his county of *Lincolnshire*. He had gathered it about the town plentifully, and preserved it."—This plant is scarcely a foot high, of a light green colour, and fleshy consistence, semitransparent, and jointed throughout. Its whole surface is smooth, showing no appearance of down, hair, scales, or other clothing. The stem therefore is a *caulis nudus aphyllus ;* a stem both leafless and naked.* See *Fig.* 19. (*b*)

12. CAULIS *bulbifer*, a bulb-bearing stem, as in some lilies, and other plants, which produce bulbs at the bases of their leaves. *Fig.* 12.

Fig. 12.

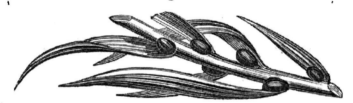

13. CAULIS *perfoliatus*, a *perfoliate* stem, (*per*, through, and *folium*, a leaf, *Lat.*) is when, instead of being clothed by leaves in the ordinary manner, the stem runs through the leaf, as at (*a*), *Fig.* 13.

Of this the common thoroughwax (Bupleurum *rotundifolium*) is a good example. The old English word *waxe* means to grow, and thorough is through; and hence Thoroughwax. " Thorowewaxe, or

* The word *nudus* has not always strictly the meaning given here, being variously modified, as the term is applied to different parts of plants. — *Vide Martyn's Language of Botany, in verbo.*

Thorowe leaf, (says Gerard,) hath a round, slender, and brittle stalke, divided into manie small braunches, which passe or grow thorow the leaves, as though they had been drawn or thrust thorowe, and every braunch doth grow thorowe, everie leafe making them like hollowe cups or sawcers." *

14. CAULIS *alatus*, a *winged* stem, (*ala*, a wing, *Lat.*) is when the angles of the stem expand into laminæ or borders of a leafy texture, as at *Fig.*13.(*b*)

Fig. 13.

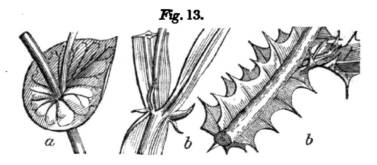

MODE OF GROWTH.

15. CAULIS *erectus*, an *upright* or *erect* stem. This term does not imply that such a stem is in no degree bent from a perpendicular line, for a stem may bend to one or other side and still be erect. But some stems are *perfectly* straight, and therefore an epithet is required to denote this in opposition to erect. The word *strictus* is adopted, and so, by the term

16. CAULIS *strictus*, is meant a stem absolutely *straight*, not pointing towards any point of the compass.

* Herbal, p. 429.

17. CAULIS *ascendens, ascending,* or bent upwards. At first lying on the ground, and then gradually bending upwards till it becomes erect. *Fig.*14. (*a*)

18. CAULIS *procumbens;* (*procumbo,* to lie down, *Lat.*) when the *whole* of the stem lies on the ground. *Prostratus* and *humifusus* are used in the same sense.

19. CAULIS *decumbens, decumbent.* Like the last, except that the *base* is erect. *Fig.* 14. (*b*)

20. CAULIS *reclinatus,* a *reclining* stem. The whole stem bent towards the ground, like an arch. *Fig.* 14. (*c*)

21. CAULIS *nutans, nodding* towards the *horizon* at top. *Fig.* 14. (*d*)

22. CAULIS *cernuus, drooping* towards the *earth* at top. *Fig.* 14. (*e*)

Fig. 14.

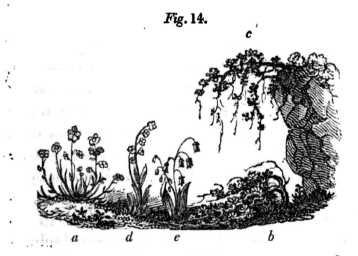

23. CAULIS *fulcratus* (*fulcrum,* a prop, from *fulcio,* to support), a supported or propped stem. When trees acquire an unusual size, they generally

become favourites with mankind. A tree especially, which from time immemorial has stood in the centre. of a village, and has been the place of evening resort for the young to frolic, and the aged to debate; is held in the light of an old friend; and when at last it is overturned by the storm, or has mouldered to a shell by the hand of time, the event is considered as a public calamity. Even the Turks are alive to, this feeling, and enjoy their coffee and tchibouque * with peculiar satisfaction under the shade of a favourite treee. The great Oriental Plane of the. island Stanchio (formerly Cos, the birth-place of Hippocrates), in the Archipelago, is remarkable for its size, and the care with which the natives have attempted to preserve it. It has stood for time immemorial in the chief town (called Stanchio also) of the island, and while it is the boast of the inhabitants, is with justice also the wonder of strangers. Earl Sandwich saw it in the year 1739, he calls it a sycamore. " Among the curiosities," he says, " of this city, is a sycamore tree, which is without doubt the largest in the known world. It extends its branches, which are supported by many ancient pillars of porphyry, verd antique, and other precious marble, in the exact form of a circle; from the outward verge of which to the trunk I measured forty-five large paces. Beneath the shade of this sycamore is a very beautiful fountain, round which the Turks have erected several

* The Turkish tobacco-pipe.

chiosks or summer-houses; where they retire in the heat of the summer, and regale themselves with their afternoon coffee and pipe of tobacco."*

Clarke saw this tree a few years ago, and although time has committed considerable ravages on it, still, as he informs us, " enough is remaining to astonish all beholders." One enormous branch, notwithstanding its being supported by pillars of granite, gave way, and this loss has considerably diminished its bulk. This author describes the branches which remain, as extending horizontally to a surprising distance, supported by granite, and marble pillars. " Some notion," he says, " may be formed of the time those props have been so employed, by the appearance of the bark; this has encased the extremities of the columns so completely, that the branches and the pillars mutually support each other; and it is probable, if those branches were raised, some of them would lift the pillars from the earth."†

Now, in some instances, Nature herself forms *props* for supporting the branches. We have an instance of this in the *black mangrove* (RHIZOPHORA *Mangle*), which grows on the shores of the West Indian islands, in places having a muddy, or soft bottom. The larger branches of the tree send out, in many places, soft lax threads, or strings, which grow rapidly, and hanging down, soon reach the

* Earl Sandwich's Voyage round the Mediterranean, p.338.
† Clarke's Travels, vol. ii. p. 198.

mud, where they immediately divide or split into roots; and when these acquire sufficient strength, they nourish the shoots or strings, which constantly acquiring by this means size and firmness, at last form trunks that prop and support the branches, from which they originally protruded. The numerous props make the groves of this tree very entangled, and by detaining the mud and other substances brought down by floods, they in time cause the land to gain upon the sea.[*]

But the most remarkable example of this kind of stem, is that of the celebrated *Banyan-tree* of India. It is named also the Arched Indian Fig-tree, or the Indian God-tree, and is the Ficus *Indica* of botanists. This famous tree increases exactly like the *mangrove*, but does not, like it, delight in sea or brackish water. Fibres are thrown out from its branches, which descend, take root, and in time are converted into great trunks, like trees, and in this manner it sometimes occupies a large extent of ground. Forbes describes and figures a Banyan-tree growing on the banks of the Nerbudda, in Hindoostan, which, in memory of a favourite saint, is named Cubbeer-burr. Although a considerable part of it has been swept off by high floods, yet it still, measuring round the chief stems, occupies a space of about two thousand feet in circumference, though the branches which have not yet sent down roots spread much farther. " The *large* trunks

---

[*] Brown's Jamaica, p. 211.

of this single tree amount to three hundred and fifty, and the smaller ones exceed three thousand: each of these is constantly sending forth branches and hanging roots, to form other trunks, and become the parents of a future progeny."[*]

This tree has given shelter to an army of seven thousand men. The Hindoos almost worship the Banyan; they plant it near their temples, and where no temple is erected, the tree itself serves the purpose: they place an image of their god against its trunk, and there perform their devotions.

Milton gives a beautiful description of the Banyan in the ninth book of the Paradise Lost. He introduces it as that tree to which Adam and Eve retired, to form for themselves garments, after having eaten the fatal fruit; the leaves, however, are certainly *not* " broad as Amazonian targe."

> So counsell'd he, and both together went
> Into the thickest wood; there soon they chose
> The fig-tree, not that kind for fruit renown'd,
> But such as at this day to Indians known
> In Malabar or Decan, spreads her arms,
> Branching so broad and long, that in the ground
> The bended twigs take root, and daughters grow
> About the mother tree, a pillar'd shade
> High over-arch'd, and echoing walks between:
> There oft the Indian herdsman, shunning heat,
> Shelters in cool, and tends his pasturing herds
> At loop-holes cut through thickest shade: those leaves
> They gathered, broad as Amazonian targe,
> And with what skill they had, together sew'd.

When the fulcra of the Banyan hang from the

* Forbes's Oriental Memoirs, vol. i. p. 26.

branches, and before they have taken hold of the earth, they are quite flexible, and wave backwards and forwards with the wind.*

It appears that other species of Fig-tree have a similar property of producing secondary stems. Labillardière saw a number of different species in the island Cocos, from the high branches of which many strings depended, in order to become fixed in the soil, and give origin to so many different trunks.

24. CAULIS *radicans*, a *rooting* stem.

Much confusion prevails in the definition of this stem.   It is, according to Willdenow, " when the stem *stands upright*, and climbs every where, sending forth small roots by which it holds itself fast, as in the ivy."†   Sir James E. Smith defines it, " clinging to any other body for support, by means of fibres which *do not imbibe nourishment ;*"‡ and

* Cordiner's Ceylon, vol. i. p. 363.
† Principles of Botany, p. 19.
‡ Introduction to Botany, p. 91.

Professor Martyn's definition is, " *bending to the earth* and striking root, but not creeping along."*

The first and last of these definitions are in direct contradiction to each other, one affirming the stem to be *upright*, the other, that it *bends to earth ;* and an essential part of the intermediate definition is, that the attaching fibres *do not imbibe nourishment ;* a thing quite beyond the power of the young student to ascertain. I think, indeed, it may be much questioned whether the *ivy*, which is given by the learned writer as an example of the *rooting stem*, do, or do not receive some nourishment by these connecting fibres. " Ivy," says the celebrated author of the Vulgar Errors, " *divided from the root*, we have observed to *live some years* by the *cirrous* parts, commonly conceived but as tenacles and holdfasts unto it."†

But, if we admit that these are holdfasts merely, and that they serve only to attach the ivy to foreign bodies, then we admit that they perform exactly the office of tendrils ; and is it not therefore an inaccuracy to bestow on them an appellation which can with consistency appertain only to roots? Were the term *clasping* used for stems whose roots are fixed in the earth, but which also adhere in the manner of ivy to trees, rocks, &c. perhaps all ambiguity would be removed. For the application of the word in this sense we have classical,

* Language of Botany, art. " *Rooting*."
† Brown's Cyrus's Garden, p. 58.

at least, if not scientific authority. In the ninth
book of Milton's sublime poem, part of an address
from Eve to Adam is to this effect: —

> Let us divide our labours, thou where choice
> Leads thee, or where most needs, whether to wind
> The woodbine round this arbour, or direct
> The *clasping ivy* where to climb, while I
> In yonder spring of roses intermix'd
> With myrtle, find what to redress till noon.

Following this idea, therefore, we have next,

25. CAULIS *amplectens*, a *clasping*, or embracing
stem (*amplector*, to embrace, *Lat.*).

Whether the fibres or tendrils of the stem and
branches of *ivy* serve in any degree for its support,
or not, one thing is very certain, that when it grows
upon level ground it never produces the fructification, nor do its leaves undergo those changes in
form which we shall attend to in another place.
When it has a firm upright body as a tree, wall,
or rock, to ascend, it grows with great luxuriance,
and sometimes acquires a very considerable thick-
ness*; but I have never seen it thicker than a twig
when growing without support.

> For when the oak denies her stay,
> The creeping ivy winds her humble way;
> No more she twists her branches round,
> But drags her feeble stem along the barren ground.†

---

* Malkin says of the castle at the village of St. Athans,
Glamorganshire, that "the trunk of the ivy that encompasses
the northern part of this castle, is of an uncommon substance.
It at least girts *five feet*, and in some years yields large quantities of gum."— *Malkin's South Wales*, p. 130.

† Lloyd's Ode to Genius.

With respect to the *rooting* stem, we have an excellent example of it, illustrative of Martyn's definition, in the tree houseleek (Sempervivum *arboreum*), which grows on rocks on the sea-shore of the Mediterranean, the branches or minor stems of which, after leaving the parent stock, make an abrupt bend downwards, throw out from the bent part a number of real radicles, and then become erect.

In Lewis and Clarke's voyage up the Missouri, there is, also, an excellent example mentioned respecting a dwarf cedar, about three or four feet high, which spreads its limbs along the ground so as almost to conceal the latter, and from the under side of these limbs, roots, every here and there, shot into the earth, while the upper side was clothed with evergreen foliage and shoots.*

26. CAULIS *scandens*, a *climbing* stem. (*Scando*, to climb, *Lat.*) A stem which ascends other plants,

* Pages 135 and 156.

&c. by means of tendrils.   Observe a *pea* climbing
up its rod, or a *passion-flower*, or a *vine*, and you
will perceive that these vegetables are supported by
a number of spiral threads which they protrude in
various directions, and entwine round such bodies
as they can approach.   These threads are named
cirri, tendrils or claspers, and will be attended to
hereafter.

27. CAULIS *volubilis*, a *twining* stem.

Observe a *hop* ascending its pole, and you may
remark that it is not supported on the latter either
by fibres like the *ivy*, or tendrils like the *vine*; but
simply by its own convolutions.   It adheres as a
snake would, by its folds.

While examining the *hop*, turn your face to the
south; the east will then, of course, be on your
left hand, and the west upon your right; and you
know that the apparent motion of the sun is from
east to west.   Now you will perceive that the hop
twines round the pole invariably from your left
hand towards your right; that is, from east to west,
or *with* the motion of the sun.

Examine next a convolvulus, or a kidney-bean,
and you will find that *their* stems as invariably turn
from the west by the south towards the east; that
is, from your right hand to your left, or *against*
the motion of the sun.*

* See Martyn's Language of Botany, art. *twining stem*;
but there is a mistake in the examples there cited, those being
represented as twining against the sun, which twine with it,
and *vice versâ*.

It may seem strange, but nothing is more true, than that twining stems are governed in their direction by constant laws. No such stem twines indifferently from right to left, or from left to right; but each species has its own natural and irresistible. tendency; and when it is by force diverted from, that, it becomes sickly, and at length perishes.

Sinistrorsum (of which this is the sign ☽) means from left to right; and

Dextrorsum (☽), from right to left.

Hence, CAULIS *volubilis sinistrorsum* (or CAULIS *volubilis* ☽) means a stem twining from left to right, or *with* the sun; and CAULIS *volubilis dextrorsum* (*c. v.* ☽), a stem twining from right to left, or *against* the sun.

Though in these islands we have many scandent and twining plants, yet we must turn our view to tropical countries, before we shall be fully able to comprehend their importance. Here, we seldom find them reaching higher than the top of a hedge; but in tropical regions they mount to the summits of the highest trees, and sometimes, by their weight, when a tree is standing alone, bring it to the earth. The climbing and voluble plants of Jamaica, especially the *convolvuli*, abound so much in reclaimed lands that have been suffered to run wild again, that it is necessary to cut one's way through them with a bill-hook.* In forests they

* Vide Sloane's Jamaica. A similar impediment occurs in. many other countries; *e.g.* — " It was difficult to get far into the Java forests, from the quantity of underwood, and the

serve to bind the trees together, and this may perhaps on many occasions prevent the latter being upset in storms. Bartram describes the Grape vines, the twining Zizyphus (Rhamnus *volubilis*), the ash-leaved trumpet-flower (Bignonia *radicans*), the cross-bearing trumpet-flower (Bignonia *crucigera*), and other climbing vegetables, as tying together the trees in the forests of Carolina and Georgia, with garlands and festoons, which form enchanting shades.* This author observes of the *grape vines*, that, " from their bulk and strength, one would imagine they are combined to pull down those mighty trees to the earth, when in fact, amongst other good purposes, they serve to uphold them. They are frequently nine, ten, and twelve inches in diameter, and twine round the trunks of the trees, climb to their very tops, and then spread along their limbs from tree to tree throughout the forest."

In some of the woods and swamps of America, the *laurel-leaved smilax* (Smilax *laurifolia*) forms a most troublesome obstacle to persons passing. It runs, by means of its *cirri*, up trees and bushes, and extends from one to another so as to bar all

---

vast number of creeping plants, which form a sort of net supported by other trees, and are impassable without an instrument to cut them. Some of them were likewise of great strength. One trailed along the ground, in the manner of some of the convolvulus kind, with a stalk about an inch in diameter throughout, and of a length exceeding a hundred feet."— *Staunton's Embassy*, vol. i. p. 301.

* Travels, p. 85.

passage, or else obliges the traveller to creep through
the interstices left near the ground, where he runs
a great chance of being bitten by serpents. It
oftens occasions the deepest shade in the woods.[*]

The *nebees*, or ligneous ropes, which Stedman
describes as being numerous in the forests of
Surinam, are very singular productions, and seem
to be the stems of some voluble plant, most probably a calamus. They not only twine around the
trees to their tops, but when arrived there, hang
down till they reach the earth, then strike root and
again climb the neighbouring trunks, and thus
spread from tree to tree, to a great extent. Sometimes they twine around each other, forming ropes
as thick as a ship's cable, which they perfectly
resemble, being at least as tough, and not presenting any appearance of foliage. When they ascend
trees in this state, the latter are often killed by their
weight and compression. The smaller *nebees* are
sometimes so interwoven and crossed, that they
resemble fishing-nets. The larger are like ropes,
of various dimensions, and make the forest, according to Stedman's comparison, look like a " fleet at
anchor." The same writer mentions that these
nebees are exceedingly tough, and may be used for
" mooring large vessels to the shore."[†] They seem,
indeed, to be in all respects similar to the *Bejucos*
of South America, which are used for lashing and
tying various kinds of merchandise, and for making

[*] Kalm's Travels, vol. ii. p. 41.
[†] Stedman's Surinam, vol. i. p. 241.

cables or hawsers for the *balzas* or small vessels of that country.*

The climbing and voluble plants often ornament, in the highest degree, the trees and shrubs around which they wind. Such are the *quadrangular passion flower* (Passiflora *quadrangularis*), whose magnificent corols hang in festoons on the trees of the Mauritius, and the *wild squash* (Cucurbita *peregrina*), whose yellow fruit, like an orange, depends from the extreme branches of the highest trees of the new continent.

The Botanist is sometimes much tantalised by these plants, especially in tropical woods and forests. He sees their blossoms, but they are far beyond his reach; and when several different species occupy the trees, he cannot determine to which the various flowers he sees belong, nor can he discriminate perhaps between them and those of the tree which supports them. Attempting to level the trees is of no use; for so securely are they tied to each other by these stems, that though a dozen were severed, not one would fall.†

28. CAULIS *sarmentosus*, a sarmentose stem.

Sarmentum means, in its original sense, the twig or spray of a vine, and is derived from *sarpo*, to

---

* Vide Ulloa's Voyage, vol. i. p. 210.

† " On the 17th we spent the forenoon in cutting down a number of very tall trees, of which we wished to gather the flowers, but all our efforts were in vain. We had no sooner cut a tree, than it hung in a thousand bindweeds and climbers from top to bottom, from which it was not in our power to disengage it." — *Forster's Cook's Voyages*, vol. i. p. 506. (New Zealand.)

prune; which latter, again, is from the Greek αϱπη (arpe), a pruning-knife. In Botany, sarmentum means what in English is called a *runner*, or a *wire*. It will be best illustrated by a figure. Let (*a*) therefore, *Fig.* 17., be a strawberry-plant; (*b*) is

Fig. 17.

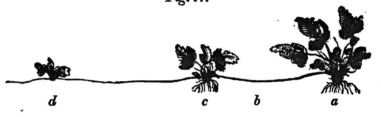

d   c   b   a

a cord-like production shooting from it, and running along upon the ground. After proceeding a considerable way, perhaps two feet or more, it protrudes a knot of leaves as at (*c*), and soon afterwards from the under side of this knot there shoots out a number of roots, and these striking into the earth nourish the knot, which, now having a root of its own, becomes an independent plant, and has no longer occasion for the runner (*b*); the latter then perishes, and thus (*a*) and (*c*) become separate plants, totally unconnected with each other. New runners proceed from (*c*), which produce other new plants, as at (*d*), and thus the species is extended far and wide.

29. CAULIS *stoloniferus.*

Stolo, means a sucker, or scion, and it differs from the runner in being leafy, which the other is not. Example: *sweet violet, common bugle.*

30. CAULIS *flagelliformis,* a *flagelliform,* or whip-like stem (*flagellum,* a whip, and *forma,* likeness). Long, pliant, and little branched, as in *periwinkle.*

31. Caulis *flexuosus, zig-zag.* As in rough bind-weed.

32. Caulis *teres,* a *round* stem; see *Fig.* 18.(*a*)

33. Caulis *semiteres, half-round,* semicylindric; *Fig.* 18. (*b*)

34. Caulis *compressus,* with the sides flattened; *Fig.* 18. (*c*)

35. Caulis *anceps, two-edged,* the sides flattened, and the edges sharp; *Fig.* 18. (*d*)

36. Caulis *trigonus,* or *triangularis,* three flat sides, with the corners or angles *rounded; Fig.* 18.(*e*) *tetragonus,* four cornered, *pentagonus,* five cornered, &c.

37. Caulis *triqueter, triquetrous,* three flat sides, with the angles *sharp; Fig.* 18. (*f*)

38. Caulis *angulatus,* or *angulosus,* an *angular* stem. When there are several angles, and the sides grooved, generally used when there are more than six angles, or when the number is variable or un-certain; *Fig.* 18. (*g*)

Fig. 18.

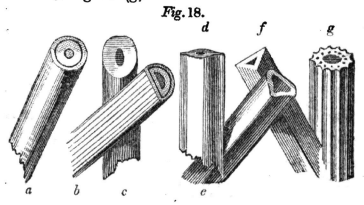

THE CULM (CULMUS).

The word Culmus literally means the straw of corn: but in Botany it is applied, not to the stem of the grasses alone, but also to that of some plants which resemble them; as the rush, bulrush, bogrush, cotton-grass, &c.

The *culm* is in general knotted (*nodosus*), but often without joints (*enodis*). Smith says justly, that it "is more easily understood than defined." It might be supposed unlikely, that this stem could under any circumstances be contemplated as a very beautiful object, yet nothing is more certain than that, in some parts of the world, the arborescent gramina constitute the most striking and beautiful ornaments of the landscape. They are sometimes above forty feet high, as in some of the bamboos; and by their airy lightness, their graceful bend, and the quivering motion into which they are thrown by the slightest breeze, they become objects of high interest, and beauty.

The Bamboo, though not very useful as an article of food, except, indeed, that its roots and young shoots are made into a pickle, is one of the most important plants of India. It serves not only for the entire construction of houses, but for furnishing them with almost every necessary utensil. In China, and many parts of the East, their tables, chairs, bedsteads, bedding, and almost every household moveable are made from it. It forms barrows, ladders, fences, and other implements of agricul-

E

ture. Sacking is made from it to hold grain. It is manufactured into cordage for rigging, and cables for mooring ships; its fibres are made into oakum for calking, and even the wicks of candles are composed of them.* In Malabar, the larger *bamboos* are trained over iron arches, and when they have assumed the curved form, are used for supporting the canopies of palanquins. Some of these bamboos, of large dimensions, and lofty arch, are valued at five or six hundred rupees.† In China, it is also manufactured into paper; and in that country it is, according to Barrow, "the instrument in the hand of power, that keeps the whole empire in awe." Thousands of bamboos are there constantly employed in the act of flagellation.

The cane-reed, which is imported into these islands from the Continent, especially from Spain, is the Arundo *Donax* of Linnæus. It is chiefly used for making weavers' reeds, and by boys, for fishing-rods. It grows luxuriantly, requiring little care in Europe; and in America it often covers whole tracts of country, forming what are called *Cane-brakes*, or meadows. In these the canes, which are as thick as walking-sticks, and ten or twelve feet high, grow so close that it is impossible to penetrate them, unless a road have been previously cut through. Some of these *cane-brakes*

* Barrow's Travels in China.
† Forbes's Oriental Memoirs.

are described as being of such great extent, that, like the ocean, they present to the eye no termin-ation, but melt insensibly into the horizon.*

The Arundo *Phragmites*, or common reed, is frequent in this country, growing in marshes and ditches, especially near the sea. It is the largest of the British gramineous plants, and rises to a height of more than seven feet. The *culm* is jointed, simple, round, and leafy; it is annual, but the roots are perennial. The species, though generally disregarded, is in some parts of consider-able value. It is much superior to common straw for thatching; and in several of the fenny counties in England, not only cottages, but houses of a better description, are covered with it. In the fenny parts of Lincolnshire it forms a valuable harvest. Pennant says, he saw a stock of reeds, the property of a single farmer, which, when harvested and stacked, was worth two or three hundred pounds. This harvest is, however, much injured by the stares, which alight upon the reeds in myriads, and break them down by their weight: hence the owners of the fens spare no pains in destroying those birds.†

The root of the Arundo *Phragmites* is repent, and hence the plant thrives best in muddy or slimy bottoms, through which the roots can work with ease. The reed may thus serve as an indication

* Bartram.
† Tour in Scotland, vol. i. p. 12.

of the state of healthiness of the soil; for where it abounds, agues and other febrile affections often prevail. Not that there is any thing deleterious in the plant itself; but the soil which is natural to it generates noxious effluvia, and hence travellers, especially in hot countries, should avoid those places in which this reed abounds.*

The different species of reed have tended much to the civilisation of the human race. In the very earliest stages of society, indeed, they furnish only implements of war or hunting; for of all substances the reed forms the lightest and best arrow. In a more advanced state of civilisation, the *reed*, in form of the Pan's-pipe, utters the first tones of instrumental music, and the signs of the metamorphosed Syrinx are breathed with equal feeling in the wild haunts of the Indian, as in the cultivated vales of Europe. But the reed presents itself as an object of peculiar veneration, when we reflect that it formed the earliest instrument, by which human ideas and all the charms of literature and science were communicated, and which has handed down to us the light of religion and the glow of genius from the remotest ages. The reed, even at the present day, forms the only pen used throughout the East.

The *epidermis* or external coat of the reeds, grasses, and most plants which have a culm, contains a large portion of siliceous earth; and hence

---

* Vide Clarke's Travels, vol. ii. p. 378.

it has been thought, I know not how truly, that they are more easily ignited by friction. Agreeable to this theory is the following beautiful description of an eastern conflagration: —

> So when the storms through Indian forests rave,
> And bend the pliant canes in curling wave,
> Grind their siliceous joints with ceaseless ire,
> Till bright emerge the ruby seeds of fire,
> A brazen light bedims the burning sky,
> And shuts each shrinking star's refulgent eye;
> The forest roars, where crimson surges play,
> And flash through lurid night infernal day;
> Floats far and loud the hoarse discordant yell
> Of ravening pards, which harmless crowd the dell,
> While boa-snakes to wet savannahs trail
> Awkward a lingering lazy length of tail;
> The barbarous tiger whets his fangs no more,
> To lap with torturing pause his victim's gore;
> Curb'd of their rage, hyenas gaunt are tame,
> And shrink, begirt with all-devouring flame.*

The culm is sometimes filled with pith, as in the rush; sometimes spongy, as in the bulrush; but generally hollow, as in most grasses. Its shape varies, but is mostly round, and often *triquetrous*. It is in general jointed, but it may be jointed in various ways, and it is necessary to have specific appellations by which such variations may be discriminated. There are three terms used in Botany for expressing the jointed structure, namely, *articulatus*, *nodosus*, and *geniculatus*.

If you find a plant, the culm or the stem of which is marked by a number of transverse parti-

---

* Leyden's Scenes of Infancy.

E 3

tions, as at (*a*) *Fig.* 19., or consisting of a number
of joints, as at (*b*), you would express it by the
word *articulatus*, which simply means jointed, and

Fig. 19.

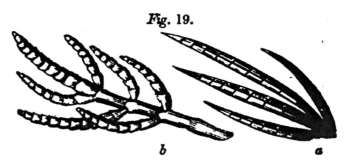

b   a

no more.   But examine a culm of wheat, or oats,
or of any of the common grasses, and you will
perceive, not only that it is jointed, but that
each joint is swelled out into a knot, thus:
nodus means a knot, and *nodosus* knotted;
and hence a culm of this description is
termed CULMUS *nodosus*, a knotted culm.
But though this is so very common, yet
some culms are remarkable for their smoothness,
and uninterrupted surface; as in the *scirpus* genus;
and hence came the old proverb applied to persons
unreasonably scrupulus, *Nodum in scirpo quæris*,
You seek a knot in a bulrush.

   The *knot* is to be considered a very important,
and by no means an accidental production: it is
designed by nature to give strength to the culm;
and hence, if we attempt to break a knotted stem,
it will be found to give way any where but at the
knot.

We have yet to attend to the meaning of *geniculatus*. There is a species of grass which is very common in moist meadows; in places overflowed in winter; and in shallow ponds, and ditches; which is named the *floating foxtail-grass* (Alopecurus *geniculatus*). If you examine the knots, you will find that, instead of being equally prominent all round, one side projects, so that the knot is bent into an angle.

Now, *genu* means the knee, and from it *geniculatus* is derived; which therefore means not only jointed, but also, that the joints are bent like a person's knee. The culm of the floating foxtail-grass is therefore correctly defined, not *articulatus*, nor *nodosus*, but *geniculatus;* which at once expresses that it is a knotted culm, and that at each knot it is bent into an angle.

The only farther observation I have to make, respecting the culm, is, that the knots are often coloured differently from the rest of the stem; and that the space between knot and knot is called the *internode* (internodium).

The next species of stem we shall attend to is

THE STIPES, OR STIPE,

which is derived from the Greek στυπος (stupos), a stake. It is proper to Palms, Ferns, and Fungi, and

is applied also to the little pillar which  *c*
supports the down of some seeds. Thus in
the seed of the *dandelion*, the column (*a*)   *a*
standing on the seed (*b*), and elevating
the star of down (*c*), is the stipe.   *b*

In Fungi it is easily un-
derstood. There is the
cap of a mushroom (*d*),
d and the stem on which it
stands is named the *stipe*.

Before noticing the stipe in Palms and Ferns,
it may be proper to explain the meaning of the
term *frond*. The word FRONS originally meant a
branch covered with leaves, or a leavy bough; but
its application in Botany is more limited. Examine
a Fern, and you will observe that the green parts,
which would *commonly* be considered as distinct
leaves, are expansions of the stem or stipe; that
there is no line of separation between them; and
that the stem, leaf, and generally the fructification,
are as one body. Like a garment without a seam,
they are all in one piece. In the *frond*, according to Sir James E. Smith, "the stem, leaf, and
fructification are united; or, *in other words*, the
flowers and fruit are produced from the leaf itself,
as in the Fern tribe."* Now, I would with all

* Introduction, p. 102.

due deference suggest the possibility of this passage leading the young botanist to pronounce the *butcher's broom*, and some other plants which bear their flowers and fruit on the leaves, to be fronds; and besides, some of the ferns bear their fructifications in *spikes distinct from the leaf*, as in the genera of *Osmunda*, and *Ophioglossum*. In the English Botany, this excellent author says, "The Linnæan term *frons* cannot *without violence* be used in the genus of Ophioglossum, as there is no necessary connection between the leaf and fructification; one species, if not more, having them on distinct stalks." I believe, however, that Linnæus never contemplated this circumstance as *essential* to the constitution of a frond. He confined the term to palms and ferns, and he illustrates his definition in the Philosophia Botanica, by a figure of a palm leaf, though no one knew better than he, that in the palms the *leaf does not bear the fructification*. In the definition alluded to, he says that the frond *frequently* bears the fructification, not that it *necessarily* does so.*

The *Stipe*, then, is the base or footstalk of the frond; and though it may in many ferns be considered as a true stem, yet in the *palms* it is only secondary, and the lofty stem which bears the frondose top of these majestic vegetables to the clouds, is nothing more than a congeries of the bases of former fronds, and of those which are con-

* Vide Philosophia Botanica, p. 42.

E 5

stantly pushing out from the summit; so that, not-withstanding their great height, and their appel-lation of Palm-*trees*, they are very different in struc-ture, and mode of growth, from trees, properly so called.   An idea of their manner of growth may be acquired from an examination of the white or orange lily, whose stems, "though of only annual duration, are formed nearly on the same principle as that of a Palm, and are really congeries of leaves rising one above another, and united by their bases into an *apparent stem*." *

The *stipe*, in most ferns, is covered with chaffy scales, and in many palms it is thorny.

SCAPUS; THE SCAPE, OR FLOWER-STEM.

Scapus means the upright stem of an herb, or the shaft of a pillar, and in Botany is used for that sort of stem which rises directly from the root, and elevates the flowers, but not the leaves. You would not, therefore, call the footstalk of a rose a scape, because the stem of the rose-tree is covered with *leaves*, as well as flowers; and the latter do not rise directly from the root.   But you would apply the term immediately to the stalk of the cowslip, because it does rise directly from the root, and bears the flower, but not a single leaf.   The hya-cinth, the lily of the valley, the snowdrop, the daffodil, the daisy, the primrose, and many other

* Smith's Introduction to Botany, p. 46.

common plants, present examples of the *scape;* and when, as in the cowslip, it divides into branchlets which support a number of flowers, these branchlets or divisions are named pedicels, or pedicles (*pedicelli*).

The *scape* is scaly in coltsfoot; spiral in cyclamen; semicylindric in lily of the valley; two-edged (*anceps*) in snowdrop; and triquetrous in Allium *triquetrum*, triangular-stalked garlic. Sometimes it has a very majestic appearance, tapering, as in the *white Strelitzia* (Strelitzia *alba*) to a height of thirty feet without a leaf; and the *great American Aloe* (Agave *Americana*), which sends up a flower-stem sometimes even forty feet high, and loaded with many thousands of flowers.

A previous knowledge of the *culm* will prevent our confounding it with the scape, which in some cases might otherwise be done; for some culms, that, for example, of the *marsh club-rush* (Scirpus *palustris*), agree perfectly with the scape in rising directly from the root; and in bearing the fruit and flowers, but not the leaves. I may mention also, that in some species, as the crocus, the meadow-saffron, &c. the part on which the flower stands is not a real scape. It is the tube of the flower which is continued down under ground; in which situation the seed is perfected.

We have now considered the *stalk*, the *culm*, the *stipe*, the *frond*, and the *scape*. The petiole or leaf-stalk, and the peduncle or flower-stalk, are yet to be described; but I have already said that these are only *parts* of the stem. I shall attend to the former when commencing the subject of leaves, and to the latter when we enter on that of flowers.

CHAPTER III.

OF THE SURFACE.

THE surface of plants is composed of a thin membrane named the Epidermis, or cuticle. The same terms are applied to the outer layer of the skin of animals, and, I doubt not, that, by taking a slight view of the latter, the nature of the former will be more clearly understood. After a blistering-plaster has been applied to the skin, a pellicle is raised from its surface, containing a limpid fluid. In other words, the skin is blistered; and the thin pellicle, which we cut to let the water flow out, is the *epidermis* or *cuticle*. To whatever part of the skin the vesicatory may be applied, a similar pellicle will rise, because the cuticle covers the whole body. It is elastic, generally transparent, insensible, and when destroyed is speedily regenerated: hence, a blistered surface becomes covered with new cuticle in a few days. In all animals it is composed of a substance whose chemical and other properties are the same as horn. It is, indeed, a modification of horn; and this material affords a remarkable example of the resources and variety of nature. *Horn* envelops the skin in form of this transparent delicate veil; it composes the shelly covering of the tortoise, the mail of the crocodile, the armour of

the porcupine, and the glassy vesture of the serpent. Modified into hair, wool, feathers, and
scales, it forms the external covering of most animals; it composes the hoof of the ox, and the
plumage of birds : the same substance which forms
the claws of the lion, beams on the neck of the
dove, and is fashioned into one of the loveliest
ornaments, the tresses of the human head.

As the cuticle in all animals is composed of the
same substance or material, it is perhaps natural
to conclude that the substance, whatever it may
be, which forms the cuticle or epidermis of any
one plant, forms that of all other plants, however
dissimilar their surface may appear. Fourcroy
supposed the epidermis of all trees to be formed
of a substance the same as cork; but the experiments which led to that conclusion have not been
related. Leaving this matter, therefore, in doubt,
we shall attend to other particulars.

The thickness of the epidermis in plants varies
considerably. On the stem and branches it is
tough, and often thick, leathery, and opaque; but
on the leaves, flowers, and fruit, it is generally
delicate and transparent. The same variety occurs
in the animal epidermis : on the lip, for instance,
it is extremely fine; on the heel, thick and horny.

In man, and many animals, it is insensibly renewed, the old cuticle falling off in bran-like or
mealy scales; in some constantly, in others only
when moulting. A similar process takes place in

many plants, but that the detached pieces are larger. Examine a full grown currant-bush, and you will almost constantly find on its stem and branches flakes of old cuticle peeling off from new cuticle underneath.

Serpents and lizards are said to change their *skins* annually, or oftener; but the cuticle only is changed; it is pushed off from the skin by a new one, splits at the head, and the animal escapes by its own exertions. But as plants have no locomotion, it may happen that a stem will be enwrapped by several cuticles at the same time; and of this the birch is a striking and familiar example. It is possible also that an inability to get rid of the old cuticle may in some instances prove injurious to the whole plant, and perhaps this is the case with the *cork-tree* (Quercus *Suber*). The cuticle, or at least the surface of the cuticle, of that species of *oak*, is thick and fungous, and of it the corks in common use are made. When the tree is left to nature, it seldom lives longer than fifty or sixty years; but when the cuticle is stripped off every eighth or tenth year, it will live above a century and a half.

If the cuticle be removed from a permanent part of a tree or shrub, as the stem or branches, a new cuticle will form in its place; but if from a leaf, flower, fruit, or any other part not permanent, or from any part of an herbaceous plant, no reproduction follows.

In the fir, and some other trees, the surface is every where cracked and scaly; and it is supposed that in this instance there is no real cuticle, but that its place is supplied by flakes of dead bark. This opinion, however, I should think very questionable, and would be inclined to consider this state of the surface as a modification of the epidermis analogous to the scaly appearance often assumed by the cuticle of animals, such as we observe on the tail of the rat and beaver.

In plants, as in animals, the cuticle is often naked: but it often also is variously clothed; being in some hairy, in others woolly, in others warty, and so on. We may now attend to these varieties of the *surface*.

Nitidus, polished and shining, as if varnished; as in *holly*, *laurel*, and *box*.

Glaber, smooth or bald.

Lævis or *levis*, smooth or even.

A surface clothed with any kind of hair, bristles, or down, or rendered uneven by furrows, lines, or risings, cannot, with strict propriety, be called smooth. A freedom from *covering*, however, and a freedom from *inequalities*, constitute different species of smoothness, which the present terms express. *Glaber* means free from any sort of covering; *lævis*, from inequalities: hence CAULIS *glaber*, means a stem free from hairs, bristles, &c.; CAULIS *lævis*, a stem free from furrows, channels, or risings of any description.

Scaber, rough.

Asper, rugged.

These terms are not exactly synonymous. The former means roughened by obscure raised clots, like shagreen; the second, a greater degree of roughness or asperity, from the dots being larger and stiffer. The one might be compared to the roughness of sandstone, the other to that of granite.

Verrucosus, warty (*verruca,* a wart, *Lat.*).

Papillosus, or *Papulosus,* papillose or pimply (*papilla,* a nipple,—*papula,* a pimple, *Lat.*).

Covered with wart-like protuberances, as in the *warted spindle-tree* (Enonymus *verrucosus*), or soft bladdery prominences, as in the *ice-plant* (Mesembryanthemum *crystallinum.*)

Striatus, striated (*stria,* a groove, *Lat.*).

Sulcatus, furrowed, or sulcated (*sulcus,* a furrow, *Lat.*).

The first term means that the surface is scored by very fine parallel lines or impressions, as in the culms of many grasses; the second, that the lines are deeper and wider, as in *Alexanders.*

Glutinosus, glutinous (*gluten,* glue, *Lat.*), covered with mucus, as in *sea-weeds,* and some *fungi.*

Viscidus, viscid or clammy (*viscum,* bird-lime, *Lat.*).

Some plants are covered with a tenacious clammy juice, which renders them very unpleasant to handle. Of this the *clammy groundsel* (Senecio

viscosus) is an example; and in it, as in most other
instances, the fluid is secreted from the hairs with
which the plant is clothed. Besides certain glandular organs in plants, which secrete a sweet, honey-
like fluid, there are also glands which elaborate a
variety of other secretions; which latter are often
resinous, viscid, and clammy. Of these glands
the most beautiful are those which are petiolate,
or standing each on the point of a hair; as in the
flower-stalk and calyx of the moss-rose. When
magnified, they generally, as in this plant and in
sundew, present a very beautiful appearance.

Their secretion in the former is resinous and
fragrant; in the latter gelatinous and inodorous.
The common Sundew (Drosera *rotundifolia*) is a
low plant, not uncommon in grassy bogs. The
leaves are round, about the size of a sixpence,
rather hollowed in, and their upper surface and
edges fringed with numerous red hairs, and on the
point of each hair stands a globule of tough fluid.
The plant is called *sundew*, because these drops,
instead of being exhaled, are most conspicuous
when exposed to the full force of the sun: " The
leaves," Parkinson says, " have this wonderful
propertie, that they are continually moist in the
hottest day; yea, the hotter the sunne shineth on
them, the moister they are, with a certain slimi-
nesse that will rise into threads or rope, as we
usually say, the small haires always holding the
moisture." *

* Theatre of Plants, p. 1052.

This secretion of the Sundew is most probably in some way highly useful to the plant. When a small insect alights on the leaf, it is immediately entangled by the viscid globules; and it has been observed that an ant so situated died in fifteen minutes, and a small fly in a shorter time.* Now here are two facts; the clammy drops entrap the insect, and next by their acrimony, or some other property, they kill it.† This is, perhaps, not merely accidental, but a snare intended for entrapping the prey; and several writers have asserted that the latter is detained, not by the viscosity of the juice alone, but that the hairs, being irritable, bend round the insect on every side, and keep it fast. This assertion, I believe, however, has no foundation in truth.

From various observations in that valuable work, Smith's Introduction to Botany, there is good reason to think, that a healthy vigorous state of some plants is sustained by the capture of insects. Almost every one knows the construction of *Venus's fly-trap* (Dionœa *muscipula*); that each leaf is terminated by an appendage of two lobes, furnished with long spines on their edges; that the centre of this appendage secretes a fluid substance attractive to flies, and has three sharp points projecting upwards; that when an insect alights,

* See Withering's Arrangement.
† The whole plant is so acrid as to remove warts, and blister the skin.

the lobes instantly close like the sides of a spring
rat-trap, and squeeze it upon the points; so that,
by pressure and impalement, it is almost instantly put to death. Plants of the Sarracenia, or
sidesaddle-flower genus, have hollow leaves, full
of water, which is sometimes so putrid, from
drowned insects, as to be offensive to persons
passing. Some plants again, by their *own* bad
odour attract flies: thus the *star-fish stapelia* (Stapelia *asterias*) smells like putrid fish; and the
Arum *muscivorum* like carrion. These odours
attract the flies, which accordingly creep into the
flower, but cannot return, as the hairs lining the
flower point towards its bottom, and prevent all
escape. The above facts are, I apprehend, very
generally known.

The method of taking flies by glandular hairs
is not peculiar to the *sundew*. The leaves of the
Roridula *dentata*, a shrub found at the Cape, are
furnished with a similar apparatus, and the people
keep it in their houses to catch flies, as we do
twigs smeared with bird-lime. On this account
they call it the *fly-bush*.

The cuticle in animals is clothed with hairs of
various descriptions, as wool in the sheep, bristles
in the hog, and fur in the sable; so in plants
there occur similar varieties. The term pubescence is applied to all sorts of hairiness on the
surface, armature, or arms (*arma*) to thorns,
prickles, and strings.

Pilosus, hairy (*pilus,* a hair, *Lat.*).

Hirsutus, rough (*hirsutia,* roughness of hair, *Lat.*).

Hirtus, a contraction of *hirsutus,* and therefore meaning the same.

These three terms denote simply that the surface is clothed with pretty long distinct flexible hairs, as is the case with a very large proportion of plants. When the hairs have a good deal of stiffness, *hirsutus,* or hirsute, is preferred to *pilosus:* but sometimes the surface is covered with bristles, which are so stiff and sharp as to make it painful to handle, and therefore

Hispidus, bristly, as in *borage;* and when the bristles are small and thickest at the base,

Strigosus, strigose.

Hairs are generally white; and sometimes, although distinct, are yet so numerous as to give a woolly appearance to the plant; hence, *Lanatus,* woolly (*lana,* wool, *Lat.*).

This term is applied to two sorts of woolliness. One is when the surface is covered with a network, somewhat like a spider's web, and is easily rubbed off, as on the upper surface of the leaves of the coltsfoot. The other is when the plant is clothed with numerous white hairs, as if it were encased in flannel, as in *Shepherd's club* (Verbascum *Thapsus*).

When the hairs are interwoven, or matted together like the felt of a hat, so that the particular hairs are scarcely discernible, the term

Tomentosus, tomentous, or cottony (*tomentum*, the nap of cloth, *Lat.*), is used.

When they are glossy, and pressed close to the surface, they often give a silky appearance to the latter, hence,

Sericeus, silky (*sericum*, silk, *Lat.*), more frequent on the under surface of leaves than else-where; as in wild tansy (Potentilla *anserina*).

That these coverings of plants are of considerable utility, there can be no doubt; though probably we are acquainted with a part only of their uses. In some species they evidently serve as a protection from the elements; and it has been observed, that Alpine plants are often characterised by woolly leaves, " as if nature had provided their foliage with an investment suited to the rigours of their situation." [*]

It is well known that the fur of quadrupeds in the arctic regions becomes much thicker in the winter, and serves as a better protection from the severe cold. A somewhat similar provision occurs occasionally in vegetables : thus, the leaves of the *silver-tree* (Protea *argentea*), which is indigenous at the Cape of Good Hope, are covered with a down which grows thickest on the parts most exposed to the winds [†]; and the same phenomenon

[*] Clarke's Travels, vol. iv. p. 209.
[†] Labillardière's Voyage, vol. i. p. 118.

is said to occur in most plants which brave the "stormy spirit of the Cape." It is generally, I believe, however, understood that the woolliness of plants more frequently defends them from too great heat, and serves to prevent an over-rapid exhalation of their juices. Few plants are more thickly clothed than the *great mullein* (Verbascum *Thapsus*); and Kalm mentions, that when the excessive drought of the spring of 1749 had completely parched up the hills and high grounds in Albany, this species alone was seen flourishing in the most arid situations, and when every other leaf was burnt up.*

The tomentum is sometimes so thick as to resemble cloth or velvet. This is observable in the husk of the almond, the skin of the peach, the outer rind of the fruit of Adansonia *digitata*, &c. When Thunberg was travelling in the south of Africa, he had an account from many of the natives of a bush on which grew various articles of wearing apparel. This bush, according to their assertions, bore very wonderful fruit indeed, such as caps, gloves, and worsted stockings. He obtained some of the leaves from the mountains, and he found them so clothed with down, as very closely to resemble white velvet. " The girls," he says, " who were used to the management of these leaves, began immediately with singular dexterity and nicety to strip off this downy coat,

* Kalm's Travels, vol. ii. p. 109.

whole and entire as it was, without rending it. After it had been taken off in this manner, it was turned inside outwards; when the green veins of the leaf appeared on one side. Accordingly, as the leaf was more or less round or oval, divers of the above-mentioned articles were formed out of it, the shape being now and then assisted a little by the scissars. The stalks of the leaves furnished stockings, and ladies fingered gloves; the smaller leaves, caps. So that the matter was not quite so wonderful as it was wonderfully related." *

Of a piece with this account is that of the caps furnished by the spathes of some palms, and the shirt-trees described by Humboldt.†

The down of plants is often deciduous, or subject to fall off, and sometimes it leaves one part,

---

* Travels, vol. i. p. 157.

† " We saw on the slope of the Cerra Duida, *shirt-trees* fifty feet high. The Indians cut off cylindrical pieces two feet in diameter, from which they peel the red and fibrous bark, without making any longitudinal incision. This bark affords them a sort of garment, which resembles sacks of a very coarse texture, and without a seam. The upper opening serves for the head, and two lateral holes are cut to admit the arms. The natives wear these shirts of marima in the rainy season : they have the form of the *ponchos* and *ruanas* of cotton which are so common in New Grenada, at Quito, and in Peru. As in these climates the riches and beneficence of nature are regarded as the primary causes of the indolence of the inhabitants, the missionaries do not fail to say, in showing the shirts of *marima,* ' In the forests of the Oroonoko, garments are found ready made on the trees.' We may add to this tale of the shirts the pointed caps, which the spathes of certain palm-trees furnish, and which resemble coarse network."—*Pers. Nar.* vol. v. p. 545.

while it remains on another; thus it falls from the upper, but continues on the under surface of the leaves of the *pearly everlasting* (Gnaphalium *margaritaceum.*) It is said that the down of the under surface of the leaves of the plane-trees in America forms a source of consumption, since by falling off through the summer it is drawn in during respiration, and keeps up an irritation in the chest. On this account the inhabitants of Kentucky are very unwilling to live in the vicinity of those trees.*

Plants often lose their pubescence by culture; thus the wild carrot is hairy, the cultivated smooth. Aquatic plants acquire a pubescent surface when deprived of a sufficiency of water.

The hairs are generally simple, but sometimes branched. The following are some of the diversities which occur in their form : —

Forked, at the point.

Set with small teeth.

Pubescent, or covered with minute hairs.

Plumose, or set with long hairs, like a feather.

Stellated, a number diverging from the same point like the rays of a star.

Bearded, or in tufts.

Uncinate, or bent like a hook.

Jointed, like the antennæ of insects.

The surface is sometimes hoary, *incanus*, arising either from a white pubescence, as in Cistus *inca-*

* Michaux in Voyages and Travels Modern and Contemporary.

F

nus (*hoary cistus*), wormwood, &c, or from a mealy scurf, as in various species of Orach. Some ferns are covered with a powder of a metallic lustre, and some palms are always powdered with dust of a greyish hue.

Glaucus, glaucous, azure-grey, or greenish-blue. " Clothed with fine sea-green mealiness which easily rubs off," according to the definition in Smith's Introduction; but though the glaucous colour is generally seated in a kind of mealiness covering the surface, yet there are exceptions, and therefore we are to consider the term *glaucus* as expressing colour alone, no matter *how* produced.

The surface of plants is often furnished with organs whose intention seems to be to defend them from the attacks of animals.

Spinosus, thorny, or spinous (*spina*, a thorn, *Lat.*).

Aculeatus, prickly (*aculeus*, a prickle, *Lat.*).

The distinction between the thorn and prickle, is very easily understood. The thorn is composed both of wood and bark; the prickle, of bark or cuticle alone : and hence, if you strip the bark from a rose-bush or bramble, you will find that the prickles come entirely away with it; but if you make the same experiment on the hawthorn or sloe you will not succeed ; you may strip the bark off, but the thorn will remain projecting from the wood. See *Fig.* 20.

Fig. 20.

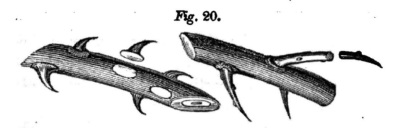

Muricatus, muricated (*murex,* a kind of shell, having many projecting points or spines). When the surface is covered with numerous subulate points or prickles, as in the capsule of the thorn-apple.

Urens, stinging (*uro,* to burn, *Lat.*).

Stimulus, or *seta urens,* are the terms by which the stings of vegetables, those of the nettle, for instance, are expressed.

There is a very close analogy between the fang of poisonous serpents, the sting of insects, and that of vegetables. In the serpent, a gland on each side of the head secretes the venom, which is conveyed by a duct into a bag placed at the root of the fangs. The latter are hollow, and the channel in each communicates with the poison. When therefore the animal wounds, the roots of the fangs are pushed against the bag, and, in consequence, the venom passes through them, and, is instilled into the wound. The channel within the fang, however, does not run to the point; that would necessarily diminish its sharpness: but it opens by a gutter or slit, at some distance behind the point, and this ensures the inoculation of the poison even better

than if it had opened at the point itself. On a
similar principle the sting of the *wasp*, nettle, &c.
is constructed; it is hollow, and has a reservoir of
venom at its root, a portion of which is conveyed
through it into the wound it inflicts.*

I think there can be little doubt, that nature has
bestowed the preceding arms on plants as means
of defence. Willdenow, however, has advanced
a theory, maintaining that the thorn " arises most

---

* The poison from the sting of the nettle, however, passes
through its very point. " The naked eye," says Curtis,
" readily perceives the instruments by which the nettle instils
its poison; a microscope of no great magnifying power more
plainly discovers them to be rigid, transparent, tubular setæ,
prickles, or stings, highly polished and exquisitely pointed,
furnished at their base with a kind of bulb, in which the juice
is principally contained, and which being pressed on when
the sting enters the skin, forces the poison into the wound:
of the venomous quality of this liquid, and of the manner in
which it is emitted, I have had ocular proof; placing the foot-
stalk of a nettle-leaf on the stage of the microscope, so that
the whole of the prickle was in the focus when horizontally
extended, I pressed on the bulb with a blunt-pointed pin, and,
after some trials, found a liquid to ascend in the prickle,
somewhat as the quicksilver does when a warm hand is applied to the bulb of a thermometer. In some of the prickles
I observed the liquid stationary. On pressing such, in particular, I saw most plainly the liquor ascend to, and flow
copiously from, its very extremity. I was the more anxious
to see this, as I suspected the poison might proceed from an
aperture in the side of the sting near the point, as in the
forceps of the spider and tooth of the viper, and where it
appears to be placed, rather than at the extremity, that it may
not take off from its necessary sharpness.

Pricking the skin of my hand with a needle, I placed some
of the juice on the wound, when it instantly inflamed, and
put on all the appearance of a part stung by a nettle. —
Curtis, Fl. Lond. Fasc. 6.

generally from an incompletely evolved bud which
has begun to form itself; but, wanting a proper
supply of nourishment, remains only in form of a
very short, sharp, and bare twig*: " and he thinks
that the thorn's arising from want of food is proved
by the circumstance of most of our fruit-trees
bearing thorns in the wild state, but losing them
when cultivated. Sir J. E. Smith thinks this
theory ingenious and satisfactory†; but in my
humble opinion it is directly the reverse, and I
would consider the change mentioned as merely
one of the numerous phenomena which culture
produces in altering vegetables *from a state of nature.* Might we not, with equal justice, apply
Willdenow's theory to other parts which are
changed, and therefore argue that stamens and
pistils are abortive petals, because they can be
converted into the latter by cultivation; and that
double and full flowers are not the monsters they
have been represented, but, on the contrary, that
single flowers are abortive attempts to arrive at
their perfection? I would ask, too, will any degree
of starvation make a plant not *naturally* thorny,
bring forth thorns; and is it not the case, that in
tropical countries many plants are remarkably
spinous, though in such countries, vegetables (with
a very few exceptions) never produce nor *attempt*

* Principles of Botany, 270.
† Introd. p. 170.

F 3

to produce buds? I would ask also, if thorns arise from defective nourishment, how comes it that they often protrude leaves similar to the other leaves of the plant, and in some instances also both flowers and fruit? These are surely very suspicious symptoms of defective nutriment. I would upon the whole consider, that it is as natural for spinous plants to bring forth thorns, as for flowering plants to bring forth flowers, though by culture we may alter the course of nature, and cause leafy twigs to be produced instead of thorns, and double flowers in place of single: but both are aberrations from nature; and thorns are no more abortive buds, than single flowers are abortive attempts to produce double ones.

Some plants are particularly distinguished by the numbers and strength of their spines; such is the *Thorn-tree*, a species of mimosa in the south of Africa, which from top to bottom is clothed with enormous double thorns, or from four to six inches in length, pointing in every direction, and forming thickets impenetrable to every animal except the rhinoceros.* The thistle which " rears in triumph his offensive head," and many other species, have almost their whole surface covered with spines or prickles; and Bartram says of the *palmetto royal* or *Adam's needle* (Yucca *gloriosa*), that its stiff leaves, standing nearly in a horizontal direction,

* Barrow's South Africa, p. 170.

are " as impenetrable to man, or any other animal, as if they were a regiment of grenadiers with their bayonets pointed." The *Prickly-pear*, according to Lewis and Clarke, renders travelling extremely difficult along some parts of the banks of the Missouri, where its spines are so strong that they will pierce a double shoe-sole made of dressed deerskin. This plant, however, is not only defended by its spines, but also by the thick consistence of its leaves or joints; and the Grecian traveller, Clarke, has suggested that in some latitudes it might serve as an outwork of fortifications; since, as he says, " artillery has no effect upon it; fire will not act upon it; pioneers cannot approach it; and neither cavalry nor infantry can traverse it." * In fact, in the Spanish colonies in America, this plant is considered as a very important means of military defence, and is propagated constantly around fortifications with that intent.

That the *sting* is intended as an organ of defence, is sufficiently obvious; yet it is singular that the soft and fleshy larvæ of several butterflies live upon the nettle with impunity. The hog is said to hunt and devour the rattlesnake with avidity, and is never injured by it; these anomalies I know not how to explain.

The sharpness of the edges of some plants serves, perhaps, a use similar to the arms mentioned

* Travels, vol. ii. p. 405.

thus, the edges of the leaves of Scleria *grandis* are as sharp as glass *; and Stedman notices the plant called *Cutty-weeree-weeree* at Surinam, which, he says, is amongst " the most serious pests of the colony, being a kind of strong-edged grass, which is in some places very plentiful; and when a man walks through it will cut his legs like a razor." †

One of the most remarkable demonstrations of the intention of nature in furnishing plants with spines and prickles, occurs in certain trees which become unarmed as soon as they have grown high

---

* Labillardière's Voyages, vol. i. p. 188.

† Stedman's Surinam, vol. ii. p. 29. — I find also in a late traveller two instances bearing on this subject, which I shall here quote. The first relates to the Poa spinosa. " I now," says the author, Mr. Burchell, " gathered, for the first time, specimens of a very extraordinary grass. Its panicle of flowers formed a bunch of strong sharp thorns, so rigid and pungent, that no animal would graze near it, nor would the naked-legged Hottentots venture to walk amongst it, though it was not more than a foot and a half high." The second relates to a shrub called the *Hookthorn.* " I was preparing," he says, " to cut some specimens of it, which the Hottentots observing, warned me to be very careful in doing so, otherwise I should certainly be caught fast in its branches. In consequence of this advice I proceeded with the utmost caution ; but with all my care, a small twig caught hold of one sleeve. While thinking to disengage it quietly with the other hand, both arms were seized by these rapacious thorns, and the more I tried to extricate myself, the more entangled I became, till at last it seized hold of my hat also, and convinced me that there was no possibility for me to free myself but by main force, and at the expence of tearing all my clothes. I therefore called out for help, and two of my men came and released me by cutting off the branches by which I was held."—*Burchell's Travels in Africa*, p. 211. and p. 309.

enough to be beyond the reach of cattle. Brown says of the *silk cotton-tree* (Bombax), that its trunk while young " is always armed with thorns; but these seldom appear after it has acquired a degree of height and strength sufficient to protect it." *

The common holly is an example still more striking.

> O reader! hast thou ever stood to see
>   The holly-tree?
> The eye that contemplates it well perceives
>   Its glossy leaves
> Ordered by an intelligence so wise
> As might confound the Atheist's sophistries.
>
> Below, a circling fence, its leaves are seen
>   Wrinkled and keen;
> No grazing cattle through their prickly round
>   Can reach to wound;
> But as they grow *where nothing is to fear*,
> Smooth and *unarmed* the pointless leaves appear.
>   SOUTHEY.

* Brown's Jamaica, p. 277,

CHAPTER IV.

OF THE LEAF.

A PERFECT knowledge of the leaves of plants is essential to the formation of a truly scientific botanist. To acquire this knowledge is indeed difficult; but as it cannot come by inspiration, it must be the reward of study: a reward, however, which will well repay the trouble and labour of acquirement. We shall first attend to the

PETIOLUS, *Petiole*, Leaf-stalk, or Footstalk, which is easily understood; it supports the leaf, and connects it to the plant. Leaves have not always leaf-stalks, however, but are fastened to the stem or branch without their intervention, and then are said to be sessile, or sitting. In some instances, but they are very rare, the petiole supports the fructification also.

1. PETIOLUS *teres*, a *round* petiole. This is very common, and every one knows what *round* means; but sometimes instead of being round, the petiole has its sides flattened, so that one edge looks up and the other down: this, of course, is a

2. PETIOLUS *compressus*, a *compressed* petiole; a good example of which is to be found in the foot-stalks of the *aspen*, or *trembling poplar* (Populus *tremula*). To this compression of the *petiole*, we are chiefly to attribute the tremulous or turning

motion of the leaves in that tree. The compression is chiefly at the end next the leaf; and as it is vertical, while the position of the leaf is horizontal, the slightest breath of wind throws the latter into agitation; so that scarcely any circumstance can be more expressive of a complete calm, than that of the leaves of the aspen remaining at perfect rest.* Thomson very beautifully adverts to this in the Seasons, when he speaks of the gradual sinking of the breeze

> Into a perfect calm; that not a breath
> Is heard to quiver through the closing woods,
> Or rustling turn the many-twinkling leaves
> Of aspen tall.

And how beautifully would Spenser's allusion to the almond-tree apply to the leaves of the trembling poplar!—

> Like to an almond-tree, ymounted hye
> On top of green Selinis all alone,
> With blossoms brave bedecked daintily,
> Whose tender locks do tremble every one
> At everie little breath that under heaven is blowne.†

The Scottish Highlanders account in a more solemn way for the tremulous motion of the leaves of the poplar. They imagine that our Saviour's cross was made of it, and that thence its leaves can never rest‡, but like troubled spirits shudder from

* The same circumstances are equally or more conspicuous in Populus *nigra*; *P. tropida*; *P. tremuloides*, and some other species.
† Faery Queene, book i.
‡ Lightfoot. Flor. Scot. p. 617.

the impression of that transaction which shook the solid earth, and made the graves give up their dead. But we cannot seriously explain the motion of the aspen by referring it to this cause; which was an event too important to require commemoration from such a trifle as the movement of a leaf. I should rather, (without wishing, however, to advance any reflections on female loquacity,) be of opinion, with the good Gerard, that the *aspen-tree* " may also be called *tremble* after the French name, considering it is the matter whereof women's toongs were made, as the Poets and some others report, which seldom cease wagging." *

3. PETIOLUS *canaliculatus*, a *channelled* petiole;

When there is a longitudinal groove on the upper surface of the leaf-stalf. This is found in many plants, and may be well seen in the petioles of the *butter-bur* and *artichoke*. The entire frond is channelled in the sea-weed named Fucus *canaliculatus*, a species common on our shores.

St. Pierre applies the term *aqueduct* to this furrow, and affirms that its use is to convey the rains to the stem and root of the plant; that it is not to be found in aquatic plants, but is general in those of the mountains. " Nature," he says, " has bestowed an aqueduct on the pedicle of the leaves of mountain plants; she withdraws it from those which grow by the side of the waters, and transforms them into aquatic plants."—" When nature

* Herbal, p. 1303.

intends to render aquatic plants susceptible of vegetation on the mountains, she bestows aqueducts on their leaves; but when, on the contrary, she means to place mountain plants by the water's side, she withdraws it."[*] He advances much more to the same purpose; and indeed the theory is pretty: but it is at the same time, as Gerard would say, " all and every part of it false and most untrue."

4. PETIOLUS *alatus*, a *winged* petiole; when, as in the winged stem, its sides are expanded into a leafy border, as in the leaves of the *Orange-tree; Fig.* 21. (*d*)

There may occur a chance of error here, of which I must warn you. There are certain appendages of plants named *stipules*, which will be described farther on. Now, sometimes these *stipules* adhere laterally to the petiole, and give it somewhat of a winged appearance, which might lead you into the error of supposing that such a petiole should be called a *petiolus subalatus*, that is, a partially winged foot-stalk. Pull the leaf of a rose-bush, and you will perceive this, as at *Fig.* 21. (*a*) is the petiole, and (*bb*) the *stipules* adhering to it.

Fig. 21.

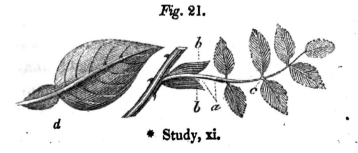

[*] Study, xi.

You will remark also, that from the principal leaf-stalk in the rose, there spring out secondary ones. The rose-leaf is *compound*, that is, not consisting of a single leaf, as in the *aspen*, but of more than one. But generally when the leaf is compound, the leaf-stalk, as in this instance, is compound also; and hence,

5. PETIOLUS *simplex*, a *simple* leaf-stalk, as in the poplar, and all plants which have simple leaves; and,

6. PETIOLUS *compositus*, a *compound* leaf-stalk, as in the rose, &c. and the secondary or partial petioles, arising from the principal, are named *petioluli;* therefore,

7. PETIOLULUS, a *partial* leaf-stalk, as at (*c*).

8. PETIOLUS *cirriferus*, a *tendrilled* leaf-stalk. When the petiole terminates in, or protrudes, a tendril, from any part of its surface.

9. PETIOLUS *vaginans*, when it invests the stem like a sheath, as in grasses.

We shall now attend to the leaves themselves; and, in the first place, it is very obvious, that they are not limited to any one part of the plant. They spring in some from the root, in others from the stem, in some from the branches, and in many from all these parts.

FOLIUM, means a leaf; FOLIA, leaves.

1. FOLIUM *radicale*, a *radical*, or root-leaf, means, of course, a leaf springing out from the root, examples of which are very frequent; familiar ones occur in the primrose, cowslip, and violet.

2. FOLIUM *caulinum*, a *stem-leaf*, equally common.

3. FOLIUM *rameum*, a *branch leaf* (*ramus*, a branch). This sometimes differs from the leaves on the stem.

4. FOLIUM *axillare*, an *axillary* leaf. When a branch leaves a stem, the angle between the two is named an *axilla;* and hence a leaf, peduncle, &c. rising from such angle, is called axillary.

5. FOLIUM *florale*, a *floral* leaf, placed close to the flower, as in Orchis, in which there is a leaf at the base of each flower-stalk. There is a leafy appendage found in some plants which has the name of *bractea* or *bracte.* This is often translated " floral leaf," but improperly; for, as is observed by Martyn, " it seems better to preserve the term *Bractea,* or *Bracte,* than to translate it : for Linnæus frequently calls leaves which are near the flower, *Floral leaves,* when they differ from the other leaves, though they are not properly bractes."

6. FOLIUM *seminale*, a *seminal* or seed-leaf (*semen,* a seed, *Lat.*).

If you plant the seed of a *lupin,* you will find that after some days it will protrude above the earth, in form of two thick orbicular fleshy leaves. These, before the seed germinated, composed its two sides, halves, or *cotyledons,* as they are called. The juices they contain in this leaf-like state go to the nourishment of the plant, and by the time that they are exhausted and dead, the root is strong enough to depend on its own exertions for support. These *temporary*, but very important, leaves are often attacked by insects, and destroyed before the root has acquired strength to perform its office, and in consequence the whole plant perishes. In this way turnip crops are blighted by the fly.

As leaves are extremely various in shape, and as they very often resemble in outline some familiar or well-known object, nothing can be more natural than to name them after such objects. If a leaf resemble a lyre, what term can be used for it more apposite than *lyrate?* or if a sword, than *ensiform;* or a lance, than *lanceolate?* By arranging leaves, whose appellations are thus taken from certain classes of bodies, together, I think the memory will be assisted, and I shall, so far as the subject will admit, adopt that plan. We shall first attend to

SUCH LEAVES AS ARE NAMED FROM PARTS OF THE ANIMAL BODY.

7. FOLIUM *cordatum*, a *cordate*, or heart-shaped leaf (*cor*, the heart, *Lat.*). This leaf bears a nearer resemblance to the heart on playing cards than to a real heart. See *Fig.* 22. (*a*). It is common, and in many plants very beautiful; as in the broad-leaved and other species of birthwort, black bryony, &c.

8. FOLIUM *reniforme, reniform,* or kidney-shaped

Fig. 22.

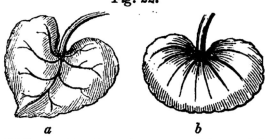

a   *b*

(*ren*, a kidney, *Lat.*), as in ground-ivy, white saxi-frage, the Anemone *palmata*, &c. *Fig.* 22. (*b*), and *Fig.* 29.

9. FOLIUM *linguiforme*, or *lingulatum;* a *lingui-form*, or tongue-shaped leaf (*lingua*, a tongue, *Lat.*); "linear and fleshy, blunt at the end, convex underneath, and having usually a cartilaginous border, as in Mesembryanthemum, Aloe, Hœman-thus *coccineus.*" *Martyn's Language of Botany.* — " Of a thick, oblong, blunt figure, generally car-tilaginous at the edges, as Mesembryanthemum *linguiforme*, Dendrobium *linguiforme*, and several species of Saxifrage." *Smith's Introduction.*

10. FOLIUM *auriculatum*, *auriculate*, or ear-shaped; *auritum* also is used (*auris*, an ear, *Lat.*); having two lobes, or two leaflets at its base. *Fig.* 23. (*a*) and (*b*).

11. FOLIUM *capillare*, or *capillaceum;* long and *hair-like* (*capillus*, a hair, *Lat.*).

12. FOLIUM *ciliatum*, *ciliated* (*cilium*, an eye-lash, *Lat.*). This term applies to the *margin* of the leaf, and means that it is set with hairs, placed at some distance from each other, of equal length, parallel, and bearing a resemblance to the eye-lashes. *Fig.* 23. (*c*).

Fig. 23.

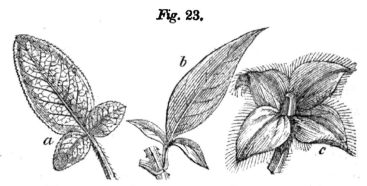

13. FOLIUM *palmatum*, a *palmated*, or hand-shaped leaf (*palma*, a hand, or the palm of the hand, *Lat.*). The leaf of the common passion-flower (Passiflora *cœrulea*) is a good example, being divided into oblong segments, resembling fingers, which arise from an entire space near the petiole that may be compared to the palm, *Fig.* 24. (*a*).

14. FOLIUM *digitatum*, a digitate, or fingered leaf (*digitus*, a finger, *Lat.*). In the palmate leaf the petiole expands into a space which has just been compared to the palm of a hand; but in the digitate leaf there is no such space, but several distinct leaflets stand immediately on the point of the petiole, as in the *horse-chesnut.* *Fig.* 24. (*b*).

Fig. 24.

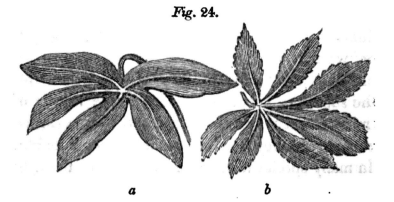

a   *b*

15. FOLIUM *pedatum*, a *pedate* leaf (*pes*, a foot, *Lat.*); the likeness in this case, however, is not to the human foot, but to that of a bird. It is not easily understood from the usual definitions which are given of it; Willdenow's is the most intelligible I have met with, and therefore I shall here quote it, but illustrate its different steps by plans. " When a leaf-stalk is divided, and in the middle where it divides, there is a leaflet, *Fig.* 25. (*a*); at both ends there is likewise a leaflet (*b*); and on each side, between the one in the middle and that on the end, another, or two, or even three leaves(*c*). Such a leaf, therefore, consists of· five, seven, or nine leaflets, that all·are inserted on one side."

Fig. 25.

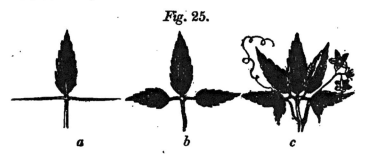

a   b   c

Whatever other uses the petiole may serve, a very principal one is, that its vessels carry nutritive fluids from the stem to the leaf; and these vessels, or, we may say the leaf-stalks themselves, if we please, ramify and divide in various ways through the substance of the leaf. In most leaves we can trace (especially on the under surface), the petiole running through their middle from bottom to top. In many species this, which is called the mid-rib,

is very prominent; and in most plants, it sends
out lateral strong divisions, which either run to
the margin of the leaf, or die away in subdivisions
like the ramifications of blood-vessels in an animal
membrane. When these divisions run to the
margin, like the ribs of an animal from its spine,
as at (*a*), *Fig.* 26. the term

Costatum, ribbed (*costa*, a rib, *Lat.*), would be
most appropriate; but unluckily it has been applied in a different way. Willdenow, indeed, defines the term in this sense; but it has, almost
universally, been considered as synonymous with

Nervosum, nerved (νευρος (neuros), a nerve,
Greek), which means that the divisions of the petiole, instead of running transversely, proceed in
straight lines from the base to the apex (*b*).

16. FOLIUM *venosum*, a *veined* leaf (*vena*, a vein,
Lat.), is when the large and prominent divisions
die off into a network of smaller ramifications, as
is the case in most plants (*c*).

Fig. 26.

a   b   c

It is to be remarked, that although these distinctions will apply strictly to the leaves of many
vegetables, yet, such is the infinite variety in nature, that we shall often be at a loss to determine

which term should be used; and we must often compound one term with another to express the exact meaning.

When a leaf has three nerves running from base to apex, it is named

17. FOLIUM *trinerve*, a *three-nerved* leaf, *Fig.* 27. (*a*), and we must take care not to confound this with the

18. FOLIUM *triplinerve*, which apparently one would suppose to be the same. In the former, the three nerves run distinct; but in the latter, the side nerves, in place of being distinct, originate from the mid-rib, above the base of the leaf (*b*).

We must be careful again not to confound these with the

19. FOLIUM *basi-trinerve*, in which the petiole splits into three great divisions at the base of the leaf, but these ramify into veins without going on like true nerves to the apex (*c*).

Fig. 27.

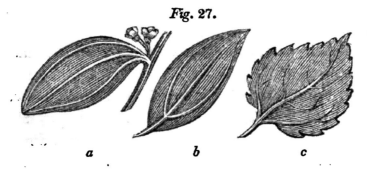

a   b   c

A leaf may have more than three nerves running distinct from base to apex, and hence FOLIUM *quin-quenerve*, a *five-nerved* leaf: FOLIUM *septemnerve*, a *seven-nerved* leaf; and more than one nerve on each side may also rise from the mid-rib: so that besides the FOLIUM *triplinerve,* we may also have a FOLIUM *quintuplinerve,* a *quintuple-nerved* leaf, a *septuple-nerved* leaf, and so on.

Fig. 28.   *b*

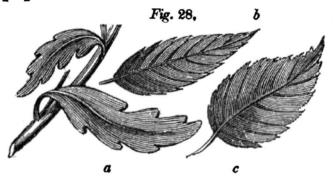

a   *c*

20. FOLIUM *dentatum,* a *toothed* leaf (*dens,* a tooth, *Lat.*). This term applies to the *margin* of the leaf. When it is divided into separate projections, like teeth, *Fig.* 28. (*a*), sometimes each tooth is itself toothed; that is, has its margin set with smaller teeth. This forms the

21. FOLIUM *duplicato-dentatum,* or *doubly-toothed* leaf. When the teeth are sharp, close together, and their points directed to the top of the leaf it is

22. FOLIUM *serratum,* a *serrated* leaf (*serra,* a saw, *Lat.*) (*b*), (*c* is *doubly serrated.*) And when in this kind of leaf the teeth are small and fine, the diminutive *serrulatum, serrulate,* is used. When the teeth are round, and do not point to either end of the leaf, it is

23. FOLIUM *crenatum,* a *crenate* leaf (*crena,* a

notch, *Lat.*), *Fig.* 29.: and this may be *obtusely* crenate, *obtuse crenatum*, *acutely* crenate, *acute crenatum*, or *doubly* crenate, *duplicato-crenatum*.

Fig. 29.

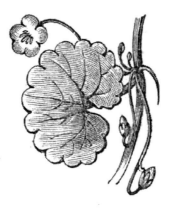

24. FOLIUM *ovatum*, an *ovate* leaf.

25. FOLIUM *ovale*, an *oval* leaf.

Ovum means an egg, and from it both these terms are derived; but they do not mean exactly the same thing. Draw the figure of an egg on paper — it will be broader at one end than the other, *Fig.* 30. (*a*). To the broad end add a petiole, and prolong it into a mid-rib, with some lateral divisions, and the representation will be that of an *ovate* leaf, FOLIUM *ovatum* (*b*).

But suppose that one end of the leaf is *not* broader than the other, but that both ends are round, and of equal breadth, then it will be a FOLIUM *ovale* (*c*). Or should the length of the latter be much greater proportionably than the length of an egg bears to its breadth, it will be

26. FOLIUM *ellipticum*, an *elliptical* leaf (*d*).

Fig. 30.

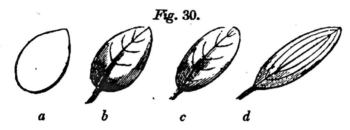

a   b   c   d

It often happens in ovate leaves, that the broad end of the egg is uppermost, the petiole being inserted into the narrow end, and hence,

27. FOLIUM *obovatum*, an *obovate*, or *inversely-ovate* leaf. The term *obcordate* is applied in like manner to heart-shaped leaves, when the base of the heart is directed outwards from the stem.

LEAVES WHICH IN SHAPE RESEMBLE INSTRUMENTS OF WAR.

28. FOLIUM *sagittatum*, a *sagittate*, or arrow-shaped leaf (*sagitta*, an arrow, *Lat.*), *Fig.* 31. (*a*).

29. FOLIUM *hastatum*, *hastate*, or halberd-shaped (*hasta*, a pike or battle-axe, *Lat.*), closely allied to the auriculate leaf (*b*).

Fig. 31.

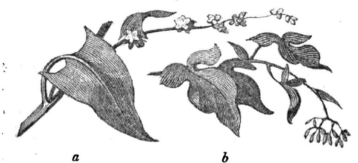

a   b

30. FOLIUM *lanceolatum*, *lanceolate* (*lancea*, a lance, *Lat.*), oblong and tapering to each extre-

mity as in *ribwort plantain*, (Plantago *lanceolata*.)
See (*b*) *Fig.* 26.

31. FOLIUM *ensiforme*, *ensiform*, or sword-shaped
(*ensis*, a sword, *Lat.*), as in *iris*.

32. FOLIUM *acinaciforme*, *acinaciform*, or scimitar-shaped (αχιναχης (*akinakes*) a scimitar,
Greek); like a Persian scimitar, one edge convex
and sharp, the other straight and thick. *Fig.* 32. (*a*)

33. FOLIUM *peltatum*, a *peltate*, or target-shaped
leaf (*pelta*, a shield, buckler, or target, *Lat.*).

In peltate leaves the petiole, in place of being
inserted into the margin of the leaf, is implanted
on its under-surface, at or near its centre. The
nasturtium, or Indian cress, cultivated every where
in gardens, is a familiar example; and also the
ivy-leaved geranium (Geranium *peltatum*). (*b*)

In many peltate leaves the upper surface is tucked
in, or hollowed towards the middle; and on this
account they have been termed FOLIA *umbilicata*,
umbilicated leaves.

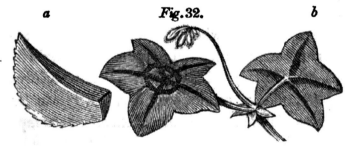

a   *Fig.* 32.   *b*

LEAVES THAT RESEMBLE MUSICAL INSTRUMENTS.

34. FOLIUM *lyratum*, a *lyrate*, or lyre-shaped leaf
(*lyra*, a lyre or harp, *Lat.*). A leaf is said to be

pinnatifid when it has a number of incisures going nearly to the mid-rib. *Fig.* 33. (*a*)   Now the lyrate only differs from the pinnatifid leaf in its terminating segment being very large and rounded. (*b*)

b   *Fig.* 33.   *a*

35. FOLIUM *panduriforme,* a *panduriform,* guitar, or fiddle-shaped leaf (*pandura,* a kind of guitar).

LEAVES WHICH RESEMBLE MECHANICAL INSTRU-
MENTS OR OTHER FAMILIAR OBJECTS.

36. FOLIUM *dolabriforme, dolabriform* or hatchet-shaped (*dolabra,* an axe, *Lat.*), like the scimitar-shaped leaf, but the sharp edge nearly orbicular. *Fig.* 34. (*a*)

37. FOLIUM *runcinatum,* a *runcinate* leaf (*runcina,* a large saw, *Lat.*), when the margin has its seg-ments and teeth acute, and pointing *backwards,* like the teeth of a large timber-saw.   It is a variety of the pinnatifid, or rather, perhaps, the lyrate leaf. Common dandelion affords an excellent example, *Fig.* 34. (*b*)

38. FOLIUM *deltoides,* or *deltoideum,* a *deltoid,* or trowel-shaped leaf (from the Greek letter Delta, Δ). (*c*)

Fig. 34.

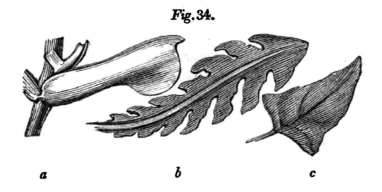

a   b   c

39. FOLIUM *subulatum,* a *subulate,* or awl-shaped leaf (*subula,* an awl, *Lat.*). The awl has generally a bend, but that is not necessary to the subulate leaf. It tapers gradually from base to point, and sometimes is hollow, forming a *tubular* leaf (FOLIUM *tubulosum*).

40. FOLIUM *acerosum,* an *acerose* leaf.

The simple inspection of the leaf of a yew or fir-tree will give a better idea of this leaf than words can. It is linear, or subulate, rigid, evergreen, and in the pine and other coniferous plants, is united at its base to the branch by a kind of articulation. Trees of the pine-tribe have been named *arbores acerosæ,* and, in the timber-merchant's phrase, *needle timber,* from their having, with only a few exceptions, acerose leaves. These trees inhabit naturally, either northern or alpine regions, which habitats explain why they have been instructed with this species of leaf. With that of any other description, they could not have been evergreens, for in winter they would be overpowered by the weight of snow, and blown down by the hurricanes. The acerose leaf enables them to evade both; the snow falls through, and the wind penetrates the interstices. The winds struggling through the boughs of these *arbores acerosæ* meet with such innumerable points and edges, as, even when gentle, to cause a deep murmur or sighing; and when the breeze is strong, or the storm is abroad, the sounds produced are like the murmuring of the ocean, or the roar of billows among rocks.

———— The loud wind through the forest wakes,
With sound like ocean's roaring, wild and deep,
And in yon gloomy pines strange music makes,
Like symphonies unearthly, heard in sleep;
The sobbing waters dash their waves and weep;
Where moans the blast its dreary path along,
The bending firs a mournful cadence keep;
And mountain rocks re-echo to the song,
As fitful raves the storm, the hills and woods among.

These sounds are highly grateful to the poet, and the lover of nature. " There is," says Burns, " scarcely any earthly object that gives me more— I do not know if I should call it pleasure,— but something which exalts me, something which enraptures me,— than to walk in the sheltered side of a wood, or high plantation, in a cloudy winter day, and hear the stormy wind howling among the trees, and raving over the plain. It is my best season for devotion: my mind is wrapt up in a kind of enthusiasm to Him, who, in the pompous language of the Hebrew bard, ' walks on the wings of the wind.' "

41. FOLIUM *pectinatum,* a *pectinate* leaf (*pecten,* a comb, *Lat.*). " A sort of pinnate leaf, in which the leaflets are toothed like a comb." *Martyn.*

Fig. 35.

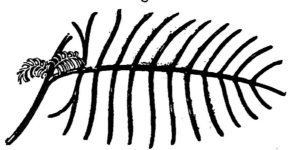

42. FOLIUM *flabelliforme,* a *flabelliform,* or fan-shaped leaf (*flabellum,* a fan, *Lat.*). This term is almost exclusively applied to the fronds of certain palms which are shaped like a fan, and split into spokes or radii. In China they are really used as fans, and form an article of merchandise.* *Fig.* 36. is a representation of the dwarf fan-palm (Chamærops *humilis*).

43. FOLIUM *spatulatum,* a *spatulate* leaf (*spathula,* an instrument formerly used for spreading salve; not shaped like the spatula now used by the apothecaries, but broad and round at the end like a battledore).

44. FOLIUM *cuneiforme, cuneiform,* or wedge-shaped (*cuneus,* a wedge, *Lat.*).

45. FOLIUM *carinatum, carinate,* or keel-shaped (*carina,* the keel of a ship, *Lat.*), when the centre

* Macartney's Embassy, vol. i. p. 413.

of the back of the leaf juts out like the bottom of a boat.

Fig.36.

LEAVES NAMED AFTER ANY OF THE HEAVENLY BODIES ARE THE CRESCENT-SHAPED, AND STELLATE OR STAR-LIKE LEAVES.

46. FOLIUM *lunulatum,* or *lunatum* (*luna,* the moon, *lunula,* a little moon, *Lat.*). We are always to understand by it that it means, *shaped like a crescent,* or horned moon. The horns in some plants point towards the stem, in others, from it. Besides the term crescent-shaped, we may use *lunate* or *lunulate ;* but, as Martyn truly observes, " *moon-shaped* is absurd, and *mooned* is abomin-

able." It is to be regretted, indeed, that *many* inelegant terms have crept into the science. This has arisen from a desire of rendering the subject plain to the mere English reader, but I believe it has had a quite opposite effect, and that it is a mistake to suppose that ideas of the different forms and appearances of the parts of plants can be acquired more easily from a nomenclature strictly vernacular. Suppose we grant that it is difficult at first to understand the more scientific terms; that very difficulty may have its use; the exertion of overcoming it fixes them steadily in the memory, and gives a precision and facility that cannot belong to common language. Those therefore who have not had the advantage of a classical education are not necessarily excluded from a participation in this delightful study. Every science must have a nomenclature of its own, to acquire which is, in general, almost as difficult to the learned student, as the unlearned; and whoever wants spirit and perseverance to make himself master of it, will never have very clear or correct notions on the subject. With respect to Botany, the terminology is, it must be confessed, very copious, and to many persons seems insuperably difficult; but when the experiment is made, the impediments will be found much less formidable than had been imagined. The practice of comparing the different parts of plants with their descriptions, will be found to be a pleasant amusement, rather than a laborious task,

and the patience of the student will be finally re-
warded by the possession of clear and precise views
of the subject.

47. Folium *stellatum,* a *stellated,* or star-like leaf
(*stella,* a star, *Lat.*); but this term is seldom used.

You have seen *mint* or *dead-nettle* in flower;
and you know that in these, as in many other
plants, the flowers surround the stem like rings.

Now, such a *ring of flowers* is called a *whorl,*
which seems to be corrupted from *whirl,* to turn
round. The botanical term is *verticillus,* which is
derived from the Latin verb *verto,* to turn. In like
manner, the leaves, in Robin-run-in-the-hedge,
woodroof, &c. surround the stem, standing out
from it like the spokes of a wheel from the nave.

Fig. 37.

Such rings of leaves however are not called whorls,
that term being restricted to flowers, but they are
named FOLIA *verticillata, verticillate,* or whorled
leaves. FOLIA *stellata, stellate* leaves, are equivalent, but the other term is now always used. We
say FOLIA *verticillata,* but not FOLIA *stellata.*

I believe there is only one species of leaf named from a resemblance to any article of clothing. This is the

48. FOLIUM *cucullatum*, a *cucullate*, or cowled leaf (*cucullus*, a cowl or hood, *Lat.*). " In shape of the paper rolled up conically by grocers for small parcels of spices, comfits, &c." — *Martyn.*

We have now considered leaves simply as they resemble in shape some well known object, but they are to be attended to in several other respects.

APEX, POINT, OR SUMMIT.

49. FOLIUM *acutum*, *acute*, sharp.
50. FOLIUM *acuminatum*, *acuminate.*

The first term means no more than that the apex terminates in form of an acute angle, *Fig.* 38. (*a*); the second, that it runs or tapers into a subulate form, as in the leaf of the common reed. (*d*)

Fig. 38.

51. FOLIUM *mucronatum*, a *mucronate* leaf (*mucro*, the point of a spear or dagger, *Lat.*), having a dagger-shaped projection at the summit, which may be soft and flexible, or spinous and rigid.(*c*)

52. FOLIUM *cirrosum*, a *cirrose* leaf, ending in a tendril (*b*), as in Gloriosa *superba*.

53. FOLIUM *obtusum*, *obtuse*, blunt.

54. FOLIUM *emarginatum*, an *emarginate* leaf.

Take a bit of paper and cut a nick in it, as at (*e*); this is what occurs in the marginate leaf (*f*); there is a portion, as it were, cut out of its point, and hence it gets sometimes the barbarous appellation of *end-nicked*. When the nick runs half down the leaf, the latter is said to be cleft, and hence we have leaves that are *bifid*, *trifid*, *quadrifid*, that is, two, three, four-cleft, and so on. But in place of making a nick, suppose you cut in the paper a shallow curve or bay; this is what occurs in the *retuse* leaf, FOLIUM *retusum* (*retusus*, blunt, *Lat.*), whose end, in place of being nicked, is of the form of *Fig.* 39. (*a*)

55. FOLIUM *truncatum*, a *truncated* leaf (*trunco*, to cut shorter, *Lat.*); as if the top of the leaf had been cut off, as at (*b*), which is a miniature representation of a leaf of the tulip-tree (Liriodendron *tulipifera*).

Fig. 39.

b   a

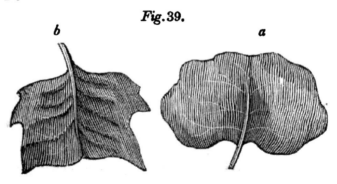

56. FOLIUM *præmorsum* truncated, and *with notches*, like marks left by the teeth.

BASE.

A number of leaves, whose peculiarities of shape depend upon the base, have already been described.*   One still remains.

57. FOLIUM *inæquale*, an *unequal* leaf, when the two sides of the base do not correspond in size, as in the elm, *Fig.*40.

*Fig.*40.

CIRCUMFERENCE.

58. $\left\{\begin{array}{l}\text{FOLIUM } orbiculatum, \text{ an } orbicular \text{ leaf.} \\ \text{FOLIUM } rotundum, \text{ a } round \text{ leaf.} \\ \text{FOLIUM } teres, \text{ also a } round \text{ leaf.}\end{array}\right.$

In common language, orbicular and round are used synonymously, but not so in botanical. A leaf which is round like a piece of money, is expressed by *orbiculatum*, but *rotundum* expresses nothing farther than that the curve of the leaf is free from angles. " By this term," says Martyn, " Linnæus does not mean a circular, or what we

---

* The cordate, sagittate, hastate, &c. leaves.

should call a round leaf in English; but one which
has a curve without any breaks for the circum-
scribing line." *Teres*, again, means round, like a
walking cane, and hence you would mention the
common rush as being furnished *foliis teretibus*,
with *round*, that is, with *cylindrical* leaves.

59. FOLIUM *subrotundum*, a *roundish* leaf, is applied to such as are nearly circular. The term
should be *suborbiculatum*, but the other has been
too long used to be now altered.

60. FOLIUM *oblongum*, oblong, " three or four
times longer than broad. This term is used with
great latitude, and serves chiefly in a specific character to contrast a leaf which has a variable, or
not very decided form, with others that are precisely round, ovate, linear, &c."—*Smith*. It is
nearly allied to the elliptic leaf.

61. FOLIUM *rhombeum*, *rhomb*, or *diamond-shaped*,
*Fig.*41. (*a*)

Fig. 41.

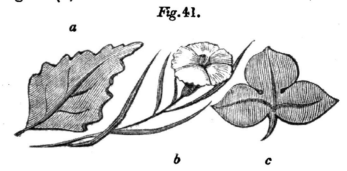

62. FOLIUM *lineare*, *linear*, all of the same
breadth, unless it be the base and points merely,
as in Convolvulus *linearis* (*b*) and most grasses.

63. FOLIUM *integrum,* or *indivisum, entire* or *undivided.* Not in any way cleft.

64. FOLIUM *lobatum, lobed.* The leaves, for instance, of the hepatica (c) are three-lobed (FOLIA *trilobata*).

65. FOLIUM *partitum, partite,* roundish and divided nearly to the base.

66. FOLIUM *laciniatum, torn.*

67. FOLIUM *squarroso-laciniatum,* " when the leaf is cut almost into the middle rib, and the incisures run in every direction, as in the thistle."*

MARGIN.

68. FOLIUM *integerrimum,* a leaf whose *margin* is entire.

As *integerrimus* is the superlative of *integer,* it would be natural to conclude that FOLIUM *integerrimum* should mean a leaf, more perfectly entire than the FOLIUM *integrum. Integrum,* however, applies to the whole leaf, the former to the *margin* only. FOLIUM *integrum* therefore means a leaf that is not in any way lobed, cleft, sinuated, or torn; its *margin,* however, may be serrated, crenate, toothed, &c., and still it will be an entire leaf. But the FOLIUM *integerrimum* may be all these; it may be notched, cleft, &c., but then the *margin* must be smooth; for if there be on the margin of a leaf any teeth or incisures whatever, it cannot be a FOLIUM *integerrimum.* The nettle, for instance,

* Willdenow.

has an entire leaf, though *serrated,* and the ground-ivy, though *crenate;* while the leaf of the blue passion-flower, though *palmate,* is a FOLIUM *integerrimum;* its *margin* being free from any kind of breach.

69. FOLIUM *repandum,* a *repand* leaf (*repandus,* bowed or bent backwards, *Lat.*). Draw a number of curves, or cut the edge of a piece of paper, as at (*a*) *Fig.*42.; (1.1.1.) are sinuses or hollows, and (2.2.2.) are segments of small circles placed between them. When the outline of a leaf describes such sinuses and intermediate circular segments, it is a repand leaf. (*b*)

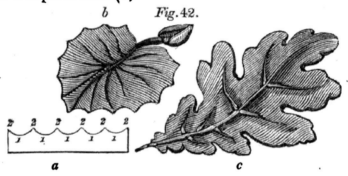

b   *Fig.42.*

a   *c*

70. FOLIUM *sinuatum,* a *sinuated* leaf (*sinus,* a bay, *Lat.*), having deep rounded indentations like an *oak-leaf.* (*c*)

71. FOLIUM *undulatum* (*undula,* a little wave, *Lat.*), when the leaf rises up and down at the margin in a *waved* direction. *Fig.*43. (*a*)

72. FOLIUM *crispum, curled.* (*b*)

73. FOLIUM *plicatum, plaited,* " folded like a fan," the plaits being acute; as in Ladies' mantle. (*c*)

Fig. 43.

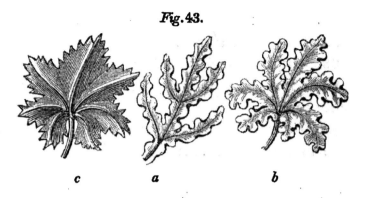

c   a   b

74. FOLIUM *erosum, gnawed* (*erodo,* to gnaw off, *Lat.*).

75. FOLIUM *cartilagineum, cartilaginous* (*cartilago,* a cartilage or gristle, *Lat.*), when the margin is composed of a substance harder than the rest of the leaf.

76. FOLIUM *glandulosum, glandular* (*glans,* a gland, *Lat.*).

SURFACE.

77. FOLIUM *rugosum, wrinkled,* as in sage.

78. FOLIUM *bullatum, blistered.*

79. FOLIUM *lacunosum, pitted* on the *upper* surface.

80. FOLIUM *punctatum, dotted,* which appearance usually arises from glands imbedded in the substance of the leaf.

81. FOLIUM *coloratum,* of any colour but *green.*

The remaining terms which we intend to notice, may be mentioned in alphabetical order.

82. FOLIUM *adpressum*, close to the stem, as if pressed to it by violence.

83. FOLIUM *alternum*, alternate.

84. FOLIUM *amplexicaule*, surrounding the stem by its base.

85. FOLIA *approximata*, or *conferta*, leaves so close to each other that they hide the stem from view.

86. FOLIUM *connatum*, a *connate* leaf (*con*, together, and *nascor*, to grow, *Lat.*).

We have seen that the perfoliate stem runs through the leaf. In the connate leaf, the stem runs through, not really a single leaf, but two leaves united at their bases, so as to seem like one. The cauline leaves of the *Fullers' thistle* (Dipsacus *fullonum*) afford good examples. It not unfrequently happens that connate leaves are concave like a kind of cup, and the rains collect in this, so that the stem is completely surrounded by water at the places from which the leaves arise. From this circumstance the generic name of the *teasel*, Dipsacus, is taken; being derived from δίψα (dipsa), thirst, " from the concave situation of its leaves, which will hold water, by which the thirst of the traveller may be relieved." *

This plant is well known in England, being cultivated on account of its heads, which the clothiers use for raising the nap on cloth. " The leaves, (Gerard says) growe foorth of the iointes by

* Parr's London Medical Dictionary.

couples, not only opposite or set one right against another, but also compassing the stalke about, and fastened togither; and so fastened, that they hold deaw and raine water in manner of a little bason." *
Parkinson says, that the water collected in these reservoirs becomes bitter, and therefore not fitted to quench, but rather to increase thirst. † This is, however, of little or no consequence in these climates, in which the traveller can have little difficulty in obtaining more satisfactory sources from which to alleviate his thirst. But there are countries where the rains fall only at very remote periods; where whole regions consist of burnt-up wastes, or the barren sand stretches like an ocean beyond the horizon's verge; where no fountain bubbles; no streamlet runs, and even the dews of night deny the solace of their tears. In situations like these we may conceive how delicious to the traveller would be even such a bitter draught as is contained in the leaf of the teasel. And, indeed, we have much cause to admire the resources which vegetables afford, from which the pain of thirst may be allayed. Sometimes a reservoir of water is formed in the base of a leaf; sometimes in the hollow of a stem; sometimes in appendages constructed for the purpose; and sometimes the sap-vessels themselves so abound in fluids, that when cut, the latter flow in abundance: while, in other instances, fruits

* Herbal, p. 1005. † Theatre of Plants, p. 985.

in the most arid soils, consist of a cool and semi-fluid pulp.

Many species of the Tillandsia, or *wild pine,* a parasitic genus, common in the West Indies, and the hotter parts of America, have their leaves so hollowed at their base as to be capable of holding above a pint of fluid. " When we find these pines," says Dampier, " we stick our knives into the leaves just above the root, and that lets out the water, which we catch in our hats, as I have done many times to my great relief."* There is a species of bamboo in dry mountainous situations in the Brazils, the young shoots of which, being filled with a cool and pleasant liquid, afford a most grateful beverage to the wearied hunter.† The Jamaica grape-vine, or water-withe, (Vitis *Labrusca,*) is still more useful. A piece of this, of the length of three feet, furnishes about a pint of clear water, " which (according to Brown,) has saved the lives of many who have wandered long in the woods, without any other refreshment of a liquid sort." Among fruits, the cocoa-nut is remarkable for affording a grateful fluid, but none, perhaps, is so extensively beneficial as the water-melon, whose growth no sterility of soil, nor defect of moisture, can retard. The peninsula of Araya, which is rocky, and sometimes for fifteen months is not re-

---

* Voyages, vol. i. p. 58.   See also Brown's Jamaica, p. 194. and Prince Maximilian's Travels, p. 81.

† Prince Maximilian, p. 147.

freshed by a single shower, produces water-melons, each of which weigh from fifty to seventy pounds.*

It has been before mentioned that the cucullate leaves of the Sarracenia genus contain water. The latter is, most probably, secreted into the hollow leaf by the vessels of the plant itself, and not, as in the Tillandsia, deposited by the rains. The species belonging to the genus grow in swampy grounds, and therefore, a provision for storing up moisture against dry weather would be superfluous; besides, the leaf is surmounted by a lid, which would prevent the intrusion of rain. These circumstances strengthen the conclusion, that the object of the fluid in the leaves of the Sarracenia is to entrap insects. But the most extraordinary receptacle of water hitherto discovered in the vegetable kingdom, is the appendage to the leaf of the *Pitcher-plant* (Nepenthes *distillatoria*). This species is a native of Ceylon and Amboyna; its leaves are lanceolate; and beyond the apex of each, the midrib protrudes, like a tendril, to the length of five or six inches. The extremity of this tendril bears the peculiar cup, or pitcher, from which the plant is named. *Fig.* 44. It is cylindrical, about six inches

Fig. 44.

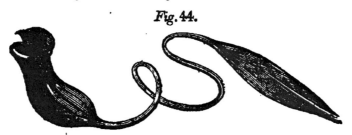

* Humboldt's Pers. Nar. vol. iii. p. 204.

long, and one and a half in diameter, and contains
several ounces of very pure water. Its top is closed
by a lid.*

The water is, unquestionably, secreted by the
vessels of the plant : insects creep into it under the
lid, and are drowned, except a small species of
shrimp, which, according to Rumphius, lives in it.
" I have no doubt," Sir J. E. Smith observes,
" that this shrimp feeds on the other insects and
worms, and that the same purposes are answered
in this instance, as in the Sarraceniæ."†

The pitcher-plant is common about Columbo,
the British capital of Ceylon, where it is called
monkey-cup; for it is said that the monkeys, when
thirsty, seek it out, and drink its contents.‡

87. FOLIA *demersa, immersa*, or *submersa*, leaves
growing under water; *emersa*, protruding above
the surface of water; *natantia*, floating.

Many plants grow completely submerged in
water, and die in any other situation. Various circumstances, however, besides the bare immersion,
are requisite for different species. Thus, some
delight in stagnant ponds; others in clear lakes;
some in slowly flowing brooks, and others are only
found in the rapid stream of mountain-rivulets. Sea-
plants, too, are in general of a very different description from those of the fresh waters. With some
exceptions, plants which grow in water emerge

* Cordiner's Ceylon, vol. i. p. 382.
† Intr. to Botany, p. 175.
‡ Maria Graham's Journal, p. 105.

from its surface, to produce their flowers and seeds
in air; and sometimes there is a very great dissi-
milarity between the *immerged* and *emerged* leaves
of the same plant. We have a striking example
of this in the *water-crowfoot* (Ranunculus *aqua-
tilis*), a species common in pools. Some of its
leaves are submerged, others floating; the latter
are broad, trilobed, and subpeltate; the former divided into many filaments, almost as fine as hairs.

The water-lily, the pondweed, the duckmeat,
and a great many other plants, have leaves which
float on the surface. Such leaves afford resting-
places, especially on their under-surfaces, for many
aquatic insects, and their larvæ; and for *helices* and
other fresh-water shells; and sometimes they serve
as floating rafts for certain birds which prey on fish
and other inhabitants of the water. In birds of
the Parra genus, the toes and nails are of a most
extraordinary length, the intention of which seems

to be to enable the bird to walk over floating leaves. Labillardière saw the *Chinese Jacana* (Parra *Sinensis*) walking on the Nymphæa *Nelumbo,* and he admired, he says, " the lightness with which it walked over the surface of the water, stepping with its long legs from one leaf to another."

COMPOUND LEAVES.

These consist of two or more leaves on one petiole, and several of them, as the digitate and pedate leaves, have been already described.

88. FOLIUM *binatum,* a *binate* leaf.

89. FOLIUM *conjugatum,* a *conjugate* or yoked leaf.

The *binate* is a species of digitate leaf, and consists of two leaflets arising from the extremity of one footstalk. *Fig.* 45.(*a*) But if a footstalk, in place of *terminating* in two leaflets, have them on its sides, then it forms a *conjugate* leaf. *Fig.* 45.(*b*) The only difference, therefore, between a binate and a conjugate leaf is, that in the former the petiole *terminates* in two leaflets; in the latter these spring from its sides; for the one is a digitate, the other a pinnate leaf. Though thus different, however, they are in general used synonymously.

If the petiole divide at the summit, and each division end in two leaflets, it is a *bigeminate* leaf, FOLIUM *bigeminatum* (*bis,* twice, and *gemini,* twins, *Lat.*). *Fig.* 45.(*c*) And if such a petiole have two leaflets at its division also, it forms a *trigeminate* leaf. *Fig.* 45.(*d*)

* Voyage, vol. ii. p. 327.

Fig. 45.

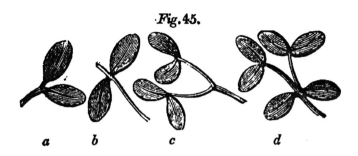

a   b   c   d

The conjugate leaf, as we have just seen, has one pair of leaflets on the petiole; but some plants have two pairs, forming a *bijugous* leaf, FOLIUM *bijugum* (*bis*, twice, and *jugum*, a yoke or pair, *Lat.*), and some three, forming a *trijugous* leaf, &c.

90. FOLIUM *ternatum*, a *ternate* leaf, when one petiole has three leaflets, as in strawberry and trefoil.

91. FOLIUM *biternatum*, *twice* ternate.

92. FOLIUM *triternatum*, *thrice* ternate.

Let us, for the sake of illustrating the biternate and the triternate leaf, have recourse to a well known object, the pawnbroker's sign. This may be called ternate, having three balls, as the strawberry leaf has three leaflets. But suppose the branch or foot-stalk of each ball to be again split into three, and each of those to be armed with a ball, then the balls will be nine, and the object will be *biternate*, as it has formed a *second* division into threes.

Suppose again each branch of this second or biternate division to be farther split into three, then the balls will amount to twenty-seven, and the object will be *triternate*, having formed a third division into threes.

Fig.46.

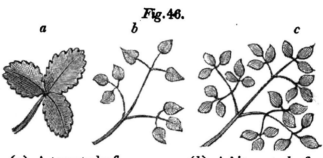

(*a*) A ternate leaf.   (*b*) A biternate leaf.
(*c*) A triternate leaf.

The leaf of the strawberry is *compound*, that is, it does not, like the leaf of the nettle, consist of one expansion only, but of more than one. It is, however, simply compound. But a leaf dividing a *second* time, as we have been explaining, is *decomposite* or doubly compound; and if it divide *thrice* or oftener, it is a *supradecomposite* leaf.

When a petiole has a number of leaflets growing from its sides it forms a *pinnate*, or pinnated leaf, FOLIUM *pinnatum*, (*pinna*, a wing or pinion, *Lat.*). The conjugate, bijugous, and trijugous leaves, for instance, are pinnate; and when there are more pairs of leaflets than in these, they may be expressed by describing the plant as being furnished *foliis pinnatis quadrijugis*, with pinnate leaves, consisting of four pairs of leaflets, *quinquejugis*, of five pairs, and so on.

If you examine a leaf of an ash-tree or of a rose, you will observe that its folioles are in pairs, except one at the end: this forms the FOLIUM *imparipinnatum*, or FOLIUM *pinnatum cum impari*, that is,

pinnated, with an odd terminal leaflet. *Fig.* 47. (*a*)
Sometimes a pinnated leaf ends in a tendril, and,
of course, is a FOLIUM *pinnatum cirrosum, Fig.*
47. (*b*); and sometimes there is neither a tendril,

Fig. 47.

a   *b*

nor odd leaflet, and then it is a FOLIUM *abrupte-
pinnatum,* an *abruptly* pinnate leaf. *Fig.* 48. (*a*)
When, as in the ash, and rose, the leaflets are
opposite to each other, the leaf is said to be *oppo-
sitely* pinnate, FOLIUM *opposite-pinnatum;* but when
they stand alternately, it is a FOLIUM *alternatim
pinnatum,* an *alternately* pinnate leaf. *Fig.* 47. (*c*)

Fig. 48.

a   *b*

H

Sometimes the leaflets grow gradually smaller from the base to the end of the petiole. This is termed a decreasingly pinnate leaf, FOLIUM *pinnatum foliolis decrescentibus. Fig.* 48. (*b*)

93. The FOLIUM *lyratopinnatum,* or *lyrato-pinnate* leaf, must not be confounded with the FOLIUM *impari pinnatum.* A beginner might easily suppose (*a*) *Fig.* 49. to be a leaf of the latter description, for it certainly is pinnate, and with a terminal odd leaflet. The great size of the latter, however, and the leaflets being gradually smaller from top to bottom, give the *lyrate* form, and make the distinction.

. 94. FOLIUM *interrupte-pinnatum,* an *interruptedly* pinnate leaf. When between every larger pair of leaflets is placed a smaller pair, or more than one. *Fig.* 49. (*b*)

a   *Fig.* 49.   b

95. FOLIUM *decursive-pinnatum, decursively* pinnate. When the leaflets are connected to each other by a leafy expansion running along the edge of the petiole.

96. FOLIUM *articulate-pinnatum, jointedly* pinnate. *Fig.* 50. (*e*)

When a petiole splits into two divisions, and

each division forms a pinnated leaf, so that *two* leaves instead of *one* are formed from the same footstalk, it is a *conjugately* pinnate leaf, FOLIUM *conjugatum pinnatum*, *Fig.* 50. (*f*); in which (*a*) shows the petiole, (*b*) its division, (*c*) one pinnate leaf, (*c*) another.

Fig. 50.

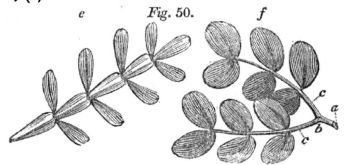

We have seen that the *digitate* leaf consists of a number of folioles standing on the point of the leafstalk. In a similar way a number of *pinnated* leaves may stand on the extremity of a petiole, so as to form a digitate, and at the same time a pinnate leaf, FOLIUM *digitatum pinnatum*, that is, both digitate and pinnate. *Fig.* 51.

Fig. 51.

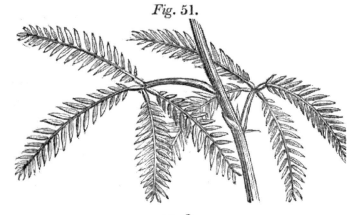

97. FOLIUM *bipinnatum,* a *bipinnate,* or doubly pinnate leaf.

98. FOLIUM *tripinnatum,* a *tripinnate,* or trebly pinnated leaf.

These terms are easily understood. The first is " when the common petiole has pinnate leaves on each side of it," * *Fig.* 52. (*a*); the second, when the common petiole has *bipinnate* leaves on each side. *Fig.* 52. (*b*)

a   *Fig.* 52.   b

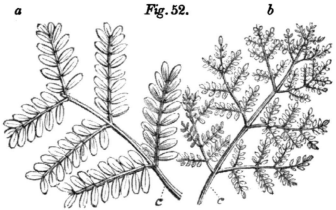

In both these figures (*c*) denotes the common petiole; and it is obvious that the leaves from its sides in the first figure are simply pinnated, and in the second bipinnate. The first is *decomposite,* the second *supradecomposite,* or *thrice* compound.

Having now considered the principal sorts of leaves, I shall make some general observations respecting them. And first, I wish to remark, that though the anatomy and physiology of plants

* Martyn.

are most interesting subjects, yet I cannot approve of the practice of introducing topics so abtruse into works *introductory* to the science. I might state several reasons for this, but shall offer one only. The study of Botany is not restricted to medical students, but, on the contrary, it may form the delight and amusement of persons of every calling, of either sex, and of almost any age; and little more previous qualification than that of a common education is necessary for its pursuit. But the functions of a leaf cannot be understood by one ignorant of the organs and physiology of animal respiration; of the composition of atmospheric air; and of the changes it undergoes in the lungs. The analogy between the animal and vegetable functions is equally strict in many other instances; and, indeed, no one is prepared to enter on the subject of vegetable physiology, who has not previously made considerable progress in a knowledge of the anatomy and physiology of the *animal* frame, and of the laws of chemistry. A person not so prepared will run the risk of being disgusted, or dismayed at the difficulties which lie before him in the very outset of his botanical enquiries.

With respect to leaves, it is very obvious that no connection exists between their size, and that of the plants to which they belong; for often the largest vegetables have leaves comparatively small. The leaf of the oak or poplar, for instance, is diminutive when compared with that of the cabbage.

Yet it may happen that plants with small leaves shall present to the atmosphere a greater foliar surface, than species in which they are very large; for *number* may compensate for smallness; and hence, the myrtle and many other species, though not furnished with large, have very numerous leaves, and expose a great surface to the air and light. From plants, however, with very large, to those with minute, or no leaves, there is every possible intermediate gradation. Among British species, those of the *Butterbur* and *Burdock* have decidedly the superiority in point of size, though this is trifling when compared to the leaves of many tropical plants, especially the fronds of the palm tribe.

The dwarf birch (Betula *nana*) is a tree of very stunted growth, not unfrequent in some parts of North Britain, and still more common in colder latitudes. Its leaves are sometimes not larger than a split pea, and the comparative diminutiveness of the whole plant is strongly marked by the opinion held among the common people in some parts of Scotland, that it is cursed with a stunted growth, because the rod was formed from it with which Christ was scourged. *

Almost all leaves sink into insignificance when compared with the size of the frond. That of the gigantic sea-weed (Fucus *giganteus*) has been

* Pennant's Tour in Scotland, vol. iii. p. 43.

found eight hundred feet long; and the frond of the majestic Rafia palm of Madagascar measures sixty feet, and is used for aprons and other sorts of wearing apparel. * The fronds of various other palms are used as coverings for huts, bags for conveying raw sugar, and baskets for holding fruit; and in Africa, the negroes, during heavy rains, use a frond of the *ciboa* palm as an umbrella. " In the afternoon (says Park) it rained hard, and we had recourse to the common negro umbrella, a large ciboa leaf, which being placed upon the head, completely defends the whole body from the rain."† In a similar way the leaf of the great fan-palm (Corypha *umbraculifera*) is used in the South Sea islands for keeping off the sun.

The great breadth of the frond of some palms renders them a substitute for paper; and they were the first material used by the Eastern nations for writing on. Hence it is with reason inferred that the Scriptures were originally committed to palm leaves.

> With fruit and ever verdant branches crown'd,
> Judea chose her emblem; on whose leaves
> She first inscribed her oracles, and all
> The fortunes of her state; herself a palm
> Still mounting from its ashes, though deprest
> Still springing unsubdued. ‡

In the *consistence* of leaves we find much variety, every possible intermediate degree, perhaps, exist-

* St. Vincent. † Travels, p. 354.
‡ Tighe's Plants, cant. iv. l. 374.

ing between the fleshy leaves of the Opuntia and other succulent species, and those of the Palis-courea *rigida*, which are large and tough, and " rustle like parchment when shaken by the winds." *

Leaves are pretty constant in their forms, though with some exceptions. The *shrubby burnet*, for instance (Poterium *spinosum*), a native of Candia and Cyprus, has pinnate leaves; but on some of these the leaflets are entire, on others pinnatifid, and on others both are intermixed, so that different branches taken from the same plant might seem to belong to totally different species.† Sometimes, as in the three-thorned acacia (Gleditschia *triacanthos*), the plant when young has its leaves, which are pinnate, doubly or even triply compound; but as the plant gets old they all become *simply pinnated.* What is more remarkable, some *mimosæ* of New Holland, when young, have leaves very compounded; when old, simple. ‡ Such instances are, fortunately for the botanist, very rare, else much confusion would be created.

The leaves of trees and shrubs, having lasted the time allotted them by nature, shrink and drop off, producing annually the phenomenon called the " fall of the leaf." With respect to the cause of this, it is sufficient at present to say, that each leaf falls

* Humboldt's Pers. Nar. vol. iii. p. 93.
† Clarke's Travels, vol. iv. p. 722.
‡ Willdenow's London Medical and Physical Journal, vol. i. p. 37.

because it is weakened or dead, and also because
it is separated by an action in the living branch
from which it grew. The bare death of a leaf is
not sufficient to cause its fall; for when both leaf
and plant are killed by lightning, by a cutting wind,
or any other sudden cause, the *dead leaf* will adhere
tenaciously to the *dead branch*. There are some
plants which it is very difficult to preserve by drying in the usual manner, because their leaves all
separate; and for this reason,—they become dead
sooner than the parts from which they grow, and
these parts retain vital action enough to throw
them off. The remedy, however, is simple: imitate
the stroke of lightning, or whatever will at once
kill the whole plant; all will then die together, and
consequently the dead branch will have no power
to cast off the dead leaf. The remedy is to dip
the specimen in *boiling water* before committing it
to paper. The heaths, especially, are said to require this treatment, as do also the succulent plants,
though on a somewhat different account; for as the
latter can live almost independent of roots, they
continue to vegetate during the usual process of
drying, and it is not uncommon to find them when
pressed in books running through the whole process of flowering, and even producing seeds. Brown
mentions that the leaves of the *smooth acacia* (which
are not succulent indeed, but sensible like those
of the sensitive plant,) will spread and contract,

after they have been in paper for a month or six weeks.

The change of temperature from hot to cold seems to be one principal circumstance connected with the death, and fall of the leaf; and hence it is, that European trees grown in the southern hemisphere cast their leaves at the approach of winter there, which is about the same period of the year that they put them forth in their own climate. *

Some birds cast their feathers all at once, and in consequence, being unable to fly, are caught in great numbers. These may be compared to most trees in our regions, which part with their leaves in a few weeks, and remain bare till the following spring. But in most birds the casting and renewing of their feathers is a gradual process, and when the change is going on, no inconvenience from want of clothing is felt by the animal; as, although it is constantly losing some of its old plumage, an equal quantity of new is coming forward to supply its place.

Now, in trees in hot countries the leaves are changed, though not so often as with us, but there is no general moulting. The trees are constantly losing leaves, but as constantly repairing the loss, so that they are always clothed, and present no change that can be denominated the "*fall of the leaf.*"

* Thunberg's Travels, vol. i. p. 104.

With respect to the *colour* of leaves, it is almost
unnecessary to say that in most plants it is green;
but in different species the green varies much in
intensity. Cowper has prettily drawn the contrasts
of shade presented by the foliage of various trees.

> No tree in all the grove but has its charms,
> Though each its hue peculiar; paler some,
> And of a wannish grey; the willow such,
> And poplar, that with silver lines his leaf,
> And ash far stretching his umbrageous arm:
> Of deeper green the elm; and deeper still,
> Lord of the woods, the long-surviving oak.
> Some glossy-leaved and shining in the sun,
> The maple, and the beech of oily nuts
> Prolific, and the lime at dewy eve
> Diffusing odours: nor unnoted pass
> The sycamore, capricious in attire;
> Now green, now tawny, and ere autumn yet
> Have changed the woods, in scarlet honours bright.

Some plants have a foliage coloured very differently from green; and many whose leaves are of
this colour on the upper surface are of a different
hue on the under. Scarcely any plant has a more
beautiful, satiny, deep green above than the shining-
leaved begonia (Begonia *nitida*); but beneath it
is universally reddish, and traversed in every direction by reticulated dark-red veins. Some species
have naturally several colours in the same leaf, and
by art and culture this circumstance is rendered
frequent, as may be observed in the many variegated
plants of shrubberies and gardens. This variega-
tion, which may be considered as a sort of disease,
is much more common in petals than in common

H 6

leaves; and hence the endless varieties of the tulip, hyacinth, &c. Red is a very common colour in the leaves of many plants, when they begin to decay, and in some long before they fall; as in the common dog-wood (Cornus *sanguinea*), the Virginian creeper (Hedera *quinquefolia*), many species of rose, &c.

Sometimes almost the same freaks are played in the colouring of a leaf as in that of a flower. In the Mauritia *aculeata*, a species of palm, Humboldt found at the centre of every frond concentric alternate circles of blue and yellow, so that it seemed coloured like a peacock's tail. *

If we include the frond of the cryptogamic plants, there scarcely exists a hue which may not be found in some of them. Many of the *Fuci* rival the crimson of the rose; the Byssus *jolithus* †, which incrusts stones, makes them appear as if stained with blood; the Byssus *lactea* is so white, that rocks on which it spreads seem whitewashed; and the Lichen *rangiferinus*, or *reindeer lichen*, is in northern countries often found spread over mountains and extensive plains, making them appear as if covered with snow. The picturesque tints acquired by aged trees and ruins are chiefly owing to the various species of lichen and moss with which they become incrusted; and the same humble

* Pers. Nar. vol. v. p. 239.
† This is now named Lichen *jolithus*. It is the cause of the blood-like stains on the stones in St. Winifred's well.

plants often give to shivered cliffs and precipices the semblance of decayed castles, and other ruins.

>   —— Rocks sublime
> To human art a sportive semblance bear,
> And yellow lichens colour all the clime,
> Like moonlight battlements and towers decay'd by time.

The changes of colour in the leaves of plants, especially of trees, which take place in autumn, are familiar to every one, but are more particularly interesting to the eye of the painter, and the contemplation of the moralist. The one finds in them some of the best subjects for the warmth and beauty of his pencil; the other contrasts these changing leaves with the races of men, which having flourished through the spring and summer of life fall at last, in the autumn of their existence, into decay, and are swept by the wintry breath of age into the tomb, and are no more found. Trees have thus been ever considered as emblems of human life, and, in all ages, affecting views and comparisons have been drawn of their progress from debility and infancy. to youth, strength, maturity, and inevitable final decay. The heathen and the atheist have found in them emblems of eternal oblivion, to which they suppose man with all his high-born hopes is to be consigned. As the leaves of the tree fall and perish for ever, so *they* represent that when man returns to his mother earth, it is only to mingle with the unthinking material elements; that never more shall he be conscious of existence; and that he, his virtues, and his crimes, sink into irrevocable annihilation.   Yet as no particle of matter is ever lost, though it may undergo a thousand changes of the most extraordinary kind, so we may rest satisfied that mind is equally indestructible; and though it be impossible for us to trace its flight or modifications after death, there is no reason for a moment to question its future existence, and its immortality.   Every thing revealed and rational teaches us that the soul is destined to survive " the wreck of elements and crush of worlds," and that it may go on in increasing knowledge and happiness for ever.

All is in change — yet there is nothing lost:
The dew becomes the essence of the flower
Which feeds the insect of the sunny hour —
Now leaf; now pinion; — though the hills were tost
By the wild whirlwinds, like the summer dust,
Would not an atom perish; — Nature's power
Knows not annihilation, and her dower
Is universal Fitness never crost.
Is all eternal save the mind of man —
The masterpiece and glory of the whole,
The wonder of creation? — Is a span
To limit the duration of the soul —
To drop ere its career is well begun,
Like a proud steed far distant from the goal?*

* Blackwood's Magazine.

CHAPTER V.

OF THE FULCRA.

LINNÆUS, in the Philosophia Botanica, enumerates seven species of FULCRA, or *props* (*fulcrum*, a
prop, *Lat.*). These are the STIPULA, BRACTEA,
THORN, PRICKLE, TENDRIL, GLAND, and HAIR; but
it is evident that of these the CIRRUS, or *tendril*,
alone can with strict propriety be called a support,
or prop. In a preceding part of this work, the
thorn, prickle, and hair, have been described. The
others are,

1. CIRRUS, *tendril*, or clasper. (*Cirrus* means a
ringlet of hair, and is derived from the Greek, κερας
(*keras*), a horn, because the horns of many animals
are spiral.) The tendril is not in general at first
convoluted; it shoots out in a straight direction,
but soon twists, and often, if it do not find a body
to lay hold of, puts on a very beautiful appearance,
its folds lying in contact with each other, and gradually contracting their diameter so as to form a
hollow cone, as in the vine and passion-flower;
and sometimes a tube, resembling such as is made
by twisting wire. *Fig. 53.*

Fig. 53.

We cannot for an instant doubt that the use of
the tendril is to support those plants which are
furnished with it; and we have already seen that
many scandent plants climb to the tops of the
highest trees, which is effected either entirely by
the help of these organs, or by the stem being at
the same time convoluted; and thus, this wise
and remarkable provision enables them, notwithstanding their apparent weakness, to scale "the
breathing steep of air," and overtop the stateliest
monarchs of the woods.

As the use of the tendril is to support the plant,
we should naturally suppose its texture to be strong
and tough; and so we find it: the tendril of a vine,
for instance, is much stronger than the footstalks of
its leaves; and as the tendril increases in rigidity
along with the growth of the plant, it is strongest
when the fruit is ripening, that is, at the precise
time when its strength is most required. In the
vines cultivated in our hot-houses, indeed, little
strength would seem necessary for the purpose, as
the clusters are not often of large size. But the
case is very different, when, as in that forest of

plane-trees seventy feet high, described by Savary, on the banks of the Platania, in Crete, the vines reach the summits of the trees, and form a magnificent canopy of verdant leaves and variously-coloured grapes, many clusters of which are two feet in length.

The tendrils of the passion-flower, and, I believe, of most of the larger scandent plants, are *simple,* or at least very little branched, and I suppose for this reason: they clamber up trees, shrubs, and other large firm bodies which are capable of bearing their weight, and therefore the tying by simple undivided tendrils answers every desired intention. But plants of a minor description, which are weak, and must often cling to stays as feeble as themselves, have generally their tendrils *much* branched or divided, so that their divisions protruding in different directions, can lay hold of a considerable number of contiguous plants or other objects; and thus the number of bodies to which they cling compensates for their individual weakness.

It has been before observed, that when voluble plants are kept turned in a direction opposite to that which is natural to their respective species, they pine, or even die; and it is not improbable that the clasping of the tendrils in scandent plants may be useful in some other ways than in barely giving a support. Pope's allusion to the vine may be more than poetical.

Man like the generous vine supported lives;
The strength he gains is from the embrace he gives.

It may happen that a plant will require the aid of tendrils when young, but not when old or arrived at certain stages of growth. Thus the vanilla plant (Epidendrum *Vanilla*), which in the West Indies rises to the tops of the highest trees, has, when young, a long winding tendril opposite to each of its lower leaves ; but when the plant has gained the top of the tree, these *cirri*, being no longer useful, drop off, and a *leaf* grows in place of each ! *

The *climbing marcgravia* (Marcgravia *umbellata*) of the West Indies, rises in a similar manner ; for the roots which Brown speaks of as attaching it to its supporter appear clearly to be tendrils. " This curious plant," he observes, " is frequent in the woods of Jamaica ; and appears in such various forms, that it has been often mistaken for different plants, in the different stages of its growth. It is but a slender weakly climber at first, and, as it rises, throws out a few leaves, somewhat of the form of a heart, on both sides: these are sustained by very short footstalks, and stand always opposite to a number of slender radical fibres, whereby it sticks and grows to its supporter. By these means the plant continues its growth until it gains the top, and lays its trunk more commodiously over some of the larger branches of the tree: then it begins to strengthen, and casts many slender, dependent, and undivided branches from the upper parts. But as it increases at the top, the stem grows thicker,

* Brown's Jamaica, p. 326.

separates from the supporter, throws off its now useless leaves and *roots* [tendrils], and appears a strong withey shrub, whose trunk is frequently no less than four or five inches in diameter."*

It appears, from the same author, that by a similar slender beginning, and a like process, the enormous Banyan originates; but the appendages it throws out in every stage of its growth at last coalesce in such a manner as completely to involve the supporting trunk, which of course dies, and is, as it were, devoured by its insidious companion.†
There is a plant also in South America which, from its destroying trees, is named *Matapalo*, that is, *Kill-timber*. This species is weak at first, but after having by its incumbrance killed the tree to which it clings, it attains so great a bulk that it serves for making canoes of a very large size.‡

The tendril is in some plants axillary; in others it terminates the leaf; in some it springs from the petiole, in some from the flower-stalk; generally it is convoluted regularly, but sometimes is *revolute*,

* History of Jamaica, p. 244. Tab. 26.
† Ibid. p. 110.
‡ " I recollect," says the author of Bracebridge Hall, " hearing a traveller of poetical temperament expressing the kind of horror which he felt on beholding, on the banks of the Missouri, an oak of prodigious size, which had been in a manner overpowered by an enormous wild grape-vine. The vine had clasped its huge folds round the trunk, and from thence had wound about every branch and twig, until the mighty tree had withered in its embrace. It seemed like Laocöon struggling ineffectually in the hideous coils of the monster Python. It was the lion of trees perishing in the embraces of a vegetable boa."

or twining first to one side and then to another. Sometimes the divisions of tendrils are armed with terminal, flat, fleshy expansions or warts, which adhere to the smoothest surfaces.

Willdenow attributes the spiral form of tendrils to their tenuity and feebleness; but this is very unphilosophical. We might as well attribute the twisting of the voluble *stem* to a like cause; but it is easy to show that numerous plants, with as long, thin, and weak stems as those of the twining tribe, show not the slightest tendency to twist. Who knows not that the woodbine is a stronger plant than the periwinkle, but who ever saw a woodbine that, when left to nature, did *not* twist, or a periwinkle that did? The twining of the voluble stems and of tendrils is a part of their economy, not originating in accident, but imposed on them by the Author of Nature for the best purposes; and it is idle to attempt explaining the phenomenon by referring it to any casual circumstances. It forms a part of vegetable economy well worthy of admiration; but its cause I believe to be as inexplicable as that of muscular contraction, secretion, and many other things going on in the " impenetrable laboratory" both of the animal and vegetable body; and which the mind of man will never, perhaps, be able to explain.

In Paley's Natural Theology there is a passage relating to climbing plants, so appropriate to our present subject, that I shall quote it. It runs thus : " In these plants, from each knot or joint, or, as botanists call it, axilla of the plant, issue, close to each other, two shoots : one bearing the flower and fruit; the other, drawn out into a wire, a long, tapering, spiral tendril, that twists itself round any thing which lies within its reach. Considering, that in this class two purposes are to be provided for (and together), fructification and support, the fruitage of the plant, and the sustentation of the stalk, what means could be used more effectual, or, as I have said, more mechanical, than what this structure presents to our eyes? Why, or how, without a view to this double purpose, do two shoots of such different and appropriate forms spring from the same joint, from contiguous points of the same stalk? It never happens thus in robust plants or in trees. ' We see not (says Ray) so much as one tree, or shrub, or herb, that hath a firm and strong stem, and that is able to mount up, and stand alone without assistance, *furnished with these tendrils.*' Make only so simple a comparison as that between a pea and a bean. Why does the pea put forth tendrils, the bean not; but because the stalk of the pea cannot support itself, the stalk of the bean can? We may add also, as a circumstance not to be overlooked, that in the pea-tribe these clasps do not make their appearance till they are wanted ; till the plant has grown to a height to stand in need of support." *

Sometimes the office of a tendril is performed

* Page 310.

by a different part; thus in the *long-leaved custard apple* (Annona *hexapetala*), a tree, native of China and the East Indies, the flower-stalk forms a hook, by which the fruit, which is very heavy and like a bunch of grapes, is suspended on the adjacent branch. *

2. STIPULA. Examine a stalk of *heart's-ease* (Viola *tricolor*), and you will find, at the base of each petiole, a pair of leaves very different from the real leaf at the other end of the petiole, as in *Fig.* 54., in which it is very obvious that the true leaf (*b*) is different from those at its base (*a, a*),

Fig. 54.

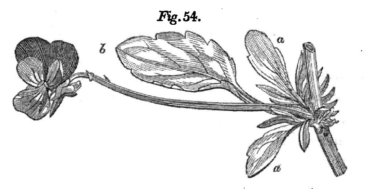

which are the *stipulas;* the former being *crenato-dentate*, the latter *lyrato-pinnatifid.* Now, this will give a general idea of what is meant by a stipula, which term is said to be derived from *stipa*, stubble, but were I to hazard a conjecture, I should rather suppose it to be from *stipatus ;* attended by a guard, as if the stipulæ were placed at the base of the leaf or petiole, as sentinels.

The stipula is generally double, one being placed

* Smith's Introduction, p. 171.

at each side of the base of the petiole, as in the last figure.

Sometimes there is only one, and in a great number of plants they are altogether wanting.

This organ varies greatly in shape in different species, and sometimes even supplies the place of real leaves, the foliage of the plant consisting almost altogether of stipules, as in yellow vetchling (Lathyrus *Aphaca*).

STIPULA *lateralis*, a lateral stipule. Placed on the sides of the petiole, as in the rose; see *Fig. 21.*

STIPULA *extrafoliacea.*

STIPULA *intrafoliacea.*

The extrafoliaceous stipula, *Fig. 55.* (*b, b*), is placed on the outside of the petiole (*a*), the intrafoliaceous on the inside, *Fig. 55.* (*c*), which represents the stipule of a species of Polygonum, in which genus it surrounds the stem.

The *stipula* in grasses was formerly named the *ligula* or strap; it is a thin whitish membrane at the top of the vaginal petiole. *Fig. 55.* (*d*)

Sometimes a thorn protrudes together with the stipules, as in the *thorny hydrolea* (Hydrolea *spinosa*).

Fig. 55.

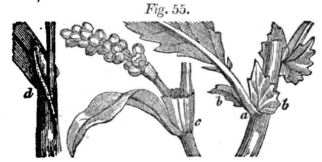

3. BRACTEA. As the *stipule* is an appendage to the leaf, or leaf-stalk, the bractea is an accompaniment of the flower, or the flower-stalk. It originally meant a plate of metal, and why it has been adopted as a botanical term I cannot conjecture. Martyn defines it, " A leaf different from the other leaves in shape and colour, generally situated on the peduncle, and often so near the corolla, as easily to be mistaken for the calyx. — The calyx, however, withers when the fruit is ripe, if not before; whereas the *bractea* is generally more permanent.

The *lime-tree* (Tili *Europæa*) is usually cited as a good example; and from the miniature figure

Fig. 56.

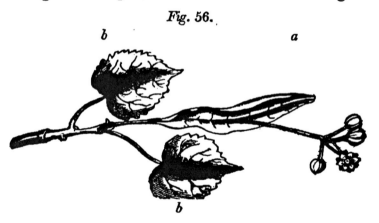

of it, *Fig. 56.*, you will at once observe that the BRACTEA (*a*) is very different from the other leaves (*b, b*). In some plants, however, as in several species of *sage*, the transition from leaves to bracteas is insensible, and a considerable part of the plant has its foliage composed of the latter.

4. GLANDULA, a gland.

We have before taken some notice of the glands of the *moss-rose*, and *sun-dew*. They are found in a great many other plants, but they are not always, as in those just mentioned, *pedicellate* or placed on pedicles. Often they are sessile, or sitting immediately upon the surface; and their forms are very various. They are like little tubercles; sometimes vesicular, or in form of hollow bladders, or like minute scales; or, as in the passion-flower, resembling little cups. They are most frequently situated on the petiole, sometimes on the leaf, and sometimes between the serratures of its margin.

The secretions from glands are very various, and in many plants they serve for forming the sweet fluids of which bees make honey.

CHAPTER VI.

OF THE FLOWER.

WE are now arrived at " the bright consummate flower," and here I use the word in its generally understood sense. There are, however, seven distinct parts in the fructification of plants, and of these the beautifully-coloured portion which, more commonly, is recognized as the flower, is scientifically named the *corolla*, and the leaves composing it are called *petals*. The four yellow leaves, for instance, of the wall-flower, the purple leaves of the gilliflower, the bell of the campanula, the snowy cup of the white convolvulus, and the sweet-scented blue petals of the violet, form the corollas of those plants.

This part is not essential to the fructification; for in many plants, even in many of the most stately trees, it is wanting, and yet they produce as perfect seeds as those in which it is most largely developed. Some, too, can dispense with the corolla at particular seasons, and thus the sweetest daughter of the spring, the *violet*, continues through he summer to produce fructifications and seeds, but has then *no* flower-leaves, and exhales *no* perfume, as though *her aid* were unnecessary when such numberless sweets are poured out from other flowers.

That the COROLLA, however, serves various useful purposes in those species that do possess it, may be very true, and often these uses can be demonstrated. But I believe that much of the beautiful vesture, and of the endless variety in the forms and colours of vegetables, has been given for the express purpose of attracting the admiration of man, and exciting him to their serious contemplation. This observation indeed may be applied to every department of nature. Why, for instance, have shells such uncommon beauty of form, colours, and polish, but that the examination of them may enlarge the field of intellect? The inhabitant of the common whelk is housed as safely in its simple residence of calcareous earth, as that of the Nautilus *Pompilius* in a chambered palace, whose walls are like pearls and silver; and the shed of the limpet serves as well for protection, as the canopy of the *haliotis* which glitters with the colours of the rainbow. Why is the goldfinch more ornamented than the sparrow; since it could fly as swiftly, though its plumage were equally dusky? and why is the peacock embellished with a combination of every hue that is beautiful and brilliant, when it could pick up its grain equally well, although it wore the unassuming dress of its more humble companions of the court-yard? Thousands of other instances might be adduced, to show that a chief part of the beauty and variety which occur in the different kingdoms of nature, have been intended for the *mind of man ;* and no where perhaps is this more conspicuous, than in the profusion of plants which clothe our globe, in which,

> No gradual bloom is wanting; from the bud
> First born of Spring to Summer's musky tribes;
> Nor hyacinths of purest virgin white,
> Low-bent and blushing inward; nor jonquils
> Of potent fragrance; nor narcissus fair,
> As o'er the fabled fountain hanging still;
> Nor broad carnations, nor gay-spotted pinks;
> Nor, showered from every bush, the damask rose:
> Infinite numbers, delicacies, smells,
> With hues on hues expression cannot paint,
> The breath of Nature and her endless bloom.

Now, what can give a more pleasing view of the benevolence of the Almighty than thus to see the earth " apparelled with plants, as with a robe of imbroidered work, set with orient pearles, and garnished with great diversitie of rare and costly jewels?" *   How little given to observation and reflection must they be, who can look on such a scene, and see in it only the workings of chance, or who feel as little impressed by it as though it were. People in general, indeed, have never thought of the extent of power, and profundity of wisdom, displayed in the formation of the vegetable world; but were we in imagination to conceive the existence of a being endued with ten thousand times the powers that any *human* mind ever possessed; and

* Gerard.

that to such an intelligence were submitted the privilege of clothing a world with organised bodies formed after its own conceptions, how comparatively miserable, how destitute, would such a creation be! how unlike that which arose when " the evening and the morning were the third day," when " the earth brought forth grass, and herb yielding seed after his kind, and the tree yielding fruit, whose seed was in itself after his kind: and God saw that it was good !"

———— The bare earth, till then
Desert and bare, unsightly, unadorned,
Brought forth the tender grass, whose verdure clad
Her universal face with pleasant green :
Then herbs of every leaf, that sudden flowered
Opening their various colours, and made gay
Her bosom smelling sweet : and these scarce blown,
Forth flourished thick the clustering vine, forth crept
The smelling gourd, up stood the corny reed
Embattled in her field, and th' humble shrub,
And bush with frizzled hair implicit : last
Rose as in dance the stately trees, and spread
Their branches hung with copious fruit, or gemmed
Their blossoms : with high woods the hills were crowned,
With tufts the valleys, and each fountain side,
With borders long, the rivers : that earth now
Seemed like to Heaven, a seat where gods might dwell,
Or wander with delight, and love to haunt
Her sacred shades.

In perusing this third volume of nature's book; whether we consider its successive pages, as they unfold through the period of a day, or through the recurring seasons of the revolving year, we shall find every line in each replete with entertainment and instruction. It is a volume in which is nothing to hurt our feelings, or excite a moment's disgust; and indeed we may with justice apply to Botany the words of the inspired writer, and assert, that " her ways are ways of pleasantness, and all her paths are peace."

As the bulk of a plant forms no standard by which to estimate the size of its leaves, neither does it with respect to the size of the COROLLA. Often, indeed, very large *trees* have no corolla; such are the oak, the pine, the beech, and many others. They have, to be sure, the essential parts of fructification, and produce seeds; but they have not what, in common language, would be called a flower;—they have no corolla, no petals. Some diminutive plants, again, have this organ very large, an example of which may be seen in the *gentianella*, or dwarf gentian (Gentiana *acaulis*), which in March and April expands its bright-blue funnel-shaped corolla to a size greater than all the rest of the plant; and in some other species it is of still more disproportionate magnitude. In the *laurel-leaved magnolia* (Magnolia *grandiflora*) of North America, the corolla, which consists of from fifteen to twenty-five thick snow-white petals, is sometimes of even the diameter of nine inches. Yet these are dwarf when compared with the blossom of a plant discovered by Sir Thomas Stamford Raffles in forests in the interior of Sumatra, in 1818. This plant, which after its discoverer has been named RAFFLESIA, is parasitic, growing on the lower stems and roots of the Cissus *angustifolia*. So gigantic is its flower, that in the bud-state it is nearly a foot in diameter; and after expansion, it measures almost three feet over, from the tip of one petal to that of another; its substance is about half an inch thick, and it weighs from twelve to fifteen pounds.* Its petals are of a brick-red colour, for we are not always to expect that most beauty is to be found in the largest flowers, since often in the smallest it is exquisite, though it becomes still more so when the flower is enlarged by a magnifying glass. In this particular few excel the little Forget-me-not (Myosotis *scorpioides*), and the flowers of the London-pride (Saxifraga *umbrosa*), whose petals are elegantly marked with the richest crimson dots.

The *number* of flowers, also, is very different on different plants. When St. Vincent was at the Mauritius, there stood in the court of the house where he lodged, an ordinarily-sized tree of the species called Acacia of Malabar (*Mimosa Lebbec*). Its flowers are white, yellow, and delicately rose-coloured, and are in bunches, each containing about thirty-six. Hence they can be easily counted; and in this tree, though not a large one, St. Vincent found the corollas to amount to thirty-two thousand seven hundred and twenty-four. †

Where there is such a profusion as this (and

* Edinburgh Philosophical Journal, Apr. 1822.
† Voyages, Modern and Contemporary, vol. ii.

often there is a much greater), it is almost impossible that the plant can fail in producing seeds; and one great object of nature in giving this exuberance of fructification, is to ensure the continuation of the species. In our orchards what innumerable flowers clothe the trees in spring, forming, in the language of the poet,

> One boundless blush, one white-empurpled shower
> Of mingled blossoms!

And *but* for this, we might plant in vain; for, by insects, cutting winds, rains, and frosts, not one blossom, perhaps, in twenty produces fruit.

The *time* at which flowers appear varies according to their species, and hence we have some in blow, of one kind or another, throughout the year. The hour of day, also, at which they expand is various. Some burst from their confinement in time to meet the dawn; some, as the water lily, do not expand until noon; and others, not till the western star sweetens with her beams the soft and dewy hour of twilight. Other plants, again, expand their flowers only in the night. Such is the great night-flowering Cereus (Cactus *grandiflorus*), which spreads its large blossoms for a few hours, and then they close to open no more. Flowers, often, however, expand and close repeatedly; and we find that their time of *shutting* is as regular as that of unclosing. In general, like

> The marigold, that goes to bed with the sun,
> And with him rises weeping,

they shut with his sinking beam, and open again to congratulate his morning ray.

> The flower enamoured of the sun,
> At his departure hangs her head and weeps,
> And shrouds her sweetness up, and keeps
>   Sad vigils like a cloistered nun,
>   Till his reviving ray appears,
> Waking her beauty as he dries her tears.

Some close regularly at mid-day, in every kind of weather, and on this account the *Goat's-beard* (Tragopogon) is vulgarly called " *John go to bed at noon ;*" others shut later, of which the *Forked marvel of Peru* (Mirabilis *dichotoma*) is an example. It is, by the Dutch, at the Cape of Good Hope, called *Vieruurs bloem,* that is, " four o'clock flower," because it invariably closes at that time. The same name is also given by the Malays to another plant; but it, instead of shutting, *opens* at four in the afternoon, and as regularly closes at four in the morning.

Flowers in general are very sensible to changes of weather, and shut up altogether, or partially, during rain, or when the sky is obscured by clouds. The daisy offers a ready example of this phenomenon. We often see it in winter, or at least in very cold weather, expanding its snow-white rays, as if regardless of the season; yet it is very sensible to impressions from dew and rain. It regularly shuts after sunset, to expand again, however, with the morning light, as is beautifully expressed by Leyden.

> Oft have I watched thy closing buds at eve,
> Which for the parting sun-beams seemed to grieve,
> And, when gay morning gilt the dew-bright plain,
> Seen them unclasp their folded leaves again.

Should the weather become moist or rainy, the time is anticipated,

> When evening brings the merry folding-hours,
> And sun-eyed daisies close their winking flowers.

And then we may examine a whole field, and not find a daisy open: unless those, indeed, whose flowering being nearly over, have in consequence lost their sensibility.

It is well known that the influence of light on plants is very great, and, with a few exceptions, even necessary to their existence. Leaves always turn to the light, and some flowers regularly follow the sun, facing him when he rises, and also when he sets. It is strange that the sun-flower is só generally supposed to possess this property, since the slightest observation is sufficient to prove its fallacy. Gerard detected the error so long ago as 1597. " The flower of the Sunne (he says), is called in Latine *Flos Solis*, taking that name from those that have reported it to turne with the sunne, the which I could never observe, although I have endevored to finde out the truth of it; but I rather thinke it was so called bicause it doth resemble the radiant beames of the sunne, whereupon some have called it *Corona Solis*, and *Sol Indianus*, the Indian Sunflower; others have called it *Chrysanthemum Peruvianum*, or the golden flower of Peru. In

English the flower of the Sunne, or the Sunne flower." *

With respect to the *duration* of flowers, we find much variety, some continuing for a long time, while others are very perishable. The flowers of the flesh-coloured sprengelia (Sprengelia *incarnata*), are so durable, that even until their seeds are ripened, they have nearly the same appearance as at their expansion.† Many flowers, on the other hand, die in a few hours, and some are so peculiarly delicate as scarcely to bear the contact of the atmosphere. Andrews says of the dull-coloured Morœa (Morœa *tristis*), that " the only means of seeing this plant in perfection is, by keeping it entirely from the air when near flowering, as it is too delicate to bear the least exposure; it begins to expand about twelve o'clock, and is quite decayed by three."‡ Of fugitive flowers, the most generally known example is the Cistus, some species of which are more perishable than the common garden, or gum cistus (Cistus *ladaniferus*). But though the individual flowers of this are very evanescent, yet they come in such numerous succession, that the shrub retains a gaudy appearance for a month or longer. The following lines, written by a friend §, (the two first excepted, which are from Darwin,) express in very poetical language their temporary stay : —

* Herbal, p. 614.
† Andrew's Botanist's Repository, p. 2. ‡ *Ibid.* p. 83.
§ Robert Williamson, Esq. of Lambeg-house, near Belfast

> " Sweet Cista, rival of the rosy dawn,
>   Put forth her buds and graced the dewy lawn :"
> Expanded all her infant charms to light,
> And fluttered in the breeze, and blessed the sight!
> But, ah! too blooming was her transient grace,
> The blush was hectic that o'erspread her face :
> One fatal morn beholds her beauties blow,
> No noon of health succeeds — no evening glow!
> Gay for that morn, a quick reverse she feels,
> The mid-day sun her fragrant essence steals ;
> A sad ephemeron, she yields her breath,
> Gives to the winds her sweets, and sinks in death.

Flowers are very attractive by the exquisiteness of their *odours*. The violet first emerges from the lap of winter, and breathes her sweetness to the rough March winds. This little flower has in all ages been a favourite, and in every country where it grows is recognised as the emblem of modesty and innocence. Shakspeare speaks of

> —— violets dim,
> But sweeter than the lids of Juno's eyes
> Or Cytherea's breath.

And indeed, scarcely a poet can be named who has not sweetly sung of

> The violet blue that on the moss-bank grows.

As the season advances, and the full power of vegetation awakes into action; every mead, thicket, lane, and hedge-row gives out its perfumes, and is garnished with blossoms. But it is in tropical countries that the animating fragrance of flowers is most exquisite. There, in the cool of the morning, or when the day declines, and the evening dews have begun to fall, the whole atmosphere is filled with balmy odours, breathed,

From plants that wake when others sleep,
From timid jasmin buds, that keep
Their odour to themselves all day,
But when the sun-light dies away,
Let the delicious secret out
To every breeze that roams about.*

The fragrance of the *starry gardenia*, or *wild Cape Jessamine* (Gardenia *Thumbergia*), when in full blow, may be perceived, in the evening, at the distance of several miles. The scent of the *swamp magnolia*, or *beaver tree* (Magnolia *glauca*), of North America, is also, when in flower, perceived at a great distance. Kalm says the whole air is filled with it, and that " it is beyond description agreeable to travel in the woods about that time, especially towards night."

* Lalla Rookh.

CHAPTER VII.

OF THE FRUCTIFICATION AND ITS PARTS.

THE fructification consists of seven parts, two only
of which are essential. These are the *stamen*, and
pistil; for without them no plant can produce seeds.
When you look into a lily you see a thick column
standing in its centre, *Fig.* 57. (*a*) and six other
bodies of smaller size ranged around it. (*bb*) The
central column is the pistil, the six others the
stamens.

Now, some plants have these parts only; they
have no flower-cup, no corolla, no petals where
" beauty plays her idle freaks;" but still they
form perfect seeds, because they possess these
essential organs. Mare's-tail (Hippuris *vulgaris*),
which grows in ditches, may be given as an example. It has indeed the rudiment of a calyx or
flower-cup, but no corolla; and the fructification
may be considered as composed of one stamen, and
one pistil. Its leaves are verticillate, and the fructifications lie in the axillæ between them and the
stem, *Fig.*57.(*c*); and each fructification, when
magnified, is found to consist of a pistil, formed
like (*d*), and a stamen, like (*e*). The base of the
pistil (*f*) is named the *germen,* and in it the seeds

Fig. 57.

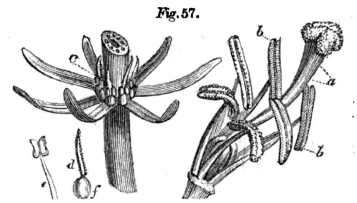

are produced and perfected.   But though they are produced by the pistil, they never would be per- fected but for the stamen; for it has been proved that the pollen, or powder, which is formed by one part of the latter, named the *anther*, must have access to the pistil before the seeds will ripen. What this power is which resides in the pollen, we know not, but we are assured of the fact; and therefore the existence of a stamen to form *pollen*, and a pistil to be acted on by it, is all that is essen- tially requisite to perpetuate a plant by seeds.

The other parts of the fructification are the CALYX, or flower-cup; the COROLLA; the PERI- CARPIUM, or seed-vessel; the SEED itself; and the RECEPTACLE.

The great use of the fructification is to continue plants by seeds; but I am not prepared to admit that " *all* other modes of propagation are but the extension of an individual, and sooner or later terminate in its total extinction." *   I believe that

* Smith's Introduction to Botany.

in many plants the reproduction by roots would perpetuate the species as effectually as that by seeds. As in plants, for example, which have tuberous roots, those especially that are gemmaceous, or furnished with eyes or buds, as the potato; in those with repent roots, as mint, and couch-grass; and also in many bulbous-rooted plants, which may be propagated apparently *ad infinitum*, by their bulbs alone. Plants, too, sometimes *prefer* increasing by roots, when in situations where they are supplied with abundance of nourishment. Thus the American arbor vitæ tree ('Thuya *occidentalis*), when growing in marshes and thick woods, is almost always barren of seeds, though these are produced plentifully when it stands accidentally on the sea-shore, or in places unfavourable to its rooting. Kalm observed a similar fact in the sugar-maple, the white fir, and a number of other trees. But it may be urged, that these are not examples in point, that they are instances even of the propagation of trees being *checked* in consequence of their roots becoming so luxuriant as to exhaust that nourishment and vital energy which should go to the branches, and promote fructification. But I apprehend that no such objection can be made to the following fact. In South America there is a species of bamboo (Bambusa *Guadua*), which forms forests in the marshes, of *many leagues* extent, and yet Mutis, who botanized for twenty years in the parts where it grows, was never able to detect the fructifications. * In addition to this, it may be stated, that viviparous grasses, &c. plants with bulb-bearing, and those with sarmentose stems, would probably continue to increase and multiply for ever, though they were never to perfect a seed. †

We shall now attend to the individual parts of the fructification.

CALYX, *flower-cup*, or empalement (from καλυπΊω (kalupto) to cover, *Greek*). A general idea of it may be expressed, by saying that it is that cup, commonly of a green colour, in which the corolla sits. *Fig.* 58. for instance, is a flower of the Campanula *mollis*, (*a*) is the blue corolla, and the green part (*b*) in which its base rests is the CALYX.

Fig. 58.

a

b

---

* Humboldt's Pers. Nar. vol. v. p. 440.

.† "On the summits of mountains, and in the frozen regions of the poles, vegetable life is necessarily languid. The parts of fructification, therefore, either are imperfectly formed, or entirely abortive. Were seeds even produced, from the deficiency of light and heat, they could scarcely be perfected: but for the evolution of buds, the stronger influence of the sun is not wanted ; and it is highly probable that the few plants that linger in a half torpid state in those dreary abodes of almost perpetual winter, are reproduced by buds only."— *Yule in Trans. Wern. Soc.* vol. i. p. 601.

In examining different plants, however, you will find that the appearance of this envelope varies greatly. It is necessary, therefore, to designate different species of calyx by different and appropriate appellations. And, in the first place, there is one great and obvious distinction arising from its situation; for generally, as in the Campanula, it is close to the corolla, and forming as it were a part of it, while in other instances it is placed *at a distance*. When close to the fructification it is named the perianth, PERIANTHIUM, περι (peri) about, and ανθος (anthos), a flower. The calyx of the Campanula, therefore, being close to the flower, is a PERIANTH.

This organ varies without end, and therefore it would be vain to attempt explaining more than its most remarkable peculiarities. Not unfrequently it is wanting, as in the crown imperial, tulip, lily, and hyacinth; and often it is found investing the fructification in plants which are destitute of a *corolla*. In some cases, the young botanist might be deceived in imagining species to want the perianth, which in reality possess it. I allude to those plants in which it is *caducous*, that is, in which it falls off before, or soon after, the flower expands. The poppy affords a ready example. Its petals before expanding are enclosed in a perianth of two large, concave, green leaves, which are not to be seen in the blown flower, having dropped off when the petals were unfolded.

In a large proportion of plants, the perianth is *deciduous;* by which is meant, that it continues with the flower, and drops off along with it, or when it begins to wither. In the greater number, however, it is permanent (*persistens*); that is, it remains after the flower has disappeared, until the fruit is perfected. At the base of a pea-pod, for instance, the perianth is as perfect as it was in the blossom; and in many species it continues, forming a sort of case or capsule, protecting the seeds, as in henbane and dead-nettle.

I suppose you have often remarked the brownish withered leaves surrounding the conical cavity on the top of an apple, or in the broad end of a pear. These are the remains of the *perianth;* and from this you learn that it had belonged to the flower, and not to the fruit, else it could not be found on the *top*, but at the bottom of the pear or apple. This is called a perianth of the flower (PERIANTHIUM *Floris*), as including the flower only. If again you examine an acorn in its cup, which is the perianth; or a hazel nut in its husk, which is the same; you will have examples of a perianth of the fruit (PERIANTHIUM *Fructus*); and if you look at a Peony, in blossom, you will see the incipient fruit in its centre, and the stamens around it, all enclosed by the calyx or perianth, and this is a PERIANTHIUM *Fructificationis*, or perianth of the fructification; as not including the stamens and pistils alone, nor the fruit alone, but all these.

The utility of these distinctions may not appear very evident, until we recollect that in some species there are two perianths; the flower having one, and the fruit a second, which may differ considerably from each other; and it is the case also that the stamen and pistil in some classes of plants do not meet together, but some flowers produce pistils only, and others only stamens, either on the same, or on different individual plants. The perianth, therefore, of the staminiferous flower may be very different from that of the flower containing pistils, and hence the necessity for distinctive appellations.

The perianth consists of one leaflet in the primrose; of two in the poppy; three in the spider-wort, and water-plantain; four in the wall-flower; five in the cistus; six in the barberry; and so on; and in many species it is common (PERIANTHIUM *commune*), that is, a single perianth contains many flowers, as in teasel and scabious; and each of these flowers also may, as often happens, have its own proper calyx, independent of the external common one. In examining holly-hock, mallow, hibiscus, and a number of others, you will find the perianth double. *Fig.* 59. (*a*)

In the perianth of a pink, or carnation, you may observe an approach to a double calyx in the small scales at its base; which form, as it were, a little cup including a larger. Such a perianth is said to be *calyculate*, or calycled (PERIANTHIUM *calyculatum*. (*b*)

Fig.59.

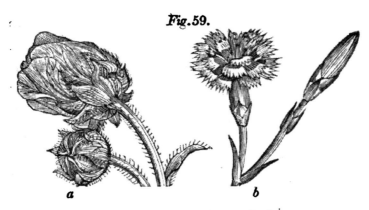

a   b

In hawk-weed, sow-thistle, and the Japan rose, you will find it imbricated; in the thistles scaly; not unfrequently it is armed with spines; and it is divided and cleft in innumerable ways.

It is coloured, or of a different hue from green, in azalea, in the pomegranate, barberry, flowering sallow, marsh cinquefoil, Japan apple, and many others, with none of which perhaps you are so familiar as with the scarlet fuchsia (Fuchsia *coccinea*), which is now very common in gardens and greenhouses. It is a native of Chili, and was introduced into England in 1788. When you look into the heart of the flower, you see lying within it a beautiful little cup of a bright purple colour; this is the real corolla consisting of four petals, while the large, monophyllous, quadripartite, or four-cleft scarlet covering that surrounds it is nothing more than a coloured perianth. In the Carolina Allspice (Calycanthus *floridus*), the perianth is composed of one leaflet divided into many scales, the inner ones of considerable size, and the whole of a deep rich purple-brown colour, exactly resembling petals. The plant however has no corolla; what to a common eye appears as such being the perianth.

The radiated marginal scales of the imbricated common calyx in the everlasting flowers, are in many species finely coloured; and as they are dry and chaffy, they resemble beautiful fresh flowers many years after they are gathered. They are particularly plentiful at the Cape of Good Hope, whence they are often sent as curiosities to Europe. Some species are much used for ornamenting children's toys.

Sometimes the perianth is bellied out like a bubble of air, as in the bladder-campion, the winter-cherry, and the yellow rattle of our meadows.

A circumstance takes place in the *thorn-apple* (Datura) which I do not recollect to occur in any other plant. Its perianth is deciduous, but not *in toto ;* the greater part drops off, but leaves an orbicular portion at the base, attached to the fruit;

a   *Fig.* 60.

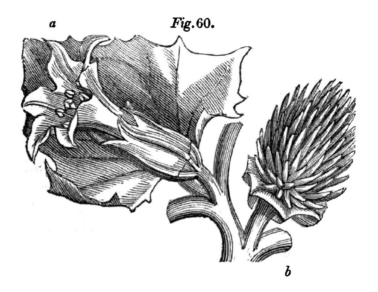

b

as at *Fig.* 60. where (*a*) represents the corolla and calyx entire, and (*b*) the young fruit with a *portion* of the calyx continuing attached to its base.

We have now paid some attention to the PE-RIANTH, which is the first of Linnæus's species of *Calyx*, after which he enumerates six others; the INVOLUCRUM, AMENTUM, SPATHA, GLUMA, CALYP-TRA, and VOLVA.

INVOLUCRUM (*involvo*, to wrap up, *Lat.*), a calyx *remote* from the flower. It therefore is not a legiti-mate calyx, though considered as such, because it is required to distinguish the genera of a very large natural order of plants, the *Umbelliferæ*. The cha-racters of genera are properly always taken from the parts of fructification; and in order not to de-part from that rule, the involucrum is admitted as a species of calyx. * We shall defer its consider-ation till, in describing the modes of flowering, we treat of the *umbel*.

The AMENTUM, or *catkin*, and the SPATHA, or *sheath*, are certainly improperly considered as species of *Calyx*, and we shall consider them as kinds of inflorescence. The CALYPTRA, or *veil*, is peculiar to the MOSSES; and the VOLVA, or *wrapper*, to the FUNGI.

* It is in reality a *bractea*, and will soon, probably, be alto-gether discarded as a part necessary for establishing the genera of the *umbellatæ*. Sir J. E. Smith has characterised them "by the parts of fructification alone, according to the wise prin-ciples taught by Linnæus, but against which he himself, in this instance, transgressed." — *English Flora*, vol. ii. p. 32. See also the preface to the same admirable work.

The GLUME, or calyx, of grasses: and the SQUAMA, or scale, which is the real calyx in amentaceous plants, are the only others to be mentioned. The latter will be described along with the *amentum*.

GLUMA, the *glume* (*gluma*, the husk of corn, *Lat.*).

The part of oats called *chaff*, and which is thrown away as useless, is what forms the calyx or glume.

In the oat it is composed of two pieces or valves, *Fig.* 61.; in some grasses, as *ray grass*, only of one; and in the Uniola, or *sea-side oat*, it is multivalve. Often it is armed or bearded.

*Fig.*61.

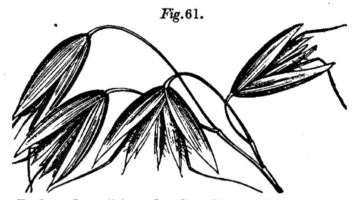

Before describing the Corolla we shall attend a little to the Peduncle, or flower-stalk; PEDUNCULUS (*pedo*, to prop or support, *Lat.*). The same terms which have been applied to the petiole are in general also applicable to the Peduncle. Like the former it may be radical, cauline, or from a branch; it may be axillary, or terminal; solitary, or in clusters; placed in a determinate order; or situated without method, here and there upon the plant. In herbaceous vegetables it not unfrequently rises from the main stem, but in trees this is unusual, though some instances occur, as in the Bilimbi-tree (Averrhoa *Bilimbi*), and the *Jaca*, or Jac, (Artocarpus *integrifolia*,) a species of bread-fruit, native of the East Indies. The fruit of the latter tree is of immense size; and perhaps the intention of nature in making the peduncle *cauline*, is to save the branches, which might suffer by the weight of this enormous fruit, or be unable to support it. *

When the Peduncle, as often happens, divides into smaller ones, the latter are called *Pedicels* (PEDICELLI). The flowers are connected by the peduncle to the plant in various ways, which by the older botanists was termed the mode of flowering (*modus florendi*), but by Linnæus the inflorescence (INFLORESCENTIA). It is of the following kinds:—

UMBELLA, an *umbel* (*umbella*, a fan or screen, *Lat.*).

The stems of many plants terminate in a number of rays, nearly all of equal length, somewhat like the spokes of an umbrella. *Fig.* 62.

Fig. 62.

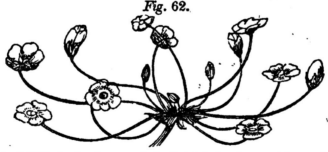

* "This is the largest fruit I think in the world; and because of its bigness, provident nature has placed its growth on the stock or body of the tree; not on the branches, lest it should not be able to bear the burthen." — *Baron's Description of Tonqueen.*

K

This forms a *simple* umbel (UMBELLA *simplex*); but generally each of these spokes or peduncles is terminated by a number of smaller spokes, forming a little umbel (UMBELLULA) on the point of each. *Fig.* 63.

The primary spokes or rays (*a*) compose what is called the universal umbel; and the secondary spokes (*b*, *b*) of the umbellulæ form the *partial* umbel. In *Fig.* 62., therefore, there is only the *universal* umbel; in *Fig.* 63. both universal and *partial*. The green leaves (*c*, *c*) at the base of the universal umbel are the INVOLUCRUM, and this, therefore, is named a *universal* involucrum (INVOLUCRUM *universale*). But there are also similar leaflets at the base of the partial umbel (*d*, *d*), which, of course, form the *partial* involucrum, or involucellum.

Fig. 63.

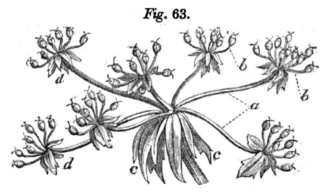

CYMA; the *cyme* much resembles the *umbel* in the primary spokes, as they all spring from one point. But the *partial* peduncles, in place of going off regularly in the same manner as the rays of the *umbellulæ*, are scattered without order upon the main peduncles.; and the flowers form a flat surface on the top. *Fig.* 64. The Laurustinus (Viburnum *Tinus*) and the common Elder (Sambucus *nigra*) afford ready examples.

In the *umbel,* then, a number of peduncles go from one point, and are terminated, each, by a flower forming the simple umbel, or by smaller peduncles from one point also, forming the compound umbel. In the *cyme,* though the primary rays start from one point, the partial ones do not, but are scattered irregularly, and this, together with the flowers, forming a flattish surface, constitutes the characteristic of the CYME.

Fig. 64.

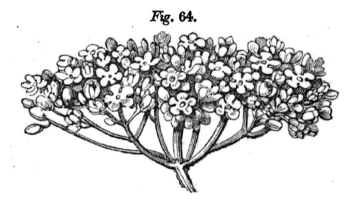

CORYMBUS, the *corymb* (χορυς (korus), a helmet), is easily understood. In it the peduncles do *not* go off at one point, but spring from the central peduncle, or stem at various heights above each other. The lower ones, however, are proportionally longer than the upper, and the consequence is that the flowers are nearly all upon a level. *Fig.* 65.

When the peduncles of a CORYMB are very crowded, so that the flowers form a dense bundle, as in sweet-william, the term *fascicle* (*fasciculus*, a bundle, *Lat.*) is used.

Fig. 65.

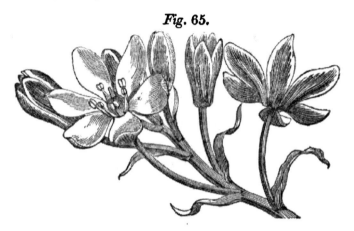

RACEMUS, a *raceme;* a peduncle, having short lateral branches. It is generally pendulous. Laburnum affords a good example.

SPICA, a *spike.* Like the raceme, it is composed of one *general* peduncle, supporting the flowers; but it has no pedicels or partial peduncles; or, at least, these are so short as not to attract notice. Wheat, barley, and lavender are familiar examples. In the raceme the flowers are all nearly blown at the same time, but in the *spike* the flowering commences at the base, and gradually goes on to the top, so that the first-blown flowers are often dead and faded long before the upper ones expand. *
Fig. 66. (*a*)

* Smith's Introduction, p. 176.

As *umbellula* means a partial umbel, so SPICULA, à *spikelet*, means the partial spike which occurs in grasses.* *Fig.* 66. (*b*)

Fig. 66.

a   b

CAPITULUM, a *head* (*caput*, the head, *Lat.*); when the flowers are sessile, and joined into a round ball, as in globe-flowered Buddlea (Buddlea *globosa*) or common clover (Trifolium *repens*).

VERTICILLUS, a *whorl.* (*Fig.* 67. See page 128.)

Fig. 67.

* " Spicula est partialis spica." — *Phil. Bot.* 223.

K 3

PANICULA, a *panicle ;* a kind of branching or diffused spike, composed of a number of small spikes, which are fixed along a common receptacle or foot-stalk. *   *Fig.* 68.

Fig. 68.

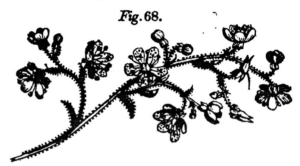

THYRSUS, a *thyrse* (Ϟυω (thuo), to burst forth). According to Linnæus it is a panicle contracted into an ovate form.   The common lilac (Syringa *vulgaris*) and the privet (Ligustrum *vulgare*) are familiar examples.   The term was "put for branches, or the flame of a lamp or torch, which have a conical form.   Hence the spear, with ivy bound about the head, carried in sacrifices to Bacchus, was named *Thyrsus.*" †

> And lo ! the love-alluring fair
> Her Thyrsus brandishes in air,
> With clustering ivy wreath'd around,
> Whose branches yield a rustling sound." ‡

AMENTUM, *ament,* or *catkin ;* the last " from the French *chaton,* on account of its resemblance to a cat's tail."   " A species of calyx, or rather of inflorescence, from a common chaffy gemmaceous

---

* Barton's Elements of Botany.   † Martyn.
          ‡ Fawkes's Anacreon, ode vi.

receptacle; or consisting of many chaffy scales, ranged along a stalk slender as a thread, which is the common receptacle." *

Let (*a*), for instance, *Fig.* 69., be the filiform receptacle. It is naked; but suppose it to be clothed on every side with chaffy scales, as at (*b*), and then you will have some idea of its usual appearance. These *squamæ*, or scales, are the calyxes of the fructification, and in the axilla of each is contained a certain number of stamens, or pistils, as magnified at (*c*), so that each scale or calyx, with these accompaniments, is to be considered as a distinct flower.

Fig. 69.

c   a   b

SPADIX.

SPATHA, *a spathe*, or sheath.

The *arum*, or *cuckoo-pint* (Arum *maculatum*), is well known to most persons. It is in fructification in the month of *May*, and then is seen frequently along the banks of rivulets shaded by trees, or on the borders of highways, about the bottoms of

* Martyn.

K 4

hedges, &c. It has a ridiculous resemblance to an image standing in a case, and hence has received the vulgar names of *Jack in a box*, and *Jack in the pulpit*. Now, the club-shaped part (*a*), *Fig.* 70., which represents the image, is the SPADIX; and the membranous enclosure (*b*), in which it stands, is the SPATHE. In the palm tribes the SPADIX is branched, and often bears an immense quantity of fruit; since on one raceme of a Seje palm Humboldt estimated the flowers at forty-four thousand, and the fruits at eight thousand.[*]

The SPATHE is found in many of the lily tribes, and in many well-known garden plants, *Fig.* 70. (*c*); for it is not necessary that it should always be accompanied by a spadix; the latter, indeed, is rather an uncommon circumstance, the *spadix* being confined to the palms, the arum, and some plants allied to the latter.

Fig. 70.

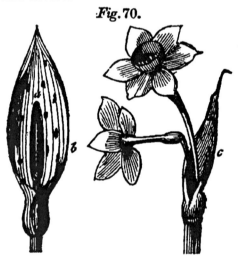

[*] Pers. Nar. vol. v. p. 152.

Sometimes the flowers grow from the surface, or from the margin of the leaves, forming a *foliar inflorescence ;* as in butcher's broom (Ruscus), and Osyris *Japonica,* in which they grow on the surface, and Xylophylla, or sea-side laurel, and Phyllanthus, in which they grow on the margin. " Most remarkable is the manner in which the flower is placed in a tree of the East Indies, called Cynometra *cauliflora.* This very leafy tree has no flowers, *but at the foot of its stem ;* its leafy top never produces any." *

COROLLA (*corona,* a crown, *corolla,* a little crown, or chaplet, *Lat.*).

It may consist of from one to any number of petals. We shall first attend to that of one petal, or the *monopetalous* corolla. Strip the perianth from a primrose, or pull off the *corolla,* and you will observe that the latter consists of a tube, *Fig.* 71. (*e*), the mouth of which expands into a broad border (*d*). TUBUS, or *tube,* is the botanical term for the former, and LIMBUS, or *limb,* for the latter. These parts vary exceedingly ; the *tube* is often extremely short, but still, as Willdenow remarks, all monopetalous corollas have a tube, except the campanulate and some of the rotate, or wheel-shaped corollas. The *tube* in the primrose is straight, but in many plants it is bent, and we might select examples of it having every degree of curvature, from a gentle inclination, to an almost

* Willdenow's Princ. p. 309.

K 5

perfect circle. In some it is very long, as in the Long-flowered Gardenia (Gardenia *longiflora*); and in many it is scarcely perceptible.

1. COROLLA *campanulata*, a *campanulate*, or bell-shaped corolla. (*Campanula*, a little bell, *Lat*.) *Fig*. 71. (*b*)

2. COROLLA *cyathiformis*, a *cyathiform*, or cup-shaped corolla. (*Cyathus*, a drinking-cup or glass, *Lat*.) (*c*)

Fig. 71.

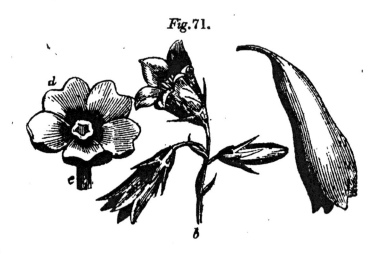

3. COROLLA *infundibuliformis*, *funnel-shaped* (*infundibulum*, a funnel, *Lat*.), as in Portlandia *grandiflora*, Fig. 72.

The campanulate corolla widens gradually from the base to the margin with a bend outwards, in form of a bell. The cyathiform differs from it in not having this bend; the infundibuliform corolla has just been explained, but the limits between it and the cyathiform are vague.

Fig. 72.

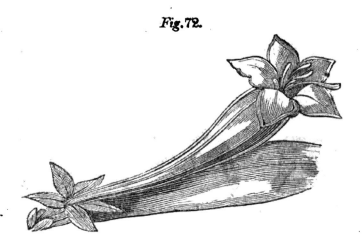

4. Corolla *hypocrateriformis* (χρατηρ (krater), an ancient cup or salver), a *hypocrateriform*, or salver-shaped corolla.

5. Corolla *rotata*, a *rotate*, or wheel-shaped corolla. (*Rota*, a wheel, *Lat.*)

These differ from each other in the *former* having a tube, the *latter* little or none. The corolla of the primrose is *hypocrateriform;* cut its tube off and you immediately make it *rotate.*

6. Corolla *ringens*, or *labiata;* a *ringent*, or *labiate* corolla (*ringo*, to gape,—*labium*, a lip, *Lat.*).

" An irregular one-petalled corolla, the border of which is usually divided into two parts, called the *upper* and *lower* lip. [*Fig.* 73. (*a, b*)] The first has sometimes the name of *Galea*, or *Helmet;* the second of *Barba*, or *Beard.* The opening between them is called *Rictus*, or the *Gape* (*c*); the opening of the tube, *Faux*, the *Throat* or *Jaws;* the pro-

minent swelling in the Faux is *Palatum*, the *Palate;*
the upper part of the tube is *Collum*, the *Neck.*" *

Fig. 73.

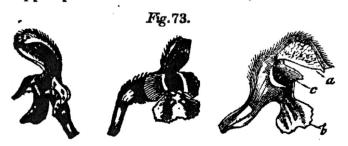

7. CoROLLA *personata*, a *personate* corolla. (*Per-
sona*, a mask, *Lat.*)   In this the lips are not *open*,
as in the ringent corolla, but *in contact ;* and when
the lower lip (*barba*, or *labellum*) is drawn from the
upper, it immediately, when let loose, springs to
its place, so as again to shut the tube.   An examination of the flower of *snap-dragon* will give a better
idea of this corolla than any description.

The leaves of the *polypetalous* corolla consist,
each, of an inferior narrow part called the *claw*
(*unguis*), *Fig.* 74. (*b*), and an upper broader portion
named the expansion, or *border* (*lamina*), *Fig.* 74. (*a*)
What, therefore, is the limb (*limbus*) in a monopetalous, is the *lamina* of the petal in a *polypetalous*
corolla.   The term polypetalous was formerly applied to such flowers only as had more than six
petals; and generally when a corolla has two petals,
it is termed *dipetalous ;* when three, *tripetalous ;*
four, *tetrapetalous ;* five, *pentapetalous ;* six, *hexa-
petalous ;* and beyond this, *polypetalous.*

* Martyn's Lang. of Botany.

8. COROLLA *cruciformis*, or *cruciata ;* a *cruciform* corolla, like a Maltese cross (*crux,* a cross, *Lat.*), as in wall-flower, stock gilliflower, rocket, &c. *Fig.* 74. (*f*)

9. COROLLA *papilionacea*, Papilionaceous, or butterfly-shaped (*papilio,* a butterfly, *Lat.*).

The blossoms of the pea, broom, or furze, afford ready examples of this. It is formed of four petals which have distinct names. The large petal (*c*), *Fig.* 74., which stands up from the rest, is the

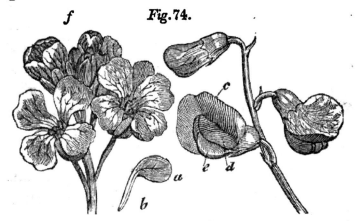

f   *Fig.* 74.

vexillum, or *standard ;* the side pieces (*d*) are the alæ or *wings ;* and the undermost (*e*), which is hollowed out like a boat, is named the *carina,* or *keel.* *
The *carina* contains the pistil and stamens, and being closed around them, defends them from the weather; while the *alæ*, which overlap its sides, serve to throw off the rain. The *vexillum,* also, has its use in protecting these parts; for when the wind is strong, the blossoms, by the intervention of

---

* The *keel* is in general composed of two petals; but in some, as Colutea, *bladder-senna,* only of one.

the standard, all turn their backs to it, by which
the more delicate parts are sheltered. The resemblance which the *papilionaceous* corolla bears
to a butterfly is pretty close, and the insect in its
turn has been compared to the flower.

> The gaudy butterfly in wanton round,
> That like a living *pea-flower* skimmed the ground.

10. Corolla *rosacea*, rosaceous, or rose-like
(*rosa*, a rose, *Lat.*).

11. Corolla *malvacea*, malvaceous, or mallow-
like (*malva*, a mallow, *Lat.*).

12. Corolla *caryophyllacea*, caryophyllaceous,
or pink-like (*caryophyllus*, a pink, *Lat.*).

13. Corolla *liliacea*, liliaceous, or lily-like
(*lilium*, a lily, *Lat.*).

14. Corolla *orchidea*, orchideous, or orchis-
like (from the plant *orchis*).

These terms will be better understood by referring to the flowers from which they are named,
than by any verbal definitions.

15. Corolla *incompleta*, an *incomplete* corolla.
When a part which we should naturally expect
to be present is wanting, as in *bastard indigo*
(Amorpha), which has " a papilionaceous flower
apparently, but consisting of the vexillum only." *

We shall treat of *compound flowers*, and of the
nectary, afterwards, and shall now attend to the
remaining parts of the fructification.

Stamen, " in the plural stamens, not stamina in

* Smith.

English." * It consists of three parts : the *filament*, FILAMENTUM (*filum*, a thread, *Lat.*); the *anther*, ANTHERA, which sits on the top of the filament; and the POLLEN, or FARINA, a sort of mealy powder which the *anther* throws out when it is ripe, and bursts; — thus, (*a*) *Fig.* 75. represents a filament and anther; and (*b*) the pollen falling from the latter.

But not unfrequently in examining flowers, you will find the stamens sessile, or immediately attached to the corolla, as at *Fig* 75. (*c*), which represents a corolla laid open, and having anthers without filaments; — the latter, therefore, are not *essential* to the formation of a stamen.

The anther is very various in form, and contains from one to four cells, but the number is in general two. It was called by the older botanists (who were not aware of its use and importance), the *summit*, *pendent*, or *tip*. As, together with the pistil, it forms the basis of the Linnæan classification, the student will, in pursuing his practical studies, have examples under his own eye of its various modifications. In some plants he will find it round; in others oblong, linear, reniform, sagittate, pilose, crested, &c.: sometimes several growing together, forming a tube; in other instances moveable or versatile, that is, turning with the slightest breath of wind; and in the tulip, in which it stands, encasing the top of the filament, he may

* Martyn.

remove it from the latter, and again replace it, when it will seem as originally situated, and will move and vibrate as though nothing had happened.

The *pollen*, which is formed by the anther, is the great agent in ripening the seeds, and if it exist, even though not formed in a regular anther as usual, the same end is answered. Thus in the *orchis* tribe, and in some other plants, the *pollen* appears in naked masses, destitute of a membranous covering. In such cases, instead of the term stamen, or anther, it is usual to speak of the *mass* or *masses of pollen* (*massa*, or *massæ pollinis*).

When we examine with a glass the individual particles of dust which compose the pollen, we find that each is a membranous bag; and it is ascertained that when these globules meet with moisture, they explode, and throw out a vapour, which coming in contact with the *pistil*, renders the seeds fertile. The form of the globules is extremely various in different plants, and in the orchis tribe, instead of being like a powder, they form *glutinous* masses.

PISTILLUM, the pistil.

This, like the *stamen*, consists, also, of three parts, the GERMEN, the STYLE, and the STIGMA. We may resemble it to a pillar, and then the first will represent the pedestal, the second the shaft, and the third the capital, as in the pistil of a lily, *Fig.* 75. where (*f*) shows the germen, (*e*) the style, and (*d*) the stigma.

Only the first and last of these, however, are *essential;* for if, instead of a lily, you examine a tulip, you will find the stigma placed immediately on the germen; or a poppy, in which it is similarly situated, radiated, and very beautiful. *Fig.* 75. (g)

Fig. 75.

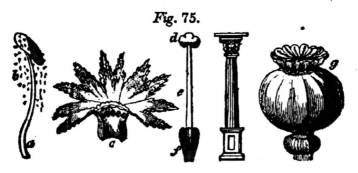

The great end of the fructification is to produce the seed; and thus to perpetuate the species. The care taken by nature to effect this, and also to disseminate the seeds when ripened, calls for our highest admiration. There is, however, another object in view than the continuation of the species merely, for multitudes of animals are to be fed and supported by them. To this source, man himself is indebted for bread, " the staff of life," and many races of animals subsist entirely on vegetable seeds; and hence, plants in general produce a much greater number of these than is necessary for their own continuance. The same observation will equally apply to animals; and it may not be uninstructive to glance at the comparative fertility of the two. In so doing, we need not advert to the multitudes of insects and miscroscopic beings which inhabit almost every department of nature;

a few observations on *fishes*, which, perhaps, more
than any other animals, carry on a constant state of
mutual depredation, will be sufficient. Their roe, or
spawn, is left to take its chance among thousands
of enemies; and were not the *ovula*, or seeds composing it, extremely numerous, not only would the
respective species be much thinned, but many
others would be deprived of a principal source of
nutriment. It might seem like exaggeration to
assert that a *smelt*, only two ounces in weight,
should have in its roe thirty-eight thousand, two
hundred and seventy-eight eggs; or that four
millions and ninety-six thousand have been com-
puted in the pea of a single *crab*, yet nothing is
more true. In the middling-sized *cod-fish*, Leu-
wenhoeck found nine millions, three hundred and
eighty-four thousand; and the following calculation
is not a little curious: " A *cod-fish* was lately sold
in *Workington* market, Cumberland, for one shilling;
it weighed fifteen pounds, and measured two feet
nine inches in length, and seven inches in breadth.
The roe weighed two pounds ten ounces: one
grain of which contained eight hundred and twenty
seeds or eggs; the whole therefore might contain
three millions, nine hundred and one thousand,
four hundred and forty seeds. — Supposing that
each of the above eggs should have arrived at the
same perfection and size of the mother-fish, its
produce would weigh twenty-six thousand, one
hundred and twenty-three *tons*, and consequently
would load two hundred and sixty-one sail of ships,

each of one hundred tons burthen. If each fish were brought to market and sold for a *shilling*, this would net a clear sum of one hundred and ninety-five thousand pounds."* Yet this comes far short of the fertility of the *sturgeon*, a single fish of this species containing in its roe one hundred and fifty thousand millions of eggs.†

Perhaps no example of such amazing increase is to be found in the vegetable kingdom, though the fertility there is still very surprising. The produce of vegetable seeds in a hundred fold degree is common, and many trees and shrubs bring forth their fruits by thousands. The grasses, which alone give food to myriads of animals, are individually much less prolific, but compensation for this is made by their universal diffusion. A single plant of the poppy will produce above thirty thousand, and of tobacco, above forty thousand; and Buffon remarks, that from the seeds of a single elm-tree, " one hundred thousand young elms may be raised from the product of one year." Some ferns, it is said, produce their seeds by millions.

By such immense produce the vegetable world is perpetuated from age to age, in undiminished bloom; for though millions of seeds are devoured, or destroyed, during the winter, on every acre,

* Daniel's Rural Sports, vol. ii. p. 34.
† " In some of the Norwegian rivers, and in Siberia, we are told the sturgeon grows to such a vast size, that the roe taken from a single fish will sometimes weigh from two to three hundred pounds." — *Donovan's British Fishes.*

yet enough are left to clothe the face of nature in its accustomed luxuriance of herbs.

> With such a liberal hand has Nature flung
> Their seeds abroad, blown them about in winds,
> Innumerous mix'd them with the nursing mould,
> The moistening current and prolific rain.

As plants have not locomotion like animals, various contrivances have been had recourse to for the dispersion, or dissemination of their seeds, to some of which we shall now advert, premising that seeds are by accidental circumstances often carried to great distances. By falling into rivers, for instance, they may be conveyed thousands of miles; and should they find their way to the ocean, may be thrown on the coasts of the most distant countries. Thus the fruits of American and West Indian vegetables are cast upon the northern isles and coasts of Scotland. Among these are the fruit of the *climbing acacia;* of the *cow-itch dolichos* (Dolichos *pruriens*); and of the Bonduc, or Nicker-tree (Guilandina *Bonduc*). The plants of Germany thus migrate to Sweden, and those of southern Europe to England. Dr. Tonning states that among other seeds of Indian and American produce, thrown on the coasts of Norway, are the *cashew-nut,* the *bottle-gourd,* the fruit of the *dog-wood-tree* (Piscidia *Erythrina*), and the *cocoa-nut.* [*]

These seeds, thrown on the shores of such ungenial climates, of course perish; but when carried to

---

[*] Barton's Elements of Botany, p. 230.

countries better suited to their nature, they will often take root, and colonise with a new race of vegetables the soil on which the ocean has cast them. The cocoa-nut, especially, is well adapted for this end, as it grows equally well, or better, when watered by salt water as by fresh, and it probably is the *first* species that vegetates on the newly formed islands of coral which are so frequent in some of the seas within the tropics. *

Another mode by which many seeds are disseminated, arises from the circumstance that they often resist the action of the gastric juice of birds, &c. and hence may be carried to great distances. Often, too, they are furnished with hooks, by which they adhere to the clothes and skins of men and animals, which carry them off; and not unfrequently, they are projected to a considerable distance by the sudden bursting of their seed-vessels.

But the winds form the great agent by which they are diffused, and nothing can be more admirable than the various wings with which they are provided for seizing on the vagrant breeze that is to waft them far from their native field. The thistle and the dandelion are known to every one,

* Forster, in describing the formation of these islands, says, " If by chance a cocoa-nut be carried by the sea to those spots, it germinates and grows into a tall tree, bearing and disseminating many nuts, some of which again germinating, soon form a palm-grove, affording shade to birds, and other animals; and supplying navigators driven to the place by stress of weather with grateful food and liquor."

and there are few who have not been amused in childhood, by blowing away the feathered seeds of the latter plant, without, however, suspecting that in so doing, they were employed in a very important part of vegetable economy. " How little," Sir J. E. Smith observes, " are children aware, as they blow away the seeds of dandelion, or stick burs in sport upon each other's clothes, that they are fulfilling one of the great ends of Nature ! " The feathered seeds of thistles, dandelions, groundsel, and other herbaceous plants, are intended, I believe, chiefly as the food of birds, and with this view we can see the reason of the great fertility and universal diffusion of these plants. It has been calculated by Dr. Woodward, that one seed of the common spear-thistle " will produce at the first crop twenty-four thousand, and consequently five hundred and seventy-six millions of seeds at the second." This profusion can only be intended as a supply of food for animals, especially the smaller birds ; and hence, even the sight of a thistle's down buffetted by the winds, inspires us with a sense of the benevolence of the great Author of nature.

The cottony plumes of some seeds are extremely delicate and beautiful; and many persons are perhaps ignorant that the important article of commerce, *cotton*, is nothing more than the down of the seeds of the cotton-tree (Gossypium). The common cotton-grass (Eriophorum) of our moors, adds great liveliness to the tracts on which it grows ; its pendulous

spikelets dance gaily in the lightest breeze, and exhibit a dazzling lustre. The whiteness, indeed, of
the down of *Cana*, which is the Irish and Gaelic
name of this plant, is often alluded to in the
poetical effusions written in those languages, as in
this beautiful passage from the Cath-Loda of Mac-
pherson's Ossian. " If on the heath she moved,
her bosom was *whiter than the down of Cana;* if on
the sea-beat shore, than the foam of the rolling
ocean. Her eyes were two stars of light. Her
face was heaven's bow in showers. Her dark hair
flowed round it like the streaming clouds. Thou
wert the dweller of souls, white-handed Strina-
dona."

The different appendages of seeds by which they
migrate have, of course, appropriate names.

PAPPUS, the seed-down. *Pappus* means a grand-
father, or an old man, and was thence applied
to the down of thistles, which resembles the grey
hairs of age. Hence we speak of the beard of
the thistle, which Ossian beautifully describes as
being pursued by "the lonely blast of ocean."
The *pappus* is either sessile, or furnished with a
stipe (PAPPUS *stipitatus*), as we have already seen. *

PAPPUS *sessilis,* — placed immediately on the
seed; not being supported (as it is in *dandelion*)
upon a pillar, or stipe, *Fig.* 76. (*f*) The *thistle,*
of which we have been speaking, affords a ready
example, but we must select specimens from the

* Page 80.

plant itself, and not trust to finding a perfect seed blowing about.   The reason is, that in the plants of this family, the *seed* and *pappus* soon separate, and thence, if we choose a flying specimen, we might, indeed, have

> The thistle's rolling wheel of silken down,

but perhaps no real seed attached to it.

The *seed-down* is also plumose, or capillary; it is the latter when the hairs are not divided, as in groundsel, and cotton-grass, *Fig.* 76. (*a*); the former when many lateral hairs go off from the main rays, like a feather, as in goats' beard. (*b*)

CAUDA (*cauda*, a tail, *Lat.*), is when the style remains and is lengthened out, as in virgin's bower, *Fig.* 76. (*c*), and Geum or *avens*. (*d*)

ROSTRUM, a beak, as in geranium.

ALA, a wing, as in the fir, &c., a membranous expansion, as at 76. (*e*)

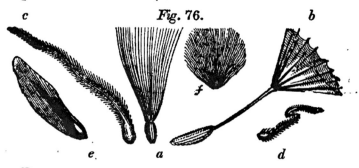

c   *Fig.* 76.   *b*

e   *a*   *d*

RECEPTACULUM, the *Receptacle* (*recipio*, to receive, *Lat.*), " the base by which the other parts of the fructification are connected;"* — it is parti-

* Martyn.

cularly conspicuous in compound flowers. It is *proper* (RECEPTACULUM *proprium*), appertaining to one fructification, *common* (*commune*), when to more than one, and it may be a receptacle of the *fructification,* or of the *fruit* only, or *flower* only, &c.

The seeds of the *dandelion* and the *thistle* which we have been attending to, stand on a receptacle without being enclosed in any kind of case, and this occurs in many other plants. But in general, the seeds are contained in a *seed-vessel.* This is named the *Pericarp* (PERICARPIUM), which is derived from πιρι (peri), about or around, and χαρπος (karpos), a seed or fruit. The pericarp is formed from the enlarged germen, which, after the flower has faded, or dropped off, continues to swell to the necessary size. " The *seed-vessel,*" says Paley, " proceeds to increase its bulk, always to a great, and, in some species (in the gourd, for example, and melon), to a surprising comparative size ; assuming in different plants an incalculable variety of forms, but all evidently conducing to the security of the seed. By virtue of this process, so necessary but so diversified, we have the seed at length, in stone-fruits and nuts, incased in a strong shell, the shell itself enclosed in a pulp or husk, by which the seed within is, or hath been, fed : or, more generally, (as in grapes, oranges, and the numerous kinds of berries,) plunged over head in a glutinous syrup, contained within a skin or bladder: at other times (as in apples

L

and pears) embedded in the heart of a firm fleshy substance ; or (as in strawberries) pricked into the surface of a soft pulp.

" These and many more varieties exist in what we call *fruits*. In pulse, and grain, and grasses ; in trees, and shrubs, and flowers ; the variety of the seed-vessels is incomputable. We have the seeds (as in the pea-tribe) regularly disposed in parchment pods, which, though soft and mem- branous, completely exclude the wet even in the heaviest rains ; the pod also (not seldom) as in the bean, lined with a fine down *; at other times (as in the senna) distended like a blown bladder; or we have seen the seed enveloped in wool (as in the cotton-plant), lodged (as in pines) between the hard and compact scales of a cone, or barricadoed (as in the artichoke and thistle) with spikes and prickles; in mushrooms, placed under a penthouse ; in ferns, within slits in the back part of the leaf; or (which is the most general organization of all) we find them covered by strong, close tunicles, and attached to the stem according to an order appro- priated to each plant, as is seen in the several kinds of grain and of grasses.

* Sometimes with an esculent powder, as in the *nitta-tree*, a species of *mimosa*, the pods of which are long and narrow, and contain a fine meal surrounding a few black seeds. — " The meal itself is of a bright yellow colour, resembling the flower of sulphur, and has a sweet mucilaginous taste : when eaten by itself it is clammy, but when mixed with milk or water, it constitutes a very pleasant and nourishing article of diet." — *Park's Travels*, p. 337.   J. L. D.

" In which enumeration, what we have first to notice is, unity of purpose under variety of expedients. Nothing can be more *single* than the design, more *diversified* than the means. Pellicles, shells, pulps, pods, husks, skin, scales armed with thorns, are all employed in prosecuting the same intention. Secondly; we may observe, that in all these cases, the purpose is fulfilled within a just and *limited* degree. We can perceive that if the seeds of plants were more strongly guarded than they are, their greater security would interfere with other uses. Many species of animals would suffer, and many perish, if they could not obtain access to them. The plant would overrun the soil; or the seed be wasted for want of room to sow itself. It is sometimes as necessary to destroy particular species of plants, as it is at other times to encourage their growth. Here, as in many cases, a balance is to be maintained between opposite uses. The provisions for the preservation of seeds appear to be directed chiefly against the inconstancy of the elements, or the sweeping destruction of inclement seasons. The depredation of animals, and the injuries of accidental violence, are allowed for in the abundance of the increase. The result is, that out of the many thousand different plants which cover the earth, not a single species, perhaps, has been lost since the creation.

" When nature has perfected her seeds, her next care is to disperse them. The seed cannot answer its purpose while it remains confined in the capsule. After the seeds, therefore, are ripened, the pericarpium opens to let them out; and the opening is not like an accidental bursting, but, for the most part, is according to a certain rule in each plant. What I have always thought very extraordinary; nuts and shells, which we can hardly crack with our teeth, divide and make way for the little tender sprout which proceeds from the kernel. Handling the nut, I could hardly conceive how the plantule was ever to get out of it. There are cases, it is said, in which the seed-vessel, by an elastic jerk, at the moment of its explosion, casts the seeds to a distance. We all, however, know, that many seeds (those of most composite flowers, as of the thistle, dandelion, &c.) are endowed with what are not improperly called *wings;* that is, downy appendages, by which they are enabled to float in the air; and are carried oftentimes by the wind to great distances from the plant which produces them."—This is a long extract, but so much to our purpose, that we need not regret that circumstance; whoever, indeed, will read the whole of what is contained, on plants, in the Natural Theology, will find many curious and interesting facts, and much useful reasoning upon them.

In general the PERICARP opens when it is completely dried up, and the seeds are ripe. But several species of *fig-marigold* in the South of Africa, when put into water, gradually open their seed-vessels, and as they dry again, as gradually close them, so as to lock up the seeds. Now, this is a very singular provision, for, contrary to the seed-vessels of other plants, these *open when wet,* and are *closed* when dry. This of course cannot arise from chance, for the latter has no share in the economy of nature, whose operations are all the result of the wisest design. And here the final cause is very apparent. These plants grow in the most arid and burning plains; and were their seeds not protected from the excessive heat by being covered, most of them would probably perish; therefore, during the heats they are locked up, but when the rainy season commences, the seed-vessels open, the seeds are discharged; and immediately commence growing in the moistened soil. Had they escaped sooner, they must during the long dry season have been tossed about at the mercy of the winds; their numbers have been dispersed to unsuitable situations, and consequently the parched tracts which they now clothe and beautify, would continue comparatively naked.

Nature, sometimes, instead of trusting to the mechanism of the seeds, or seed-vessels, for the migration of plants, contrives that the mother-plant herself shall migrate, and bear along with her the seeds, her offspring. Thus we learn from Pallas * that most of the plants of the Russian

* Travels, vol. i. p. 158.

L 3

Steppes are so organized, that when arrived at full maturity they become very light, and breaking off near the root, are carried away by the breeze. Some of these also, are assisted in their migration by growing into the form of a globular bush, which rolls under the slightest impulse of the wind.

Linnæus enumerates seven species of PERICARP: the *capsule* (CAPSULA); *pod* (SILIQUA); *legume* (LEGUMEN); *drupe*, or stone-fruit (DRUPA); *pome* or apple (POMUM); *berry* (BACCA); and the *cone* (STROBILUS).

CAPSULA, the *capsule* (*capsula*, a little chest, or casket, *Lat.*). This is a pericarp opening generally by valves, or pieces, but variously in different plants; sometimes bursting at the top, sometimes at the bottom, and occasionally it divides at the middle, forming the CAPSULA *circumscissa*, as in the *pimparnel* (Anagallis). Sometimes, as in the *poppy*, instead of splitting, there are pores or holes through which the seeds escape. See *Fig. 75.*

The number of valves is various, as is also the number of cells for containing the seeds; each cell is called a *loculamentum*, which means a little box, *Lat.*; and hence the capsula may be *unilocular*, *bilocular*, &c. according to their number. The capsule (*d*), for instance, *Fig. 77.*, is *quadrilocular*, or four-celled; the partitions, dividing the cells from each other, are called dissepiments (*dissepimenta*); and the central column or thread from which they go off is named the *columella.*

Fig. 77.

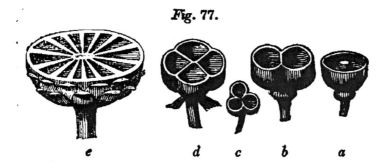

e   d   c   b   a

(*a*) Section of a *unilocular* capsule.   (*b*) A *bilocular.*
(*c*) A *trilocular.*   (*d*) A *quadrilocular.*
(*e*) A *multilocular* capsule.

Siliqua, a *Silique,* or Pod.
Silicula, a *Silicle.*
Legumen, a *Legume.*

Suppose that you compare the seed-vessel of the plant called *Honesty,* with that of any kind of *pea,* and you will find certain differences. You know that the pieces which compose a *pericarp,* or seed-vessel, are named valves, therefore, when you open a pea, you observe that it is *bivalve,* or composed of two pieces. You naturally open it at the edges, because there the two halves or valves are joined to each other; this joining is named a *suture,* or seam (συω (suo), to sew together.) Now, in this instance, the seeds are attached to only one of these seams, as you will find on examination; or, imagine the valves to be transparent, and then the seeds would be seen lying as in *Fig.* 78., connected to the *suture* (*c*) only, and not at all to (*a*).

This is a *Legume,* or that species of pericarp

which consists of two valves, united by two sutures, and having the seeds connected to *one* suture only.

On examining the pericarp of *honesty*, something more than this is found. It apparently seems, like the *Legume*, to consist of two valves; but on separating these, a third layer presents itself lying between them, so that besides the two valves there is also the intermediate partition (*e*), *Fig.* 78. To the

Fig. 78.

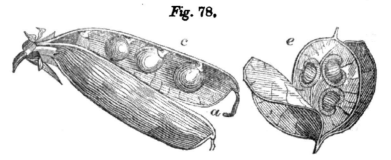

latter the seeds are attached, and therefore, it is the receptacle, and you may observe that they are attached to *both* sutures or edges, and not to one only as in the Legume. This will give a general idea of the SILIQUA, which is *a bivalve pericarp,* having the seeds attached to both sutures. The *intermediate* receptacle is generally present, but is not essential, and therefore in some siliquose plants it is wanting. When this pericarp is long, as in *wallflower*, it is a *silique;* when its breadth is equal, or nearly equal to its length, it is a *silicle;* the pericarp of *honesty*, therefore, is of the latter description, it is a silicle not a silique.

DRUPA, a *Drupe*, or stone-fruit. A pericarp

without valves, containing a *nut* or *stone*, in which
is a kernel. It is generally pulpy as in the plum,
peach, and cherry; in the almond and walnut it
is dry; and in the cocoa-nut, fibrous.

POMUM, a *Pome*, or Apple. A pulpy pericarp,
containing, not a stone, but a *capsule*.

The husky part in the centre of a pear or apple,
which is called the heart or core, is a membranaceous capsule, of five cells, in which are contained
the pippins or seeds. The pulp *surrounding* this
capsule is the part which we eat.

BACCA, a *Berry*. " A succulent or pulpy
pericarp or fruit, without valves, containing naked
seeds." *

Cut an orange or a lemon in two, and you will
find its seeds, neither in a *stone* like the cherry, nor
a *capsule* as in the apple, but lying naked in the
pulp. The orange and lemon, therefore, are *berries*;
so are the gooseberry and currant; " and also,"
perhaps you might say, "the strawberry;"—give
this fruit, however, a moment's attention, and you
will discover that it is *not* a berry, for its seeds instead of being immersed *in* the pulp, are placed
on it. It is in reality a large, soft, coloured,
deciduous, common receptacle bearing the seeds,
which are the dots that render the surface of the
strawberry so beautiful. *Fig.* 79. (*a*)

The *blackberry*, on the contrary, is a true berry,
but being composed of many smaller ones joined

* Martyn.

L 5

together, is a BACCA *composita,* or *compound berry.*
Each of these small ones contains a seed, and is
named an *acinus.*   *Fig.* 79. (*b*)

Spurious or false berries occur in several plants,
the calyx or corolla becoming of a fleshy consistence, and investing the seeds. *

Fig. 79.

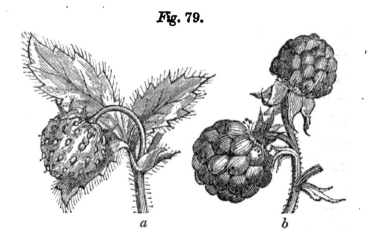

a   *b*

STROBILUS, a *Strobile,* or *Cone.*

A pericarp composed of the hardened scales of
an amentum, as the cones of the pine-tribe; such
as the larch, the Scotch fir, &c.

* For a variety of examples, see Smith's Introduction,
p. 217. and Willdenow's Principles of Botany, p. 117.

CHAPTER VIII.

OF THE NECTARY.

We have now taken a pretty comprehensive view of the different parts composing a plant, but still another remains — the NECTARY. No species, perhaps, either of plant or animal, is made for itself alone; and hence, as vegetables produce a superabundance of seeds for the nourishment of certain races of animals, they also secrete fluids for the sustentation of others. Every one knows that the industrious bee collects the nectar or sweet juice of flowers; but besides it, the numerous tribes of butterflies. and thousands of other insects, live also on the same substance. It may be, that this saccharine juice serves some useful purpose in the economy of the plant itself; and certain philosophers who have a ready explanation for every thing, however inexplicable, point out its uses in this respect, with great confidence. But the truth is, we can see no farther than this, and perhaps it is enough, that without injury to the plant it serves for the maintenance of a large portion of animated beings, and I am inclined to believe that this is its chief, if not sole object. Nature, however, is a rigid economist, and never loses an opportunity of

converting her means to as many uses as possible;
and hence, though the honey be created for the
sake of the insect, the latter, in collecting it, may
confer a favour on the flower by disturbing the
pollen, and thus applying it to the stigma.   As
this application, however accomplished, is absolutely indispensable to the production of fertile
seeds, we find the greatest anxiety, if I may use
the expression, in Nature to have it accomplished.
In the generality of instances, the anthers and
stigmas are so near, or so relatively placed with
respect to each other, that no art is necessary;
for when the former burst, their pollen infallibly
reaches the latter.

But, suppose you examine the *Tiger-lily* at the
time its corolla opens; you will observe the pistil
in the centre, and the six stamens with their points
all turned away from it, so that you might conceive
the possibility of the pollen not reaching the stigma
in any degree.   Look at the plant some hours
afterwards, and you will observe that the pistil, as
if endued with intelligence, has bent itself towards
the circumference in pursuit of the stamens, and
that the stigma is covered with pollen, and on re-
peating the examination from time to time, you
will find that the pistil not only thus bends, but
that also, having done with one anther it leaves it
to get to another, which it again deserts for a third;
so that on no two successive days will you find the
stigma turned to the same stamen.   Instances of

this kind are numerous, and indeed in most, if not all plants in which the stamens and pistils meet in the same flower, the application of the pollen to the stigma is completely provided for, independent of foreign aid. But in those species where the stamens only appear in one flower, and only the pistils in another, the pollen must be conveyed to the latter by the winds, or by insects, or in aquatic plants by the waters in which they reside. Most persons, I believe, have read of the very curious contrivance for this end, which occurs in the Vallisneria *spiralis.* It is diœcious, and the *pistil- liferous* flowers float on the surface attached to a spiral stalk by which they rise or fall according to the height or lowness of the water. The *stamini- ferous* flowers are produced *under* the surface, but when the pollen is ready, they separate from the stalk, rise to the top, and sailing about impelled by the winds or borne by the current, bring the pollen to the pistilliferous flowers, which remain fixed.

As, however, in only a small part of the veget- able world, the stamens and pistils are on different plants, it is obvious that the requisiteness of insects to convey the pollen is very limited. Now, were the fertilization of the germen by their means the *final* object of the nectareous juice, the latter would be wanting in more than nine-tenths of the veget- able kingdom, because in not a tenth part of that kingdom is any such assistance required; for we know that almost all plants possess this fluid. We observe also that often, as in the *crown-imperial*, the sweet juice is produced in great abundance, though the intrusion of insects is totally unnecessary; while in diœcious plants where, in our present point of view, there is most occasion for them, its quantity is by no means remarkable.

We may drop this discussion, and attend to the NECTARY itself. It is commonly, in English, called the Honey-cup, but as it is often any thing but a cup, and as it frequently has nothing to do with honey, the term *Nectary* is better; and by it we are to understand any organ which may occur in a flower over and above the seven regular parts of fructification, whether we have evidence of such organ forming a sweet fluid or not. " Linnæus usually called every supernumerary part of a flower, Nectary, from analogy alone, though he might not in every case be able to prove that such parts produced honey. This is convenient enough for botanical distinctions, though perhaps not always right in physiology; yet there is nothing for which he has been more severely and contemptuously censured. He was too wise to answer illiberal criticism, or he might have required his adversaries to prove that such parts were not Nectaries. Sometimes possibly he may seem to err, like L'Heretier, in calling abortive stamens by this name. Yet who knows that their filaments do not secrete honey, as well as the tubes of numerous flowers? And though abortive as to Anthers, the Filament, continuing strong and vigorous, may do its office." *

It being the case then that every supernumerary part of the flower is called the nectary, we may readily conceive its varieties to be very great. It is only indeed by practice and observation that an extensive knowledge of it can be acquired, though it will be necessary at present to point out some of its forms.

On opening the corolla of a honeysuckle you find at the bottom of the tube a quantity of sweet juice, but there is no gland nor extra-organ by which it could have been secreted, and therefore, we must take for granted that it was formed by the tube itself, and such is generally the case in monopetalous flowers. In the *crown-imperial* (Fritillaria *imperialis*), there is a deviation from this extreme simplicity. The petals of its corolla are six, and in the claw of each is a pit of a white colour, large enough to hold a grain of hempseed, and full of a transparent sweet fluid. "In the bottom," says Gerard, " of ech of these bels there is placed sixe drops of most cleere shining sweete water, in taste like sugar, resembling in shew faire orient pearles; the which drops if you take away, there doe immediately appeere the like, as well in bignes as also in sweetness: notwithstanding if they may be suffered to stande still in the flower according to his owne nature, they will never fall away, no, not.

* Smith's Intr. p. 205.

if you strike the plant, untill it be broken." *   In *Fig.* 80. (*a*) shows the nectaries in the base of this flower, the upper parts of the petals having been cut away.

Fig. 80.

a   g   d

In *Ranunculus* the nectary is also a pit or pore in the claw of the petal; but in a considerable number of the species of this genus it is much less simple than that of the crown-imperial, being shut in some by an emarginate scale placed before it (*b*), and in some surrounded by a cylindrical margin. In *Hellebore* the nectaries are numerous, ranged in a circle, tubular and bilabiate. *Fig.* 80. (*c, c*). Frequently the corolla, as in *violet*, and larkspur, and

* Herbal, p. 153.

sometimes the calyx, as in nasturtium, is prolonged into a spur (*calcar*), which is the nectary. (*d*) And in *Aconite* the nectaries resemble two horns, each bearing on its point a hollow kind of box. *Fig.* 80.(*g*) A flower of the *grass of Parnassus* (Parnassia *palustris*) is represented at (*e*), and one of its nectaries separate at (*f*).

CHAPTER IX.

OF THE LINNÆAN CLASSIFICATION.

WE shall now turn our attention to the Linnæan classification, and I may observe that in most of the popular publications entitled Botanical Guides, Conversations, &c. the explanation of this system is almost the only thing aimed at, and the student who trusts to them imagines that when he can distinguish the class and order of a plant, he has become an accomplished botanist. Without a knowledge, however, of the different kinds of roots, stems, leaves, &c. such as we have been explaining, he never will be able so to profit by any classification as to find out the name of a strange plant, or give an intelligible account of any species which he might wish to describe. I do not mean to say that the preceding pages contain *all* the technological terms used in the science; for it was not intended that they should ; but if the student render himself master of those they do explain, he will have no difficulty in clearly comprehending by a simple reading, such farther terms as are defined in Martyn's Language of Botany, and other works of similar import.

Linnæus took the stamens and pistils, as the

basis of his celebrated system, founding the CLASSES on the number, situation, connection, or comparative length of the former; and the ORDERS, in general, on the number of the latter. These organs vary greatly in quantity in different species, and often are out of all proportion to each other. The *poppy*, for instance, has only one pistil but hundreds of stamens, and the *mouse-tail* (Myosurus), only five stamens, but hundreds of pistils. The fructification in some plants contains one stamen, in some two, in others three, four, five, six, and so on; but in examining flowers for the purpose of ascertaining their number, or that of the pistils, you must, if possible, always examine several of each species, especially in garden flowers, because culture, and sometimes other causes, produce deviations from the natural quantity. You are to remember also, not to trust to double flowers, because in them these organs are changed to petals, and often so completely that no vestige of them is to be seen. In a few instances, independent of this, in cultivated plants, they are not produced; as in *hydrangea*, and common *guelder-rose* (Viburnum *Opulus*).

We may assume the liberty of translating the Greek word ανηρ (aner), into *stamen*, or *anther*, and γυνη (gune), into *pistil*, or *stigma*. When we speak, therefore, of a *monandrous* flower, we mean that it has only one stamen; of a *diandrous*, that it has two; of a *triandrous*, three, and so on: and in the same way of a *monogynous* flower, that it has one pistil; *digynous*, two; and *trigynous*, three. If then I say that such a plant is of the *Monandria* class, and *Monogynia* order, I express at once that its fructifications contain, each, one stamen and one pistil; and could all plants be thus classed, merely from the *number* of these parts, the matter would be very simple, though perhaps not so practically useful as the classification (of which the following is a table,) now stands.

TABLE OF THE TWENTY-FOUR CLASSES.

1. MONANDRIA; one stamen.
2. DIANDRIA; two stamens.
3. TRIANDRIA; three stamens.
4. TETRANDRIA; four stamens, provided the two outer do not overtop the others, as in ringent corollas of the fourteenth class.
5. PENTANDRIA; five.
6. HEXANDRIA; six, provided the flowers are not cruciform.
7. HEPTANDRIA; seven.
8. OCTANDRIA; eight.
9. ENNEANDRIA; nine.
10. DECANDRIA; ten, provided the filaments are *separate* from each other.
11. DODECANDRIA; eleven to nineteen or twenty.
12. ICOSANDRIA; twenty, or more, provided that they *grow out of the calyx*.
13. POLYANDRIA; twenty to a thousand *growing from the receptacle*.

14. DIDYNAMIA; four, *two* long, and *two* short.

15. TETRADYNAMIA; six, *four* long and *two* short flowers *cruciform*.

16. MONADELPHIA; when, whatever may be their number, the filaments *unite below into a tube*.

17. DIADELPHIA; when the filaments are joined like the last, provided that the corolla is *papilionaceous*, or else that instead of being in *one* set so as to form a perfect tube, they are in *two*.

18. POLYADELPHIA; filaments united in *more than two sets*.

19. SYNGENESIA; anthers *united* so as to form a tube, provided the flowers be *compound*.

20. GYNANDRIA; stamens connected to, or growing out of, *some part of the pistil*.

21. MONŒCIA; stamens and pistils in *separate flowers*, but both growing on the *same plant*.

22. DIŒCIA; do. but on *separate* plants.

23. POLYGAMIA includes such plants as produce *three* different kinds of flowers, namely, some with *pistils* only, some only with *stamens*, and others with *both*, either on the *same*, or on *two*, or *three* different plants.

24. CRYPTOGAMIA includes the Ferns, Mosses, Liverworts, Flags, and Mushrooms or Fungi.

I shall now attempt farther to explain the above by making a few observations on each class separately. I shall describe the Orders as I proceed.

CLASS I.

MONANDRIA.   *One* stamen.

Its ORDERS are two, *Monogynia* and *Digynia.*

This is a small class but contains a number of very valuable plants, among which are ginger, cardamom, turmeric, and the Indian arrow-root (Maranta *arundinacea*).   The arrow-root of commerce is nothing more than the starch prepared from the root.   It is manufactured in the usual way, and I believe is not better than that made from the roots of potato or wake-robin.   The white and black ginger are the roots of the Amomum *Zingiber* *, but the second is lower priced, and not so good as the first, because after being dug, it is dipped in boiling water before drying.   The use of this scalding is, I presume, that it destroys the *life* of the root, after which it is dried with much less time and trouble.

The British plants of this class are few and unattractive, and will therefore most likely not come under your review till after some experience in the examination of others, whose fructifications are more conspicuous.   Let me suppose, however, that you walk into the garden, and examine the flowers of *red valerian* (Valeriana *rubra*), which

* In stating the scientific names of plants, I shall in future follow Turton's Edition of the System of Nature.

is a common plant; you will find in each blossom *one* stamen, and no more. "Here," you will say, " is a plant belonging to the MONANDRIA class." But before deciding, let me ask a question. If there were *thirty* different species of valerian, and *twenty-five* of these had flowers containing *three* stamens, would it not be preposterous to place the genus in any other than the TRIANDRIA, or third class, although the *remaining five* should have only *one* stamen, or *two*, or *four*? Now, this is exactly the case with valerian; the red, the narrow-leaved, and the cut-leaved species are *monandrous*, the purple valerian is *diandrous*, and the Siberian *tetrandrous*, but still the genus is in the TRIANDRIA class, the great majority of its species being *triandrous*. This is a kind of difficulty you will sometimes, but not often, meet with in your investigations, and it is well that you should be aware of it.

CLASS II.

DIANDRIA. *Two* stamens.

Its ORDERS are three.

1. *Monogynia.*

Among the plants in this order are the sorrowful-tree (Nyctanthes *Arbor-tristis*), of the East Indies, which during the day droops all its boughs and seems about to wither, but after sunset raises them again, and through the night appears fresh and flourishing; the olive (Olea), which still, as in the days of the Prophets, asserts its paternal right to the rocks of Palestine *; the jessamine (Jasminum),

—— with which the queen of flowers,
To charm her god, adorns his favourite bowers;

the lilac (Syringa); the privet (Ligustrum), common in our hedges; the Verbena, or vervain, one species of which (Verbena *triphilla*) is a universal favourite on account of the delicious fragrance of its leaves. We have here also the beautiful speedwell (Veronica); the water-horehound (Lycopus), which is sometimes called the *gipsy-herb*, "because those strolling cheats called *gipsies* do dye themselves of a blackish hue with the juice of this plant, the better to pass for *Africans*, by their tanned looks, and swarthy hides, to bubble the credulous and ignorant by the practice of Magick, and Fortune-telling, they being indeed a sink of all nations, living by rapine, filching, pilfering, and imposture." † We find also here the rosemary, sage, and some other plants with ringent corollas, but you will recollect that most vegetables having

* " It is truly a curious and interesting fact, that during a period of little more than two thousand years, Hebrews, Assyrians, Romans, Moslems, and Christians, have been successively in possession of the rocky mountains of Palestine; yet the olive still vindicates its paternal soil, and is found, at this day, upon the same spot which was called by the Hebrew writers *Mount Olivat* and *the Mount of Olives*, eleven centuries before the Christian æra."— *Clarke's Travels*, vol. ii. p. 588.
† Threlkeld.

flowers of this kind, belong to the *fourteenth* class.

2. *Digynia* contains two genera, and

3. *Trigynia* only the genus Piper, which is very extensive, and from one species of which (Piper *nigrum*) the pepper of our tables is procured. In this genus there is neither calyx nor corolla.

CLASS III.

TRIANDRIA.   *Three* stamens.

ORDERS three.

1. *Monogynia* contains many plants, among which are the beautiful crocus, the iris, the corn-flag, the ixia, &c., and numerous grassy species, as the cyperus-grass, the cotton-grass, the bulrush, the bog-rush, &c.

2. *Digynia.* Here are the sugar-canes, and, with a very few exceptions, the true grasses, so many of which, as the wheat, barley, rye, oat, &c. are serviceable to man. One, only, the Lolium *temulentum*, is injurious. It is the *infelix lolium* of Virgil, and the *darnel* of English writers, stigmatised as the "fellest of the weedy race." It is very poisonous, producing vertigo, sickness, delirium, and even death. In the first volume of the London Medical and Physical Journal, there is a very interesting case of the injurious effects produced by darnel, in a family of the name of Edmonds. It was used in form of bread, half

composed of tarling wheat, which is the refuse that passes the sieve. The symptoms were, giddiness, sickness, and vomiting, pain and tightness in the calves of the legs, with redness, swelling, and itching of the skin. In one patient the vomiting did not take place till the third day, and in him the pain and inflammation of the legs continued to increase, till they both mortified, and had to be amputated. This patient was thirteen years old; the others, three children and their father, recovered. The writer of the account saw a number of other cases, and he mentions that a universal symptom was violent pain in the calves of the legs, as if they were tightly bound with cords.

3. *Trigynia* contains about eleven genera.

CLASS IV.

TETRANDRIA.   *Four* stamens.

ORDERS three.

1. *Monogynia.* In this order there are above a hundred genera, many of which, as the Protea, Banksia, &c. are very magnificent vegetables.

One species of Protea (Protea *argentea*) has leaves as soft and rich as satin, and resembling silver, whence it is called the *Silver Tree.* Its foliage, when thrown in motion by the breeze, forms a most beautiful appearance, especially if there stand near, to contrast with it, some of the Golden Proteas, whose foliage is yellowish-green, and each leaf edged with scarlet, so that, when agitated in the sunbeams, they resemble waves of fire.*

The Silver Tree is a native of the Cape, and is remarkable in being confined to the base of the Table Mountain, having never been found in any other situation.† The localities, indeed, of animals and plants often afford curious matter of reflection to the naturalist. The worms, for instance, which inhabit the intestines of animals, will not live in any other situation; and, generally speaking, each animal has one or more species of these peculiar to itself. One sort of shell, the Lepas *Testudinarius*, is found attached to the turtle, and no where else; and another, the Lepas *Diadema*, is never observed living any where but on the whale: there are many similar examples. The Silver Tree, in like manner, grows only in one particular part; and Thunberg found some other plants at the Table Mountain on a single spot, but never could discover them in any other. Tournefort found a species of Origanum (Origanum *Tournefortii*) on a rock on the little island Amorgos, in the Archipelago, and Sibthorp detected it afterwards on the same, but it has never been observed elsewhere.‡ We see, also, that plants which are very abundant in one country are unknown in

* Forbes's Oriental Memoirs, vol. ii. p. 168.
† Barrow's Travels in Africa, vol. ii. p. 35.
‡ Willdenow's Princ. of Bot. p. 386.

another: thus, no species of Rose has been discovered indigenous to South America; nor can
the whole New World boast of one native heath,
though it possesses many vegetables which are
equally strangers to the old. We need not, however, be surprised at this; for not unfrequently the
plants growing on one side of a brook, which you
might step over, are totally different from those
on the opposite. * The geography of plants is
a very interesting subject, and has of late years
gained much attention, and received considerable
illustration. Every day, indeed, brings forth new
facts and observations on the subject; but to attend
to these would be foreign to our present purpose.

There is not, I presume, a great probability of
your ever seeing the silver or golden Proteas; but
there is a little humble plant, belonging to this
Class and Order, which you will find plentifully
in flower, about the shaded banks of rivulets, in
mountain woods, &c., during May, and often in
the latter end of April. I mean the Asperula
odorata, or Sweet Woodroof; which in English is
also called *Woodruff, Woodrowe,* and *Woodrowel.*
Perhaps you may recollect a rhyme, which often
forms an amusement of children at school, and is

---

* "I have often observed with astonishment, on my travels,
the great difference between the plants and the soil, on the
two opposite banks of brooks. Sometimes a brook, which
one can stride over, has plants on one bank widely different
from those on the opposite. Therefore, whenever I came to
a great brook or a river, I expected to find plants which I had
not met with before." — *Kalm's Travels,* vol. ii. p. 61.

taken from the ancient method of spelling the
name of this plant. It runs thus : —

> Double U, double O, double D, E,
> R, O, double U, double F, E,

the old English word being *Woodderowffe*.

In order to become better acquainted with this
species, you may look in the Index to Withering's
Arrangement of British Plants for the word Asperula; and then turning to the page referred to, you
will find its description. It nearly resembles some
species of the Galium genus which follows it; and
should you be in any doubt, wait a little till your
specimen withers, and begins to dry, when, if it be
really the Woodroof, it will emit a very delightful
scent, exceeding in sweetness that of new-mown
hay. This fine odour it retains for many months,
I may indeed say for years, after it is dried ; and
hence the leaves are often put into books, watch-
cases, &c., for the sake of their fragrance.

The *Plantain* (Plantago), of which there are six
British species, is another of the genera belonging
to this class. The great plantain, Plantago *major*,
and the rib-wort plantain, Plantago *lanceolata*, are
so common, that they may be found in almost every
field. The latter species was once much celebrated
in the cure of wounds. In Romeo and Juliet,
I believe, it is said, that "your plantain leaf is
excellent for your broken shin;" and Shenstone,
among the plants enumerated in his School-mis-
tress, includes

The plantain ribbed, that heals the reaper's wound.

I may observe, that when this and other herbs were in repute as *vulneraries,* the principles which should regulate the treatment of wounds were little understood. The supposed virtues of the herb, however, produced this good effect; it was firmly bound over the cut, so that the raw edges came in contact, adhesion followed, and the wound healed nearly as well as though the plant had not been used. The real secret of the cure, was the application of the lips of the wound to each other; but this was not understood, and the supposed vulnerary bore off the credit.

The *plantain* is known in Teviotdale by the name of *Wabret,* or *Wabron,* a word of Saxon origin, which sometimes occurs in the early English poets, as in the following ludicrous description of a Bee's Pilgrimage : —

> He made himself a pair of holy beads :
> The fifty *aves* were of gooseberries:
> The paternosters, and the holy creeds,
> Were made of red and goodly fair ripe cherries :
> Blessing his marigold with *ave-maries,*
> And on a staff made of a fennel-stalk
> The beadroll hangs, whilst he along did walk.
>
> And with the flower monkshood makes a cowl;
> And of a grey dock got himself a gown ;
> And looking like a fox, or holy fool,
> He barbs his little beard, and shaves his crown;
> And in his pilgrimage goes up and down ;
> And with a *wabret-leaf* he made a wallet,
> With scrip, to beg his crumbs, and pick his sallet.[*]

---

[*] Cutwode's Caltha Poetarum.—Leyden's Remains, p. 302.

The leaves of the sea-plantain (Plantago maritima) are used by the French during voyages,
either as a salad, or boiled in broth; and sometimes they are pickled like samphire.* Another
species, Plantago *tricuspidata*, which Labillardière
discovered near Rocky Bay, in New Holland, is
one of the most useful plants of that country, its
leaves being very tender, and forming a grateful
refreshment to the weary voyager. †

 Some plants are contained in this first order of
the fourth class, which are useful in the arts, as the
Teasel, already mentioned; the Rubia *tinctorum*,
whose roots form the valuable dye called *madder;*
and the Santalum genus, which affords the red and
white *sandal-wood.* There is, however, a shrub,
very generally known, which will well serve for ex-
emplifying this class. I allude to the Cornus *sanguinea*, common *dogwood*, or *cornel-tree.* It will
readily attract your notice in the shrubbery, especially in autumn, by its leaves, which are then
changed to a blood-red colour, and at all times by
its branches, especially the younger, which have
the same hue; whence the shrub has, in some
places, the name of *"bloody-twig."* There are about
fourteen species of Cornus, two of which, the present, and the Cornus *suecica*, or *dwarf-cornel*, are
found wild in Britain. You can consult Withering
for their descriptions. The *Virginian dogwood*

* Kalm's Trav. vol. ii. p. 345.
† Labillardière's Voy. vol. ii. p. 18.

(Cornus *florida*), sometimes, in America, usurps large tracts of country, excluding almost every other plant from the soil. Bartram describes a wood of these trees, which extended nine or ten miles. They were about twelve feet high, their branches stretching horizontally, and interlacing each other so thickly, as to form one vast cool grove, impenetrable to the sun-beans at noon-day, and affording a delightful shade. A similar mode of growth takes place in the Egyptian thorn (Mimosa *nilotica*): its stems grow far asunder, but the tops are flat, and spread abroad so as to touch each other and form a verdant canopy, under which the traveller may walk many miles undisturbed by the rays of the most burning vertical sun.*

There are three other orders in the fourth class, viz. *Digynia*, *Trigynia*, and *Tetragynia*, which contain few genera.

CLASS V.

PENTANDRIA. *Five* stamens.

This class is of such vast extent, that a bare catalogue of the plants it includes would occupy many pages. I shall, therefore, select from the great mass a few examples, the comments upon which will, I hope, stimulate you to examine the class further, and to become acquainted with the arti-

* Bruce's Trav. vol. iv. p. 236.

ficial and natural divisions under which its genera are arranged.

Its ORDERS are seven.*

1. *Monogynia.*

Read Withering's description of the British species of Pulmonaria (*Lungwort*), and you will find that, in them all, the blossoms are, on first expanding, pink-coloured, but soon afterwards change to blue. This is a circumstance apparently very unimportant; yet, I would have you to keep it in remembrance : for, by connecting it with similar phenomena, you will find it to be one of the ways in which nature indulges her insatiable thirst for variety. I shall add one or two more examples of flowers changing from one colour to another during their time of blowing. I must request your attention, however, to a few previous remarks. You are aware, I suppose, how necessary the presence of light is to vegetation; you know that the whiteness and tenderness of the celery brought to table is produced by heaping mould about the plant so as to keep off light and air; and that the *outer* leaves of a cabbage are green, but those of the heart white, because they are shut up. This influence is often as conspicuous in the animal kingdom, and I scarcely know a more interesting sight than is afforded by the changes of colour which take place in some flies after bursting from the chrysalid state. At first

* See Turton's edition of the System of Nature.

M 5

they are greyish white, with a waxy transparency;
in a few seconds they become bluish; in a few
more, like the mainspring of a watch; and after
some minutes, great part of them is grown quite
black.   In examining bivalve shell-fish, you will
generally find that one valve is more highly and
beautifully coloured than the other, and when this
is the case, you may take for granted that the *dull-
coloured* side had been turned towards the bottom,
and of course did not receive the full influence of
the light.

You may observe many similar phenomena in
plants, the underside of leaves in general being
much paler than the upper, and most flowers, even
the " thousand-coloured tulip," being green until
they expand, and experience the contact of the
sun's rays.   Let me warn you, however, never for
a moment to forget that plants are *living* bodies,
and that if light, air, and water, produce in them
important changes, they do so through the vital
energies of the plant, and not from bare chemical
affinities, such as exist between dead or inorgan-
ical objects.

We are not, therefore, to refer the changes from
one colour to another in plants to chemistry alone;
but to those energies which belong to living organised beings, whose effects we see, though their
manner of acting is inexplicable by our limited
faculties.

The colours of plants have with some apparent
ingenuity been referred to the predominance of

acids and alkalis over each other, or to their various admixture, but we need not dwell on this theory. I think we may lay it down as an undoubted fact, that every species of animal and plant has a mode of vital action peculiar to itself. They all breathe air in one form or another, and they all use food, but very different results follow. The self-same heap of earth that nourishes the most wholesome vegetables, gives vigour, also, to the most deadly.

> The drops which morning sheds
> With dewy fingers on the meads,
>   The pinks' and violets' tubes to fill,
> Alike the noxious juices feed
> Of deadly hemlock's poisonous weed,
>   And gives them fatal power to kill.

The same soil from which the violet scarcely lifts her head, gives growth to the aspiring pine whose high top tapers to the clouds, and to the monarch oak whose giant limbs bid defiance to the storm. Let us not, then, attempt to explain the colours of flowers by any specific theory; but admit, that while light is necessary to their production, yet, that the vital action, whatever that may be, of the individual species, is the agent which modifies the light so as to produce that colour which nature has intended the plant to assume. Food is as necessary to animals, as light to plants; but a portion of food may be swallowed by a bird and converted into feathers, which, were it digested by a fish, would form scales, by a quadruped, hair, by a serpent, perhaps, a deadly poison, and so on.

Although light, therefore, is necessary to vegetables, it is not it, but the vegetable itself, which is the operator in producing the variety of colour; and when we say that light causes such or such phenomena in plants, we are merely to understand that the plant makes use of the light for its own purposes, reflecting some of its rays to produce colours, or absorbing and digesting others to form various vegetables products.

Admitting, then, that the variety of colours in vegetables is produced, not by the light acting on the plant, but by the latter acting on the light, we shall return to our more immediate subject.

There is a plant nearly allied to the *Lungwort*, now common in gardens, which being more stately and of much larger dimensions, exhibits more strikingly the same change of blossom from red to blue. This is the *prickly Comfrey* (Symphytum *asperrimum*), a native of the Caucasus. The *Japanese Honeysuckle* (Lonicera *japonica*) has its flowers at first of a bright silvery white, but they afterwards change to a golden yellow, so that on the same raceme some corollas are pure white, and others like gold; whence in China and Japan it is named *kin gin qua*, which means " gold and silver flowers."* A more remarkable example occurs in the *changeable rose Hibiscus* (Hibiscus *mutabilis*) of the East Indies and China; whose corollas on opening in the morning are green: they soon be-

* Kæmpfer, vid. Bot. Reg. 70.

come white; towards noon change to a reddish hue, and in the evening are bright crimson. The *changeable Corn-Flag* (Gladiolus *versicolor*) is still more remarkable, as in it the colour changes from morning till night, but on the morning succeeding, the original hue has returned, and the same alterations are again gone through. This continues for nine or ten days. In the morning the colour is brown, in the evening bluish. Andrews mentions that a figure of this plant was begun at ten in the morning, but before the drawing was finished, the plant was so totally changed in colour, that there was an absolute necessity of waiting till the next day to complete it.*

The Lithospermum, or *Gromwell*, is another genus in this Class and Order. Its name is taken from the hardness of its seeds (λιθος (*lithos*), a stone, and σπερμα (*sperma*), a seed). You will observe in Withering a remark from Linnæus, that the seeds of the *common Gromwell* (Lithospermum *officinale*) are as hard as bone. This leads me to mention to you a few examples in which the hardness of seeds is very remarkable. You are acquainted with the stone or seed of the *tamarind*, in which this quality is rather conspicuous, and you are familiar with the black beads worn by ladies under the name of *Soap-berries*. They are the produce of the Sapindus *Saponaria*, and in the West Indies the Spaniards use them as buttons.†

* Andrews's Bot. Repos. pl. 19.   † Brown's Jamaica, p. 207.

The seeds of several other plants are applied to a similar use, and when not globular they are sometimes formed by art into a proper shape : thus, in Barbary the stones of the *date* are turned by the natives into handsome beads *, and in the West Indies the seeds of the *prickly Cocos*, or Macaw-tree (Cocos *aculeata*), which are black, as large as walnuts, and bear a high polish, are made into similar ornaments by the negroes. †

, The seeds of the *red Bead-vine* or *Jamaica wild Liquorice* (Abrus *precatorius*), are used by the inhabitants of the Malacca coast for setting into rings in place of stones. ‡ Those of the *Nicker-tree* (Guilandina) are employed by the boys in Jamaica as marbles, and those of the *Indian Reed* (Canna) serve not only as prayer-beads, but as organs of destruction ; being used as a substitute for large shot, which, in appearance, they exactly resemble.

Let us now turn our attention a little to a flower, which we all know and admire; for who does not acknowledge the *Primrose* as a favourite ? All plants, indeed, which herald in the spring, are more or less so. They are the sure signs of that coming season which is to replenish the multifarious lap of nature, and restore the delights of smiling fields, and tranquil skies. The botanic name, Primula, is derived from *primus*, first, prime, or early, and

---

* Hasselquist's Voy. p. 261.
† Brown's Jamaica, p. 343.
‡ Toreen's Voyage.

hence *prime-rose* contracted into *primrose*. It is not, indeed, the very first flower of the opening year, for the *snowdrop* precedes it, though, in gardens and sheltered situations, some species of Primula may be seen all the year round. Added to the early appearance of the *primrose*, its scent is very delicate, and its pale colour gives it a striking expression of modesty and sweetness.

> Welcome, Pale Primrose! starting up between
>   Dead matted leaves of ash and oak, that strew
>   The every lawn, the wood, and spinney through,
> 'Mid creeping moss and ivy's darker green;
>   How much thy presence beautifies the ground!
> How sweet thy modest unaffected pride
> Glows on the sunny bank, and wood's warm side!
>   And where thy fairy flowers in groups are found,
> The schoolboy roams enchantedly along,
>   Plucking the fairest with a rude delight:
> While the meek shepherd stops his simple song,
>   To gaze a moment on the pleasing sight;
> O'erjoyed to see the flowers that truly bring
> The welcome news of sweet returning spring.*

The root of the common primrose (Primula *vulgaris*), in powder, is said to be a safe and effectual emetic, as was "experimented," according to Gerard, "by a learned and skilfull apothecarie of Colchester, master *Thomas Buckstone*, and singular in the knowledge of simples."

Another British species of Primula, the Primula *veris* or *cowslip*, has been immortalised by Shakspeare. The bases of the segments of its corolla are within of a deep orange colour, and these spots

* Clare.

the unrivalled bard has endowed with the office of
giving out the delicious fragrance of the flower,
and supposes them to have been the gift of the
Fairy Queen. In the Midsummer Night's Dream*,
Puck, meeting a fairy, asks,

> How now, spirit!   Whither wander you?
> *Fairy*. Over hill, over dale,
>   Thorough bush, thorough briar,
>   Over park, over pale,
>   Thorough flood, thorough fire,
>   I do wander every where,
>   Swifter than the moone's sphere;
> And I serve the fairy queen,
> To dew her orbs upon the green;
> The *cowslips* tall her pensioners be;
> In their gold coats spots you see;
> Those be rubies, fairy favours,
> In those freckles live their savours:
> I must go seek some dewdrops here,
> And hang a pearl in every *cowslip*'s ear.

The snow-wreath excepted, I can scarcely conceive a more perfect emblem of purity than a wild
plant, native of the glen or mountain, whose flowers,
gemmed with liquid diamond, sparkle to the morning sun, and shiver in the breeze. Or should
the orb of day be concealed, still, each simple cha-
lice, impearled with the dews of night, seems equally
pure and interesting; and when "ilk cowslip-cup
has kepped a tear," we may profitably commune
with those children of the wild, and from their
apparent dejection learn to moralise on the un-
certainties and sorrows attendant on the lot of
mortality. As in Herrick's exquisite address

* Act ii. Scene I.

TO PRIMROSES FILLED WITH MORNING DEW.

Why do you weep?   Can tears
   Speak grief in you
   Who were but born
Just as the modest morn
Teem'd her refreshing dew?

Alas! you have not known that shower
   That mars a flower;
   Nor felt th' unkind
Breath of a blasting wind;
Nor are ye worn with years;
   Nor warped as we,
   Who think it strange to see
Such pretty flowers like to orphans young,
To speak by tears before ye have a tongue.

Speak, * * * * and make known
   The reason why
   Ye droop and weep;
Is it for want of sleep,
Or childish lullaby?
Or that ye have not seen as yet
   The violet?
   *   *   *   *   *   *
   *   *   *   *   *   *   *

No, no; this sorrow, shown
   By your tears shed,
   Would have this lecture read,
That things of greatest, so of meanest worth,
Conceived with grief are, and with tears brought forth.

The common Buckbean, or Marsh Trefoil (Menyanthes *trifoliata*), which you will find in flower during June and July, in pits and marshes, is worthy your examination on account of its beautifully fringed corolla.   About the same time you may in some places gather the *Thorn-apple* (Datura *Stramonium*) among rubbish, ruined cottages, &c.

You will find a description of this plant in Withering; for although not originally a native of Britain, it is become so completely naturalised as to claim a place in the British catalogue. It is an American, but has spread itself over the greater part of Europe. This plant affords a remarkable example of how much the growth of vegetables is promoted or retarded by the nature of the soil they grow in. It flourishes in great quantities near all the villages in Pennsylvania, and in a rich soil rises to a height of eight or ten feet, but in hard poor ground seldom exceeds six inches.*

To the Pentandria class, and Monogynia order, belong the several species of tobacco (Nicotiana), whose leaf has almost equally fascinated the savage and the philosopher. I have known more than one respectable person who I believe held it nearly in as high estimation as was ever done by Captain Bobadil himself, by whom it is thus eulogised: " Sir, believe me, upon my relation; for what I tell you, the world shall not reprove. I have been in the Indies, where this herb grows, where neither myself, nor a dozen gentlemen more, of my knowledge, have received the taste of any other nutriment in the world, for the space of one-and-twenty weeks but the fume of this simple only. Therefore, it cannot be, but 'tis most divine, especially your Trinidado. Your Nicotian is good too. I do hold it, and will affirm it before any prince in Europe,

* Kalm's Trav. vol. i. p. 119.

to be the most sovereign and precious weed that
ever the earth tendered to the use of man." * Its
history would occupy a volume.

We can only notice farther in this Order, the
violet and *ivy*. What the origin of the word Viola
is cannot be precisely determined. It has been
fabled, however, that the Greek name of the plant
Ιον (ion) is taken from the circumstance, that, when
the nymph Io was changed by Jupiter into a cow,
this plant sprang from the earth to become her
food. From the same fable the term Viola is supposed to have had its origin, *viola* being formed
from *vitula* (which means a young cow), by drop-
ping the *t*.

The syrup of the sweet violet is employed by
chemists as a delicate test of the presence of acids
and alkalies; and the flowers are highly esteemed
by the Egyptians and Turks on account of their
colour and fragrance, especially for making sher-
bet, which is composed of violet-sugar dissolved in
water.† They are also said to give a very agreeable odour and taste to vinegar. The flowers of
the violet are frequently white, which is a change
that blue and purple flowers are peculiarly liable to,
though, could we believe in the fancies of poetry,
the violet was originally of that colour.

> Not from the verdant garden's cultured bound,
>   That breathes of Pœstum's aromatic gale,

---

* Jonson's Every Man in his Humour.
† Hasselquist, p. 254.

We sprang; but nurslings of the lonely vale,
'Midst woods obscure, and native glooms were found:
'Midst woods and glooms whose tangled brakes around
　Once Venus sorrowing traced, as all forlorn
　She sought Adonis, when a lurking thorn
Deep on her foot impressed an impious wound.
Then prone to earth we bow'd our pallid flowers,
　And caught the drops divine; the purple dyes
　Tinging the lustre of our native hue;
Nor summer gales, nor art-conducted showers,
　Have nursed our slender forms, but lovers' sighs
　Have been our gales, and lovers' tears our dew.*

The Dog-violet (Viola *canina*)† is very common about ditches and banks from April to June. It is a pretty plant, but is destitute of the delightful odour of the *sweet violet*. At the first opening of the flower there is no stem, but one grows afterwards bearing fruit-stalks. The flower is sometimes white. The circumstance of this species being without fragrance has been made use of in the following pretty little address to the scentless violet: —

Deceitful plant, from thee no odours rise,
　Perfume the air, nor scent the mossy glade,
Although thy blossoms wear the modest guise
　Of her, the sweetest offspring of the shade.
Yet not like her's, still shunning to be seen,
　And by their fragrant breath alone betray'd,
Veil'd in the vesture of a scantier green,
　To every gazer are thy flowers display'd.
Thus Virtue's garb Hypocrisy may wear,
　Kneel as she kneels, or give as she has given;
But ah! no meek retiring worth is there,
　No incense of the heart exhales to heaven! ‡

---

* Roscoe, from Lorenzo de Medici.

† "The epithet *canina* seems to have been given to it, as to the hedge-rose, to express a degree of inferiority or unworthiness, as if a dog were always a less respectable or useful animal than his master." — *Sir J. E. Smith.*

‡ Chauncy Hare Townsend.

" The Pansy freaked with jet " is another species of Viola which is very common. It is the Viola *tricolor* of botanists, but it has a great variety of provincial names, of which Heart's Ease is the most common. Pansy is a corruption of the French *pensée*, a thought, " by which name," says Gerard, " they became knowen to the Brabanders and those of the Lowe Countries that are next adjoining." Ophelia (in Hamlet) says,

> There's rosemary, that's for remembrance;
> Pray you, love, remember: and there is pansies,
> That's for *thoughts*.

It is also called " Three faces under a hood," " Cull me to you," and " Love in idleness," under which latter appellation it has been immortalised by Shakspeare in The Midsummer Night's Dream. The origin of this name has been thus fancifully explained : —

> It was at the noontide hour
> A lady reposed in a bower,
>   Where, shaded between
>   The branches of green,
> Blossom'd and blush'd a fair flower;
> Not a pinion was moved, nor a breeze was heard,
> As with curious hand the lady stirred
>   The leaves of this unknown flower.
>
> She saw in its cradling bloom
> A Cherub, with folding plume,
>   And a bow unstrung,
>   And arrows, were flung
> O'er the cup of this opening flower;
> And the lady fancied she much had need
> Of the light of his wakening eyes to read
>   The name of this unknown flower.

She placed it too near to her breast,
And the cherub was charmed from his rest;
Then he winged a dart
At the lady's heart
From the leaves of this treacherous flower.
Ah! cruel child, said the lady; I guess,
Too late, that *Love in Idleness*
Is the name of this unknown flower.

The Heart's Ease is much improved by culture, and forms endless varieties. It is a curious circumstance that a number of the violets produce occasionally their fructifications without the petals. Withering observes from Curtis, of the *hairy violet* (Viola *hirta*), that " after the first flowers are withered, the plant continues, for a month or more, to throw out others entirely destitute of petals, or with only the rudiments of them, which never appear beyond the calyx, but with all the other parts of fructification perfect, and producing, as the first crop, perfect seeds."

There are about eighty different species of Viola, several of which, besides the Viola *odorata*, are sweet-scented. One species, the *subterraneous violet* (Viola *subterranea*), grows in beech-woods on the mountains of Pennsylvania. Its flowers are very small, and of a chocolate colour, and are always covered either with fallen leaves or rotten wood, and the seed-vessels penetrate into the ground. *

Ivy (Hedera *Helix*) adds much to the beauty of many parts of the landscape, as old turrets, broken arches, ruined bridges, &c.; and when age

* Rees's Cyclopædia.

has destroyed the vigour of the monarchs of the wood, the Ivy wreathes its evergreen foliage around them, and gives them an appearance of beauty even when in ruin.

> Hast thou seen in winter's stormiest day
>   The trunk of a blighted oak,
> Not dead, but sinking in slow decay
>   Beneath Time's resistless stroke,
> Round which a luxuriant *ivy* had grown,
> And wreathed it with verdure no longer its own?
>
> Perchance thou hast seen this sight, and then,
>   As I at thy years might do,
> Passed carelessly by, nor turned again
>   That scathed wreck to view.
> But now I can draw from that perishing tree
> Thoughts which are soothing and dear to me.
>
> O smile not! nor think it a worthless thing
>   If it be with instruction fraught;
> That which will closest and longest cling
>   Is alone worth a serious thought!
> Should aught be unlovely which thus can shed
> Grace on the dying, and leaves on the dead? *

The *Ivy* often under other circumstances assumes a beautiful appearance. We learn from Hasselquist that it is very common at Smyrna, forming the greatest part of the hedges, and ornamenting every garden. He mentions several fine combinations of this plant; " but the handsomest of all," he says, " was a gateway nature had made of Ivy, which had twisted itself together over a miserable garden-gate, to the thickness of three feet, and the length of eight. The gate consisted of some unplaned and rough deals nailed together, ordinary enough

* B. Barton.

for a common stable-door; but the covering might have been an ornament to the entrance of a royal garden." *

That this plant is injurious to trees is well known; and hence, though often praised, it has as often been vilified, and that to a degree much beyond its desert. We can scarcely condemn it so decidedly as is done by Langhorn, in one of his Fables of Flora: —

> No flower can bear the Ivy's shade,
>   No tree support its cold embrace.
>
> The oak that rears it from the ground,
>   And bears its tendrils to the skies,
> Feels at his heart the rankling wound,
>   And in its poisonous arms he dies.

An error, however, is often committed in removing Ivy from trees which have been long covered with it; for they are apt to perish by exposure to sudden colds, being no longer protected by their accustomed clothing. The roots of Ivy make beautiful cups, boxes, and even tables. †

I shall conclude our slight sketch of this first order of the PENTANDRIA class with the following beautiful and appropriate lines, for the insertion of which I am sure I need make no apology: —

TO THE IVY.

> Oh! how could fancy crown with *thee*,
>   In ancient days, the god of wine,
> And bid thee at the banquet be
>   Companion of the vine?

---

* Voyage, p. 24. † See Evelyn.

Thy home, wild plant, is where each sound
   Of revelry hath long been o'er,
Where song's full notes once peal'd around,
   But now are heard no more.

The Roman on his battle plains,
   Where kings before his eagles bent,
Entwined thee with exulting strains
   Around the victor's tent.
Yet there, though fresh in glossy green,
   Triumphantly thy boughs might wave, —
Better thou lovest the silent scene
   Around the victor's grave.

Where sleep the sons of ages flown,
   The bards and heroes of the past —
Where through the halls of glory gone,
   Murmurs the wintry blast;
Where years are hastening to efface
   Each record of the grand and fair,
Thou in thy solitary grace,
   Wreath of the tomb! art there.

Thou o'er the shrines of fallen gods
   On classic plains dost mantling spread,
And veil the desolate abodes
   And cities of the dead.
Deserted palaces of kings,
   Arches of triumph long o'erthrown,
And all once glorious earthly things,
   At length are thine alone.

Oh! many a temple, once sublime,
   Beneath the blue Italian sky,
Hath naught of beauty left by time,
   Save thy wild tapestry:
And, rear'd 'midst crags and clouds, 'tis thine
   To wave where banners waved of yore;
O'er mould'ring towers, by lovely Rhine,
   Cresting the rocky shore.

High from the fields of air look down
   Those eyries of a vanished race,
Homes of the mighty, whose renown
   Hath pass'd and left no trace.

But thou art there — thy foliage bright
   Unchanged the mountain-storm can brave,
Thou that wilt climb the loftiest height,
   And deck the humblest grave.

The breathing forms of Parian stone,
   That rise round grandeur's marble halls,
The vivid hues by painting thrown
   Rich o'er the glowing walls;
Th' Acanthus, on Corinthian fanes,
   In sculptured beauty waving fair;
These perish all — and what remains?
   Thou, thou alone, art there!

'Tis still the same — where'er we tread,
   The wrecks of human power we see,
The marvels of all ages fled,
   Left to decay and thee!
And still let man his fabrics rear,
   August in beauty, grace, and strength,
Days pass — thou *Ivy*, never sere,
   And all is thine at length!*

2. *Digynia.*

This Order, though not nearly so numerous as the first, contains some important plants, among which I may mention the *Gentian*, useful as a bitter; the *beet*, whose roots afford a large quantity of sugar; and the *elm*, which serves better for the keels of ships, and the naves of carriage-wheels, than wood of any other description. This Order also contains the copious tribe of umbelliferous plants, to describe which would require a volume. Some of them are aromatic and esculent, but many nauseous and extremely poisonous. It is said that the latter grow in watery places, the former in dry, but this rule, I believe, is not infallible.

            * Mrs. Hemans.

Sir James E. Smith observes that "Botanists in general shrink from the study of the *Umbelliferæ*, nor have these plants much beauty in the eyes of amateurs; but they will repay the trouble of a careful observation. The late M. Cusson, of Montpellier, bestowed more pains upon them than any other botanist has ever done ; but the world has as yet been favoured with only a part of his remarks. His labours met with a most ungrateful check, in the unkindness, and still more mortifying stupidity of his wife, who, during his absence from home, is recorded to have destroyed his whole herbarium, scraping off the dried specimens for the sake of the paper on which they were pasted ! " *

3. *Trigynia.*

In this Order stands the poisonous genus Rhus (*Sumach* or *Poison-oak*), one species of which, Rhus *Vernix*, is said to be the true Varnish-tree of the Japanese. It is so deadly, that a swarm of bees which alighted on a branch of it was destroyed by its effluvia. † The smooth *sumach* (Rhus *glabrum*), which is not unfrequent in gardens, has a most beautifully feathered leaf that in autumn becomes of a bright crimson colour. In this order also is the beautiful *Laurustinus* (Viburnum *Tinus*), which renders itself extremely valuable by blooming through most of the winter. It is a native of the south of Europe, and exhibits many varieties. Here also

* Smith's Intr. 317.
† Mease's Description of the Productions of America.

are the *elder* (Sambacus); the *Tamarisk* (Tamarix);
the common species of which (Tamarix *gallica*) is
rendered of a fine glaucous colour by a hoary down
covering its leaves and branches; the *bladder-nut
tree* (Staphylea), remarkable for its inflated capsules; and several others.

4. *Tetragynia* contains only two genera, Parnassia and Evolvulus.

4. *Pentagynia.* Of the plants in this Order,
there are two with which I think you must be acquainted; the *sea-pink*, or *thrift* (Statice *Armeria*),
and flax (Linum). The former is remarkable for
growing in almost any soil or situation, from which
circumstance, the name *thrift* is supposed to have
been given to it. It is a good example of a simple
scape bearing a *capitulum*, or head of flowers.
There are many species of *flax*, but the most important is the *common* (Linum *usitatissimum*), to which
we are indebted for that valuable commodity, Linen,
and the still more useful article, Paper. Materials
of various kinds had, from the earliest ages, been
used by mankind on which to commit their thoughts
and observations; but the discovery of the mode
of manufacturing paper, from a plant growing in
the Nile, formed a new and important æra in the
affairs of literature. This plant was named *Papyrus*. It is the Cyperus *Papyrus* of modern botanists, is contained in the TRIANDRIA class, *Monogynia*
order, and may be considered as a gigantic species
of grass. From it the word *paper* is derived, and

as it was also in the Greek tongue called *biblos*, the latter term came to mean a book, and thence the word Bible, or *the book*, applied exclusively to the Scriptures; they being the volume of all others most valuable to man. *Liber* in Latin means the bark of a tree, but it means a book also, because paper was made of the bark of various trees, and books formed of it; and the reason of the term *leaf* being applied to paper, is, that formerly leaves, especially the fronds of the palms, were used for writing on. Hence we as familiarly speak of the leaf of a book as of the leaf of a tree. The art of making paper has been long known in China, and there it is manufactured from a great variety of vegetable substances. It is said indeed that every province has a paper of its own, and that it is prepared in that empire of such dimensions that a single sheet is large enough to cover one side of a moderately sized room.*

6. *Polygynia* contains *Mousetail* (Myosurus), and Zanthorhiza, or *Yellow-root*.

CLASS VI.

HEXANDRIA. *Six* stamens, flowers *not cruciform.*
This class abounds in beautiful plants, especially of the liliaceous tribes, called by Linnæus the "nobles of the vegetable kingdom."—Its orders are six.

* Barrow's Travels in China, p. 310.

1. *Monogynia.*   We have here the *Pine-apple*
(Bromelia),

> Pride
> Of vegetable life, beyond whate'er
> The poets imaged in the golden age;

the Tillandsia, one species of which (Tillandsia *usneoides*), named "Old Man's Beard," resembles bunches of hair, and waves in festoons,
fifteen or twenty feet in length, from the branches
of trees in the American woods. — Here also, is
the fair *Snowdrop*, that "morning-star of flowers,"
pure as the virgin drift from which it seems to take
its birth, and which it almost outrivals in apparent
chillness.

> As Flora's breath, by some transforming power,
> Had changed an icicle into a flower;
> Its name and hue the scentless plant retains,
> And winter lingers in its icy veins. *

In this Order is the extensive and beautiful
genus, Narcissus, some species of which appear
almost as early as the *snowdrop.* The Pancratium
is another beautiful genus, the roots of one species
of which, called the *white lily* of *Jamaica* (Pancratium *caribæum*), being acrid, are, as Brown
most ungallantly asserts, "sometimes used in
poultices by antiquated and pale-faced ladies, to
raise a forced bloom in their fading cheeks."†
The Crinum and Amaryllis are also beautiful
genera ; the *lily* (Lilium) and the *tulip* (Tulipa)
are known to every one. For an interesting ac-

* Mrs. Barbauld.   † Brown's Jamaica, p. 195.

count of the latter, and of the *tulipomania*, which existed in Holland in the middle of the seventeenth century, I refer you to the first volume of Beckman's History of Inventions. Some species of *garlic* (Allium) are very pretty, but many of them possess the offensive odour of the cultivated kind. The *bear's garlic*, or *ramsons* (Allium *ursinum*), is in these countries sometimes felt as a noxious weed, the milk of cattle, which get into places where it grows, being infected with the garlic smell. This is an evil frequently experienced in America, the milk and butter being rendered quite useless by the quantities of different species of garlic which spring up in the pastures. The Allium *canadense* sometimes makes even the flesh unfit for eating. The *guinea-hen-weed* (Petiveria *alliacea*) produces the same effect; for the garlic flavour is not limited to the Allium genus, but is found in many other plants. The *squill* (Scilla) is a fine genus, one species of which, the *harebell* or *wild hyacinth* (Scilla *nutans*), is among the earliest beautifiers of our woods and glens, and when it appears all nature is breaking forth into life and beauty.

A thousand hues flush o'er the fragrant earth,
Or tinge the infant germs of every tree
That bursts with teeming life. Her various vest
The gentle Spring assumes, refulgent less
Than Autumn's robe, but O! how soft, how gay,
The pleasing tints that steal upon the eye!

How white the fields with countless *daisies* drest!
Fair too the leafless hedge with the prime sweets
Of early thorn; the while the *hawthorn* bursts
With tender green. How blue the devious dell,
The rivulet's winding banks, the tangled copse,
With *harebell* flowers!

The *harebell* of Scotland is a very different plant from the present. It is a species of *Campanula*, common in dry mountainous pastures, and has a wiry elastic stem, instead of the soft brittle scape of the Scilla *nutans*. The description of Ellen's step in the fine poem of The Lady of the Lake would be quite absurd, were the flower there mentioned intended to be the English harebell:

A foot more light, a step more true,
Ne'er from the heath-flower dash'd the dew;
E'en the slight *hare-bell* raised its head
Elastic from her airy tread.

When applied to the *campanula*, it is very intelligible.*

The Cyanella genus, found at the Cape, is singular on account of its stamens resembling the fingers, nails, and thumb of the human hand. — The *Asphodel* genus (Asphodelus) affords some fine plants, especially the majestic *king's spear* (A. *ramosus*); as does also the extensive Anthericum. Asparagus is much less showy, but contains the useful Asparagus *officinalis*, which is the species

* " We suspect poets sometimes take this (CAMPANULA *rotundifolia*) for the harebell. We have somewhere read of ' the trembling rye-grass, and the hare-bell blue,' growing on mouldering turrets, which could scarcely be the real harebell." — *Sir J. E. Smith, in Eng. Bot.*

brought to table. In its native place of growth by the sea-shore, it arrives at the height of only a few inches when full grown. A number of species of Asparagus are armed with spines or prickles, which render them, especially the *Cape Asparagus*, very troublesome. " Round the hills near the Cape," says Thunberg, " grew the Cliffortia *rusci-folia*, and the Borbonia *lanceolata*, much resembling juniper-trees, and like the Polygala *Heisteria*, with their sharp leaves pricking the foot-passengers; while the Asparagus *capensis*, with its recurved thorns, tore their clothes, and retarded their passage, for which reason it has received from the inhabitants the name of *wakt en beetje*, Stop a bit." *

Of the Convallaria genus, the *lily of the valley* (Convallaria *majalis*), termed by Churchill the " silver mistress of the vale," is generally known, and on account of its sweet perfume, and the beauty of its drooping snow-white bells, is a general favourite. There is something indeed peculiarly sweet and delicate in the odours of this, and the other early flowers of spring; and the botanist, in his researches by woods, glens, and streams, is often surprised by the gentle breeze laden with fragrance exhaled from primrose banks, or lurking violets, or deepening shades,

Where scatter'd wild, the *lily of the vale*
Its balmy essence breathes.

* Trav. vol. i. p. 243.

The perfumes of summer are often too strong to be agreeable, and sometimes cause oppression and head-ache. By distance, indeed, they become blended and softened, so as to be highly grateful; and I shall never forget an admixture of this kind which I experienced on first sailing into the Bay of Palermo. It was on a lovely summer morning, with a gentle breeze off the land; but it was a breeze impregnated with a thousand odours, blended together into the most exquisite sweetness. It seemed to be wafted rather from some heavenly, than earthly residence. It was such as Milton so beautifully describes in the fourth book of Paradise Lost,

> As when to them who sail
> Beyond the Cape of Hope, and now are past
> Mozambic, off at sea north-east winds blow
> Sabæan odours from the spicy shore
> Of Araby the blest; with such delay
> Well pleased they slack their course, and many a league
> Cheered with the grateful smell old Ocean smiles.

Those species of Convallaria whose corollas are campanulate, are called *lilies of the valley;* but those in which it is funnel-shaped are named *Solomon's seal.* The common *Solomon's seal* (Convallaria *multiflora*), is found in most old gardens. The English name is taken either from its former reputation in sealing up or healing fresh wounds, or from certain marks on its root left by the old stems which resemble the impressions made by a seal.*

* Dr. Thomson's Lect. on Bot. vol. i. p. 141.

It was formerly much celebrated in the cure of fractured bones, and was thought to disperse inward bruises, and effusions of blood ; and if the following assertion go not beyond the truth, this plant would in some families still prove highly valuable : " The roote of Solomon's Seale stamped, while it is fresh and greene, and applied, taketh away in one night, or two at the most, any bruse, black or blew spots gotten by fals or womans wilfulness, in stumbling upon their hasty husbands fists, or such like." *

In this Order is the sweet tuberose (Polianthes *tuberosa*),

> That in the gardens of Malay
> Is called the Mistress of the Night,
> So like a bride, scented and bright,
>   She comes out when the sun's away.

Also the *hyacinth* (Hyacinthus) ; the *New Zealand flax* (Phormium) ; the great family of the Aloes ; the *great fan palm* (Corypha *umbraculifera*), one frond of which is large enough to cover twenty men ; the Calamus, whose different species produce the walking canes and ratans of commerce ; the barberry (Berberis), whose filaments being touched on the inside, immediately contract, and strike the anthers against the stigma ; the *bamboo* (Bambusa) ; and many others.

2. *Digynia* contains *rice* (Oryza), and some more.

* Gerard, p. 758.

3. *Trigynia.* *Dock* (Rumex), one species of which, *common sorrel* (Rumex *acetosa*), is much used in Lapland for making a sort of cheese with the milk of the rein-deer.*— The *meadow saffron* (Colchicum), for an interesting account of which I refer you to Paley's Natural Theology.

4. *Hexagynia.*

5. *Polygynia.*

CLASS VII.

HEPTANDRIA. *Seven* stamens.

ORDERS four.

1. *Monogynia.* The horse-chesnut (Æsculus *Hippocastanum*) stands in this order; and when in blossom, it presents a remarkably fine appearance. " No flowering shrub is rendered more gay by its blossoms than this tall tree; hence it combines beauty with grandeur, in a degree superior to any other vegetable of these climates." †

You must have often observed the hawthorn and other trees putting forth their buds in spring, but perhaps you have not been aware that those very buds were formed in the preceding summer; and being protected by a number of enveloping scales, unmolestedly braved the cold and storms of winter. I shall not detain you with a description of them, and their economy here; you may find the subject amply discussed in many works, especially in Dr.

---

* Vide Lachesis Lapponica, vol. i. p. 102.

† Aikin's Woodland Companion.

Thomson's " Lectures on Botany." Let me recommend to you, however, to commence a series
of observations, early in spring, on the *flower-buds*
of the horse-chesnut; you will know them from
the *leaf-buds* by their greater size, though you had
better examine both. In considering the resinous
varnish which covers the young bud; the multiplicity of scales forming its walls; the beds of woolly
fibres surrounding the infant flowers, and the
gradual expansion, from day to day, of its spikes
from their first Lilliputian dimensions to their
complete development, you will find much matter
for admiration and reflection.

2. *Digynia.*

3. *Tetragynia.*

4. *Heptagynia.* Septas *capensis* has a calyx of
seven segments, a corolla of seven petals, seven
stamens, seven pistils, and seven capsules.

This class is the smallest in the system.

CLASS VIII.

OCTANDRIA. *Eight* stamens.

ORDERS four.

1. *Monogynia.* Many plants stand in this order,
of which I shall enumerate a few; *nasturtium*, or
Indian cress (Tropæolum), cultivated for its pungent seed-vessels which are used in pickles; *tree
primrose* (Œnothera); *willow herb* (Epilobium);
the elegant Fuchsia; the copious genus Vac-

cinium, of which the *bleaberry* (Vaccinium *Myrtillus*), the *great bilberry* (Vaccinium *Uliginosum*), the *red whortle-berry* (Vaccinium *Vitis idæa*), and the *cranberry* (Vaccinium *Oxycoccos*), are natives of Britain. Many species of Vaccinium are extremely common in North America, and great quantities of the berries are sent to Europe under the names of whortle-berries, huckle-berries, and cranberries; it is said, too, that dried bilberries are imported into England from Germany, under the name of *berry-dye,* for the purpose of giving a fictitious colour to port-wine.* In China the Vaccinium *formosum* is held sacred, and at the commencement of the new year its flowers are placed in the temples as an offering to the gods.†

It has already been stated that no species of *heath* (Erica) has hitherto been discovered in the new world; and what is no less strange, so abundant is this genus in Southern Africa, that one botanist found above one hundred and thirty distinct species between the Cape and the nearest range of mountains.‡ Nothing can surpass the beauty of these *Cape-heaths,* as they are found in collections in Europe; but it appears that they are by no means so attractive in their native soil. Sometimes one or two species jagged by the winds, or shrivelled by drought, spread over large tracts

---

* Accum on Culinary Poisons, p. 72.
† Abel's China, p. 221.
‡ Barrow's Trav. in Africa, vol. ii. p. 35.

of country, giving it the appearance of our barren heaths; and even those which grow in boggy situations, though larger, are not near so beautiful as when cultivated.* Much, however, may depend on seeing the plants in full blow; for what can be more beautiful than even our wildest moors, when in July and August they glow empurpled with innumerable heath-bells?

In this order is the fine genus Daphne, one species of which *mezereon* (Daphne *Mezereum*), I suppose you have often admired, on beholding it in March,

> Though leafless, well attired, and thick beset
> With blushing wreaths, investing every spray.†

Daphne *Laureola*, or *Spurge-Laurel*, is also common, and will be worth your examination, as its corolla (or calyx, if you will) is always green. These two are natives, but a number of exotic species, as the *Neapolitan Mezereon* (Daphna *collina*), the *trailing Daphne* (Daphne *Cneorum*), &c. are common in gardens. The *Lace-bark-tree*, (Daphne *Lagetto*) of Jamaica, is remarkable for the layers composing its bark, which are above twenty in number, and resemble white gauze, or lace, for which they are said to be sometimes used as a substitute.

2. *Digynia* contains about five genera.

3. *Trigynia.* Among the plants in this order is

---

* Barrow's Trav. in Africa, ed. 2d. Pref. vii.
† Cowper.

the *Soap-berry* (Sapindus), whose fruit is so elastic that when thrown on a stone it rebounds several times to the height of seven or eight feet.*

4. *Tetragynia.* Few genera.

CLASS IX.

ENNEANDRIA. *Nine* stamens.

ORDERS three.

1. *Monogynia.* Among the numerous species in the Laurus genus are the *cinnamon-tree* (Laurus *Cinnamomum*), the *wild cinnamon-tree* (Laurus *Cassia*), the *camphor-tree* (Laurus *Camphora*), the *sweet bay* (Laurus *nobilis*), and the *sassafras-tree* (Laurus *Sassafras*), all very valuable, — also the *Acajou* or *Cashew-nut* (Anacardium *occidentale*), &c.

2. *Trigynia.* *Rhubarb* (Rheum), only.

3. *Hexagynia.* *Flowering rush* (Butomus), only.

CLASS X.

DECANDRIA. *Ten* stamens.

ORDERS five.

1. *Monogynia.*

You know that the plants of the seventeenth class (DIADELPHIA) have *papilionaceous* corollas, and that all plants whose corollas are such belong to it, provided their filaments be united. But, suppose you saw a papilionaceous flower with ten sta-

* Humboldt, Pers. Nar. vol. iii. p. 198.

mens *all separate and distinct,* you would not refer it to the seventeenth class, but to the present, it being an indispensable requisite that in the former, the filaments shall be united. Now in the first order of the class DECANDRIA there are many species with papilionaceous flowers ; and they are placed there, because, their stamens being separate, it would be quite improper to arrange them in the seventeenth.

This Order contains many plants useful in medicine and the arts, as for instance the Cassia *Senna,* whose leaves form the Senna of the druggist ; the Cassia *Fistula,* the pulp of whose pods was formerly in much estimation ; Guaiacum *officinale,* whose wood is known by the name of *Lignum vitæ,* and whose gum resin is the *Gum Guaiacum* of the shops ; Toluifera *Balsamum,* balsam of Tolu-tree ; Myroxylon *peruiferum,* balsam of Peru-tree ; Hæmatoxylon *campechianum,* Logwood ; Swietenia *Mahagoni,* Mahogany ; and Quassia *amara,* which affords the purest bitter perhaps that is produced.

Here also are the *Fraxinella* (Dictamnus), which in dry still evenings emits an inflammable gas, or vapour ; the singular *Venus's fly-trap* (Dionæa *Muscipula*); and the beautiful genera of Andromeda, Kalmia, Rhododendron, Arbutus, and many others.

You will find here, too, the genus Ruta (*Rue*), with which you can scarcely fail to be acquainted. You probably abhor the smell of this plant ; though perhaps not, for we cannot account for tastes. A very ingenious friend of mine is quite enamoured with the odour of assafœtida, and in Persia, a young assafœtida plant is considered, when *fried in oil,* as one of the greatest delicacies.   Peyrouse mentions a hut which he visited on the island Sagaleen or Tchoka, in the Sea of Ochotsk.   It was seated in a thicket of rose-trees in blossom, that emitted a delicious fragrance; not sufficient however to overcome the stench of the fish and oil about the hut. " We wished (he says) to know whether the pleasures of smell, like those of taste, depended on habit; I gave one of the old men a phial of very sweet-scented water, which he put to his nose, and for which he testified the same repugnance as we felt for his oil." *

Without multiplying instances of this kind, it will be easy to conceive that the olfactory organs may occasionally be pleased even with the perfume

> That breathes from vulgar *rosemary* and *rue.*

Madam Piozzi relates, that being delighted with the beauty and fragrance of the numerous flowers at Florence, she enquired for some scented pomatum; and two pots being brought her, she found one to smell strongly of garden-mint, the other of *rue* and *tansy.*   But this was a slight matter to what happened afterwards.   She was introduced by the Venetian Ambassador to a party at Rome, but to

* Voyages, vol. ii. p. 375.

her great confusion, the conversation soon ceased, and all the ladies shrank from her, and stopped their noses with *rue*, which a servant handed about upon a salver. The cause of this was her having some scented powder in her hair! She was led sinking with shame and distress from the company, to which of course she did not return; but she very naturally asks, " What can make these Roman ladies fly from *odori*, so that a drop of lavender-water in one's handkerchief, or a carnation in one's stomacher, is to throw them into convulsions thus? Sure this is the only instance in which they forbear to *fabbricare su l'antico* (build upon the old foundation), in their own phrase; the dames' of whom Juvenal delights to tell, liked perfumes' well enough if I remember; and Horace and Martial cry *carpe rosas* perpetually."*

2. *Digynia.*

This order contains about twelve genera.

You know the plant called *London Pride*, or *None so pretty;* it belongs to the extensive genus Saxifraga†, another species of which, Saxifraga *granulata*, or *white saxifrage*, is common in gardens; but its flowers are generally double, and consequently you will not find the stamens and pistils,

* Travels, p. 291.
" The Italians in general dislike perfumes, and the Pope (Pius VII.) has a particular antipathy to musk. On the last presentation, one of the company was highly scented with this odour, and Pius was constrained to dismiss the party almost immediately." —*Diary of an Invalid*, p.164. *Feb.* 1817.
† It is the Saxifraga *umbrosa*.

they being changed into petals. You are acquainted also with the *Hydrangea* (Hydrangea *hortensis*), and, perhaps, have observed that its flowers are first green, and change gradually to a rose or a bluish-purple colour. Should you examine one of these in order to count the stamens, you will probably be disappointed, for this part of the fructification, as well as the pistils, is in the cultivated hydrangea almost always wanting. In the *guelder-rose* (Vibernum *Opulus*) of the fifth class a similar circumstance is observable: the flowers in the centre of each cyme are perfect, but those in the circumference abortive. When cultivated, they *all* become abortive, grow much larger and whiter, and the cymes assuming a globular shape, the plant gets the name of the *snowball-tree*.

The only other genus in this order which I shall mention is the Dianthus, some species of which, as the Dianthus *barbatus* (*Sweet William*), Dianthus *plumarius* (*Pink*), and Dianthus *Caryophyllus* (Carnation), are in general estimation.

3. *Trigynia.*

Here is the extensive genus Silene (*campion* or *catch-fly*). The latter appellation arises from the circumstance of the stems of some species being varnished with a viscid substance, that entraps flies and other insects. The Silene *noctiflora*, and some others, flower in the night. Stellaria, the common *chickweed*, belongs to this genus; it is the Stellaria *media;* and another species, Stellaria *Holostea*, or *greater stitchwort,* beautifies almost every hedge in April and May, with its large, snowy, and star-like blossoms. There are also, in this order, Arenaria (*sandwort*), Malpighia (*Barbadoes cherry*), and a few more.

4. *Pentagynia.*

Among plants in this order are the *bilimbi-tree* (Averrhoa), the *hog-plumb* (Spondias), the *navel-wort* (Cotyledon), *stone-crop* (Sedum), *corn-cockle* (Agrostemma), *lychnis* (Lychnis), and *wood-sorrel* (Oxalis).

The *sedums* are extremely tenacious of life, and grow, or continue fresh, long after being separated from the roots. On this account the *orpine* (Sedum *Telephium*), has been named " live-long." Its vivaciousness had attracted the notice of Spenser, since he sings of

Cool violets, and *orpine growing still,*
Embathed balm and cheerful galingale.

Of the Oxalis, which is a very copious genus, we have one species very common and very beautiful, the *common wood-sorrel* (Oxalis *Acetosella*). You will find it in blossom during April and May, in sheltered moist situations, in woods and thickets, along the sides of rivulets, and almost, indeed, in every shade,

Where lowly lurks the violet blue,where droops,
In tender beauty, its fair spotted bells
The cowslip.*

----

* Langhorne.

5. Decagynia.

Phytolacca, and Neurada, only.

CLASS XI.

DODECANDRIA.

The plants belonging to this class have from eleven to nineteen stamens. Its ORDERS are six.

1. *Monogynia.*

Contains among others the *asarabacca* (Asarum), the genus Tomex, a species of which (Tomex *sebifera*) is named the *tallow-tree*, as the Chinese extract a species of tallow from its kernels; Bocconia (*tree-celandine*), Blakea (*Jamaica wild-rose*), Garcinia (*Mangosteen*), a native of Java and the Molucca islands. It is a tree twenty feet high, and bears fruit the size of an orange, which is delightfully flavoured, and said to be the most salubrious in the world. Halesia (*snowdrop-tree*), Canella whose bark is highly aromatic, Cratæva (*garlic-pear*), Peganum (*Syrian rue*), Portulaca (*purslane*), Rhizophora (*mangrove*), Lythrum (*willow-herb*), &c.

2. *Digynia.*

Heliocarpus (*sun-seed-tree*), Agrimonia (*agrimony*), only.

3. *Trigynia.*

Reseda. To this genus the charming *mignonette*, originally a native of Egypt, belongs: it is the Reseda *odorata*. Euphorbia (*spurge*). This is a

very extensive genus, and of so peculiar a conform-
ation, that when the student gets acquainted with a
very few species, he will afterwards, on the slightest
glance, recognise any native and most foreign plants
belonging to it.   Almost all the species abound in
a milky juice possessed of great acrimony, on which
account some of the more common species are in
Ireland named "*devil's churns.*"   This milk seems
often as rich as cream, and its quantity is astonishing.   There is a tree-like species in Egypt, named
the *Kol-quall:* and Bruce asserts, that on cutting
off two branches with his sabre, there flowed out
not less than *four gallons* of a bluish watery milk.
"When," he says, "the tree grows old the branches
wither, and, in place of milk, the inside appears to
be full of powder, which is so pungent, that the
small dust which I drew upon striking a withered
branch, seemed to threaten to make me sneeze to
death; and the touching of the milk with my fingers
excoriated them as if scalded with boiling water;
yet I every where observed the woodpecker piercing
the rotten branches with its beak, and eating the
insects, without any impression upon its olfactory
nerves." *   The milk of our native *spurges* is dread-
fully acrid, a proof of which, as respects the juice
of the *sea-spurge,* is given by Gerard from his own
experience.   "Some," he says, "write by report of
others, that it inflameth exceedingly, but myself
speake by experience; for walking along the sea-

* Trav. vol. vi. p. 53.

coast at Lee in Essex, with a gentleman called
Master Rich, dwelling in the same towne, I tooke
but one drop of it into my mouth, which neverthe-
lesse did so inflame and swell in my throte that I
hardly escaped with my life: and in like case was
the gentleman, which caused us to take our horses,
and poste for our lives unto the next farme house
to drinke some milke to quench the extremitie of
our heate, which then ceased." * He advises against
the internal use of these plants as medicines, because, " Deere is the. honie that is lickt out of
thornes, and that health is deere bought which is
procured with such danger."

I may remark, that the milky juice of plants is
almost always acrid, bitter, or narcotic; but there
are exceptions. Sir J. E. Smith mentions, that
Dr. Afzelius met with a shrub at Sierra Leone, the
milk of whose fruit was very copious, and so sweet,
that he used it as a substitute for cream. This
however, might be rather an emulsion formed by
a union of the fixed oil and mucilage of the fruit,
than real sap : and here let me observe, that vegetable fixed oil is furnished by seeds only. The bark
and other parts may produce waxy secretions, or
resins, gums, essential oils, &c., but no *fixed* oil.
Hence it so often happens, that seeds, when bruised
alone, or with water, afford a milk or cream-like
fluid; a circumstance noticed by Milton in his enu-

* Herbal, p. 407.

meration of the materials of the banquet prepared
by our first mother for her angel guest.

> ——— fruit of all kinds, in coat
> Rough or smooth rin'd, or bearded husk, or shell,
> She gathers, tribute large, and on the board
> Heaps with unsparing hand; for drink the grape
> She crushes, inoffensive must, and meaths
> From many a berry; and from sweet kernels press'd
> She tempers dulcet creams.

I formerly attempted to show that Nature has
ordained vegetables to produce an exuberance of
seeds for the support of animals, independent of
the extension of their own species. I might perhaps go farther, and assert, that this is the final
object of the fixed oil they contain; and certainly
there are few combinations more nutritive than an
admixture of fatty with farinaceous matter, such as
is found in a large proportion of seeds. I have not
sufficiently, however, considered this subject to
speak with great confidence, and shall therefore
but drop a hint or two.

There are very few instances of a fruit abounding
in juices, as the orange and lemon; in pulp, as the
grape and gooseberry; in flesh, as the apple, pear,
and melon; or saccharine matter, as the date and
fig; whose seeds are capable of affording oil, and
so far as the feeding of animals is concerned, it
would, in these cases, be quite superfluous. In
fruits, on the other hand, whose husks, having none
of these supernumerary parts, are coriaceous and
inedible, the seed or kernel generally abounds in
oil, and forms a rich and fattening food. Of this

o

kind are the walnut, almond, filbert, chocolate nut, cocoa nut, &c. There are undoubtedly exceptions, for nature is not limited to precise rules : and we have a remarkable example in the *olive*, of a seed invested with a pulp abounding in oil. The importance of this oil of the olive to man in all ages, is well known; but however advantageous it may be to him and other animals, it is said to be absolutely injurious to the olive-seed itself, by hindering the moisture from penetrating to it, and thereby preventing germination. Hence the *olive-tree* is not propagated by planting its fruit, unless the oil be first destroyed. This is effected in the great economy of nature by birds; they swallow the fruit, the oily part serves them as nutriment, and the seed being freed from this incumbrance, germinates, and is developed into a growing plant. An inhabitant of Marseilles, in imitation of this process, made turkeys swallow ripe olives, and produced plants from their kernels which had passed the alimentary canal. He found also, that maceration of the fruit in an alkaline lixivium was, by destroying the oiliness, equally successful.*

To return to our more immediate subject. The milky juice of vegetables is not, I have said, always acrid, narcotic, or bitter; and I believe we have an example of this even among the *spurges;* for there is a species at the Cape whose centre contains about a pint of milk, so grateful to cattle, that they

* Vide Blackwood's Mag. vol. iii. p. 219.

pierce the plant with their teeth for the sake of drinking it. But the most remarkable example of a nutritive vegetable milk is afforded by the *palo de vaca*, or *cow-tree* of South America, which you will find amply described in the fourth volume of Miss Williams's translation of Humboldt's " Personal Narrative." A general idea may be formed from this quotation. " On the barren flank of a rock grows a tree with coriaceous and dry leaves. Its large woody roots can scarcely penetrate into the stone. For several months of the year not a single shower moistens its foliage. Its branches appear dead and dried; but when the trunk is pierced, there flows from it a sweet and nourishing milk. It is at the rising of the sun, that this vegetable fountain is most abundant. The blacks and natives are then seen hastening from all quarters, furnished with large bowls to receive the milk, which grows yellow, and thickens at its surface. Some employ their bowls under the tree itself, others carry the juice home to their children. We seem to see the family of a shepherd, who distributes the milk of his flock."

4. *Tetragynia.* Calligonum and Aponogeton only.

5. *Pentagynia.* Glinus and Blackwellia only.
6. *Dodecagynia.* Sempervivum (*houseleek*) only.

CLASS XII.

ICOSANDRIA.   *Twenty* or *more* stamens inserted in the *calyx.*

It is a singular and important fact, that the fruit of every plant whose stamens grow from the calyx, may be eaten with impunity, even though the rest of the plant should be highly poisonous. " No traveller," says Sir J. E. Smith, " in the most un-known wilderness need scruple to eat any fruit whose stamens are thus situated; while, on the other hand, he will do well to be cautious of feeding on any other parts of the plant." *   The present class is characterised by this mode of insertion of the stamens; but it is necessary that their number be twenty or more. If in examining a flower you found five, eight, or ten stamens, even although they were inserted into the calyx, you would still refer it to the fifth, eighth, or tenth class. But whenever you meet with a plant having *twenty*, or any greater number of stamens thus situated, you must refer it to the class ICOSANDRIA.

Its ORDERS are five.

1. *Monogynia.*

In this order is the beautiful Cactus genus, the different species of which have in English a diversity of names. When of a round form, they are called *Melon Thistles ;* when erect and strong, *Torch Thistles ;* when creeping with lateral roots, *Cereuses ;*

* Introd. p. 298.

INDIAN FIG. — MOCK-ORANGE.

and when compressed with proliferous joints, *Prickly Pears*, or *Indian Figs.** Philadelphus (*Syringa*, or *mock-orange*). The common syringa of gardens is the Philadelphus *coronarius ;* it is a native of the south of Europe, and its leaves taste like cucumber. — Leptospermum (*South-sea Myrtle*). — Psidium (*Guava*). — Myrtus (*Myrtle*). — Punica (*Pomegranate*). — Amygdalus. The *peach* is the Amygdalus *Persica*, and the *nectarine* is merely a variety of the peach, having a smooth, instead of a downy skin; the *almond* is the Amygdalus *communis*, and the sweet and bitter almonds are not distinct species. Prunus. — Prunus *Padus*, bird-cherry; P. *Lusitanica*, Portugal laurel; P. *Laurocerasus*, common laurel; P. *Armeniaca*, Apricot-tree; P. *Cerasus*, cherry-tree; P. *domestica*, plum-tree; P. *spinosa*, sloe or blackthorn.

2. *Digynia*, Waldsteinia only.

3. *Trigynia*, Sesuvium only.

4. *Pentagynia*. Some authors make this the second order, and include in it all the genera of the class having from two to five styles. Mespilus. — "the *haw-thorn*" (Mespilus *Oxyacantha*) "should not be entirely passed over amidst the minuter plants of the forest, though it has little claim to picturesque beauty. In song, indeed, the shepherd may with propriety,

—————— tell his tale
Under the hawthorn in the dale :

————————————————————

* Vide Turton, Syst. Nat.

but when the scenes of Nature are presented to
the eye, it is but a poor appendage.—Its shape is
bad.   It does not taper and point, like the holly,
but is rather a matted, round, heavy bush.   Its
fragrance indeed is great: but its bloom, which is
the source of that fragrance, is spread over it in too
much profusion.   It becomes a mere white sheet—
a bright spot, which is seldom found in harmony
with the objects around it.   In autumn the hawthorn makes its best appearance.   Its glowing berries produce a rich tint, which often adds great
beauty to the corner of a wood, or the side of
some crowded clump." *

However true these remarks may be, there are
very few persons, I believe, who do not admire
this species, particularly at that season,

When wheat is green, when hawthorn buds appear;

or when, farther on,

The gorse is yellow on the heath,
　The banks with speedwell flowers are gay,
The oaks are budding, and beneath
The hawthorn soon shall bear the wreath,
　The silver wreath of May. †

In this genus is the *medlar* (Mespilus *germanica*),
a fruit which is only eatable after having undergone
a kind of putrefactive fermentation.   " You'll be
rotten (says Rosalind to Touchstone, in *As You
Like it*) ere you be half ripe, and that's the right
virtue of the medlar."

* Gilpin's Forest Scenery, vol. i. p. 99.
† Charlotte Smith.

Pyrus.—You are acquainted with several species belonging to this genus, as the *pear-tree* (Pyrus *communis*), the *apple* (P. *Malus*), the *Japan apple-tree* (P. *japonica*), the *quince* (P. *Cydonia*), the *mountain-ash* or *rowan-tree* (P. *aucuparia*), &c. In this order is the immense genus Mesembryanthemum, *Fig Marigold,* of which the *ice-plant* (M. *crystallinum*) is a species.—Spiræa. One species of this, the Spiræa *Ulmaria,* or *meadow sweet,* I am sure you are acquainted with.

5. *Polygynia.*

Rosa.—To pass over the "queen of flowers," the Rose, without particular attention, may perhaps seem little short of sacrilege: yet that censure we must incur, for so much has been said, and is to say of this lovely plant, that no ordinary limits could do it justice. You will find much information respecting it in the first canto of Tighe's Plants, and its explanatory notes. You may read the "Light of the Haram," also, in Lalla Rookh; and in the several volumes of that most elegant and instructive work, "Time's Telescope,"* you will find many poetical tributes to this sweetest flower,

> that ever bloom'd in any bower.

---

* I am indebted to this excellent publication for many poetical illustrations taken from recent or living authors, which I should not otherwise have had an opportunity of seeing. I know of no work so well calculated to spread and improve a taste for Natural History in these kingdoms; and I would most strenuously recommend it to the attention of every student and lover of Nature.

Rosa is an extensive genus, and its varieties are very numerous, for the goodness of Providence has given to it, and many other plants, which the human eye delights to contemplate, a capability of being varied into endless forms, and freaks of colour. The most beautiful species is undoubtedly the *Moss Rose* (Rosa *muscosa*). Its bloom is delightful, and the mossy vesture gives it an indescribable elegance and simplicity. Of the origin of this moss-like covering there is a very fanciful and poetic idea in a German writer, which has been thus translated: —

> The Angel of the flowers one day,
> Beneath a rose-tree sleeping lay,
> That spirit — to whose charge is given
> To bathe young buds in dews from heaven;
> Awaking from his light repose,
> The Angel whisper'd to the Rose:
> ' O fondest object of my care,
> Still fairest found where all are fair,
> For the sweet shade thou'st given to me,
> Ask what thou wilt, 'tis granted thee.'
> ' Then,' said the Rose, with deepen'd glow,
> ' On me another grace bestow.'
> The spirit paused, in silent thought,
> What grace was there that flower had not!
> 'Twas but a moment — o'er the Rose
> A *veil of moss* the angel throws,
> And, robed in nature's simplest weed,
> Could there a flower that rose exceed? *

The *sweet-briar*, Rosa *rubiginosa*, on account of its perfume, forms a general inmate of the garden. Eglantine is another appellation by which

* Blackwood's Magazine.

it is commonly known, and which is applied to it
in several parts of Shakspeare, as thus in Cym-
beline : —

> With fairest flowers,
> Whilst summer lasts, and I live here, Fidele,
> I'll sweeten thy sad grave: Thou shalt not lack
> The flower that's like thy face, pale primrose ; nor
> The azured hare-bell, like thy veins ; no, nor
> The leaf of eglantine, whom not to slander,
> Out-sweeten'd not thy breath:

Milton confounds it with the woodbine.*

The common *briar* or *dog-rose* is the Rosa *canina*,
and you know how pure and beautiful its flowers
come from the hand of nature, adorning ditches,
banks, rocks, and ruins with their blushing honours.
We often perceive in flowers, even independent of
beauty of colouring and sweetness of scent, certain
undefinable charms which strike a secret influence
to the heart, and turn us with gratitude to that
great Being who has so constituted our minds as
that they can experience such sweet sensations
from the contemplation of external things.

> Who can have watched the *wild rose*' blushing dye,
>   And seen what treasures its rich cups contain ;
> Who, of soft shades the fine variety,
>   From white to deepest flush of vermeil stain ?

---

* To hear the lark begin his flight,
  And singing startle the dull night,
  From his watch-tower in the skies,
  Till the dappled dawn doth rise ;
  Then to come in spite of sorrow,
  And at my window bid good-morrow,
  Through the sweet-briar or the vine,
  Or the *twisted* eglantine.

Who, when impearl'd with dew-drop's radiancy,
    Its petals breathed perfume, while he did strain
His very being, lest the sense should fail
    To imbibe each sweet its beauties did exhale?

Who amid lanes on eve of summer days,
    Which sheep browze, could the thicket's wealth behold?
The fragrant *honeysuckle*'s bowery maze?
    The *furze-bush* with its vegetable gold?
In every satin sheath that helps to raise
    The *fox-glove*'s cone, the figures manifold
With such a dainty exquisiteness wrought?
    Nor grant that thoughtful love they all have taught?

The *daisy, cowslip*, each have to them given —
    The *wood-anemone*, the *strawberry* wild,
Grass of Parnassus, meek as star of even;
    Bright as the bright'ning eye of smiling child,
And bathed in blue transparency of heaven,
    Veronica; the *primrose* pale, and mild; —
Of charms (of which to speak no tongue is able)
Intercommunion incommunicable. *

Rubus. — A number of species belonging to this genus are British, as the *rasp-berry,* Rubus *Idæus;* the *dew-berry,* Rubus *cæsius ;* the *hazel-leaved bramble,* Rubus *corylifolius;* the *common bramble,* or *blackberry,* Rubus *fruticosus;* which is sometimes called *scald-berry,* under an idea that the fruit causes the head to ulcerate, and thus children are terrified from eating it too copiously: "but," says Threlkeld, "I look upon this as a vulgar error, and that after Michaelmas the Devil casts his club over them, which is a fable: For the earth is the Lord's, and the fulness thereof."— Other British species are the *stone bramble,* Rubus *saxatilis;*

* Lloyd's Desultory Thoughts.

the *dwarf crimson bramble*, Rubus *arcticus;* and the *mountain,* or *cloud-berry,* Rubus *Chamæmorus.*

Fragaria, *Strawberry.*—It has been already explained that this fruit is not really a berry, but a fleshy receptacle, on which the seeds are placed; and I shall mention a few similar examples. The *Cashew-nut* (Anacardium *occidentale*), which belongs to the ninth class, is a native of both Indies. It is a tree seldom exceeding twenty feet in height, having crooked branches; and oval leaves like those of the pear-tree. After flowering, the receptacle, which is fleshy, and full of acid juice, swells to the size of a lemon, and has the seed or nut itself growing on its extremity. This nut is *reniform,* about an inch and a half long, and an inch broad; its shell very hard, the kernel sweet, but between the two is a thick black liquor, so caustic, that it burns the skin like *aquafortis.* It is said that the young West-Indian ladies, when too much tanned, sometimes peel off the coat or pellicle of the kernels, and rub their faces with it. The skin immediately swells and blackens, but falls off in a few days, and in two or three weeks they appear in public with a face as fresh and fair as that of an infant. In America the acid juice of the receptacle is used for acidulating punch.

There is a tree also in the fifth class, (Semicarpus *Anacardium*), which bears a nut in a similar manner on a fleshy receptacle, and it is remarkable that in this also a black caustic juice is interposed between the shell and kernel.   It is used for marking linen,. &c. and the letters formed with it never wash out; on which account it is called the *marking-nut tree.* In Gomphia, Exocarpus, and several other genera, the seed is, in a similar manner, placed upon a fleshy receptacle much larger than itself.

Other genera in this Order are Potentilla, *cinquefoil;* Tormentilla, *tormentil,* or *septfoil;* Geum, *avens;* Dryas, *mountain avens;* Comarum, *marsh cinquefoil,* and Calycanthus, *Jamaica allspice.*

CLASS XIII.

POLYANDRIA.   *Twenty* to one *thousand* stamens placed on the *receptacle.*

1. *Monogynia.*

This is a tolerably copious Order, containing amongst others the Sanguinaria, or *bloodroot,* so called from the copious bloodlike juice which flows from the root when cut; Chelidonium, *celandine,* a pretty plant, common in gardens, whose stem and leaves abound in an orange-coloured sap; Papaver, the *poppy,* worthy your examination on account of the style being wanting, and the stigma being peltate, flat, and radiated.   The Opium of commerce is prepared from the Papaver *somniferum,* or white poppy, so named from the whiteness of its seeds.   Opium is merely the milky juice of the plant inspissated, and blackened by drying. It is obtained by making incisions in the capsules every evening, and in the morning the sap, which has distilled from the wound, and become thickened, is scraped off, and being afterwards worked by the hand in the sunshine, is formed into cakes of about four pounds weight each. The quantity of this drug used for medical and other purposes is immense. Six hundred thousand pounds are said to be annually exported from the Ganges alone.

Whatever be the mysterious link connecting mind to matter, we are certain that during this " mortal coil " the former is influenced by the condition of the latter, especially of that part which seems to be the soul's peculiar habitation, the nervous system. A human being may linger under disease of the lungs or other viscera, and be worn to the last thread of debility and emaciation, and still, the brain remaining sound, the intellectual faculties may continue in as full force as at any former period of life. Let the brain, however, be diseased, and then, whatever be the state of the other organs, the mental fabric generally falls into disorder or ruin. Those substances called narcotics act with peculiar influence on the mind through the medium of the nerves, and of these narcotics opium is one of the most powerful. I pretend not to explain how it acts; the gratuitous assumption of spirits, nervous oscillations, and all that tissue of conjectural doctrine which once formed the pride and boast of physiology, having, though late, sunk at last into deserved neglect. That opium, however, exerts a powerful influence on the mind as well as body, is obvious to almost every one's experience. It allays pain, and lightens sorrow, diffuses a pleasing languor over the frame, and gives unusual serenity to the mind, dispelling from it every apprehension of sublunary evil, and steeping it in scenes of elysium. It is indeed an agent which can, for a period at least,

> Raze out the written troubles of the brain;
> And, with a sweet oblivious antidote,
> Cleanse the full bosom of that perilous stuff,
> Which weighs upon the heart.

But this is only for a time, and the charm being dissolved, the soul awakes from its trance only to experience aggravated woe, in those at least (and even in Britain the number is not small,) who have fallen into the habitual use of this drug. If there be on earth a misery that approaches what we might be allowed to conceive as among the worst sufferings of a future place of punishment, it is the state of an opium-eater, after the action of his dose has subsided. Unhappy and trembling, his head confused, and his stomach sick, remorse at his heart, but his resolution too feeble to attempt a reformation; feeling as an outcast from every thing that is good or great, he returns despairing to a repetition of his dose, and every repetition adds confirmation to the evil habit. His constitution becomes exhausted in a few years; he grows prematurely old, and dies of palsy, dropsy, or some disease as fatal; he dies, having by his own

weakness and imprudence lived a life of wretched-
ness in this world, and looking forward at his
exit to the darkest scenes of misery in the next.
How often does man turn the greatest blessings
into the greatest curse!

In the first Order of the Polyandria class is the
Sarracenia (*Side-saddle flower*), whose singular tu-
bulate leaves have been before noticed; and here
also is the Nymphæa (*water-lily*), some, if not all
of whose species, close their flowers in the evening,
and recline them on the water, or sink under it,
till the brightness of the succeeding day stimulates
them to rise again to an elevation of several
inches above its surface.

> Those virgin lilies, all the night
>   Bathing their beauties in the lake,
> That they may rise more fresh and bright,
>   When their beloved Sun's awake.

Bixa *Orellana*; the pulp surrounding the seeds
of this American shrub forms the dye-stuff called
arnotto; Mammea, the *mamme-tree*, whose fruit is
much esteemed in Jamaica; Grias, *anchovy-pear*;
Calophyllum, *Tacamahac-tree*; Tilia, *lime-tree*;
Thea, *tea*; Cistus, &c. &c.

2. *Digynia.*

Pæonia, *Pæony*; and a few others.

3. *Trigynia.*

Delphinium, *Larkspur*; Aconitum, *Aconite,
wolf's-bane*, or *monk's-hood.*

4. *Tetragynia.*

Wintera. The true *winter's bark* is produced

by the Wintera *aromatica;* Caryocar, "whose large, rugged, woody nuts contain the most exquisite kernel ever brought to our tables,"* and one or two more.

5. *Pentagynia.*

Aquilegia, *columbine ;* Nigella, *fennel-flower ;* the plant common in gardens, called *Devil in a bush,* or *Love in a mist,* is the Nigella *Damascena.*

6. *Hexagynia.*   Stratiotes, *water-soldier.*

The number of styles in the preceding five orders is very variable, and Sir J. E. Smith judiciously advises their coalition into one.   That is, letting the Order *Hexagynia* be the second, and embracing all plants in the class, having from two to six styles, in which case,

7. *Polygynia,* would form only a third, instead of a seventh order.   We find in it many fine plants, as the Dillenia, a genus consisting of eight or ten species of East Indian trees; the *tulip-tree,* Liriodendron; the beautiful Magnolia; Illicium, the *Aniseed-tree,* one species of which grows in Japan and China, and another in Florida.   Clarke mentions that bread and brandy, two of the most important articles in the diet of the Swedes, " are made very unpalatable to strangers by the quantity of *aniseed* with which they are flavoured,·and to which flavour the *Swedes* are as partial as the *Chinese,* who use the Illicium *anisatum* for seasoning dishes.   In *Japan* they place bundles and garlands of the *ani-*

* Smith's Introd. p. 328.

seed-tree in their temples before their idols, and on the tombs of their friends. They also use thè powdered bark, as incense to their idols. — Indeed, *Linnæus* himself, as a native of Sweden, has left a curious memorial of his national taste in this respect, by naming this genus *Illicium*, signifying an allurement." Annona, *custard-apple* ; Anemone, *wind-flower* ; Clematis,

——— the favoured flower,
Which boasts the name of *virgin's bower*.

Thalictrum, *meadow rue* ; Adonis, *pheasant's eye* ; Ranunculus, *Crowfoot*. The plants belonging to this genus are extremely acrid; " all and every of them (says Gerard) do blister and cause paine wheresoever they be applied, and paine doth draw unto itself more paine : for the nature of paine is, to resort unto the weakest place, and where it may find paine ; and likewise the poison and venemous qualitie of that disease is to resort unto that painful place"— not a bad anticipation this of the more modern doctrine of counter-irritation, or of contiguous sympathy. The British crowfoots are generally called *butter-cups*. The Ranunculus *Ficaria* (*lesser celandine*) is one of our earliest flowering plants, and is quite common on moist ditches, in damp woods, along the banks of streams, and wherever there is a tough and moist clay soil. It often contrasts beautifully its bright, glossy, yellow corollas with the cream-coloured and more modest complexion of the primrose, adorning

the bare ground before a bud has burst from bush
or tree.

> Ere a leaf is on a bush,
> In the time before the thrush
> Has a thought about its nest,
> Thou wilt come with half a call,
> Spreading out thy glossy breast
> Like a careless prodigal;
> Telling tales about the sun,
> When we've little warmth, or none.*

The *wood-crowfoot* (Ranunculus *auricomus*), which
flowers in woody glens, &c. in April and May, is a
very beautiful plant. Trollius, *globe-flower*, Helle-
borus, *hellebore;* Caltha, *marsh-marigold*, or *May-
flower*. In Irish it is named *Bealtaine*, which,
says Threlkeld, " seems to imply it was used
(perhaps in a garland) in their feasts in May, (as
Baaltine signifies a feast to *Baal*), in the darkness
of heathenism." The practice of strewing *May-
flowers* about the doors and in the houses on May-
day is still followed in some parts of these kingdoms,
and the May-pole still celebrates in a few villages
the return of this merry month.

> —————— faire May, the fairest Mayd on ground,
> Deck't all with dainties of her season's pryde,
> And throwing flowers out of her lap around.

But these are faint relics of the festivities and jocund
ceremonies, which formerly obtained at this season,
and employed the attention of all ranks. " Now,
there is scarcely a garland to be seen: the song is

* Wordsworth.

silent, and the dance is over: the revelry has ceased; and vulgar pursuits usurp the place of those pleasant pastimes, which seemed a sort of first offering to gentle skies, and were consecrated by the smiles of the tender year."*

In consulting Withering for the description of Caltha, you will find it mentioned that the un-expanded corollas are used as a substitute for *capers.*† Capers are themselves the flower-buds of the Capparis *spinosa*, which are annually pickled for exportation on the Continent. We have several other instances of flowers being used as articles of diet; those of the marigold are still employed in country places in soups, and the receptacle of others is in much estimation, as the bottom of the artichoke, the carline thistle, and the sun-flower. But the *Mahwah-tree* (Bassia *latifolia*), found in some parts of India, is in this respect of very great importance. It belongs to the Dode-candria class; its corollas, when dried, are like raisins, and the produce of one tree in this state will weigh above three hundred pounds. They are eaten raw, or in curries, or boiled with rice; a spirituous liquor is distilled from them, which, on account of its cheapness, is very mischievous. The kernels of one tree afford about sixty pounds of good oil.‡

* Time's Telescope, 1821.
† They are named *Swedish capers.*
‡ Hamilton, in Asiatic Researches.

CLASS XIV.

DIDYNAMIA. *Four* stamens, *two* long, and *two* short.

For the essential and natural characters of this class, consult the first volume of Withering.

ORDERS two.

1. *Gymnospermia;* seeds naked in the bottom of the calyx.

Many common plants will serve to illustrate this order, as *bugle* (Ajuga); *lavender* (Lavendula); *mint* (Mintha); *ground-ivy* (Glechoma); *dead-nettle* (Lamium); *wound-wort* (Stachys); *horehound* (Marrubium); *marjoram* (Origanum); *thyme* (Thymus); *balm* (Melissa); and *self-heal* (Prunella.)

2. *Angiospermia;* seeds enclosed in a capsule.

Here also you will find many familiar specimens, as *cock's-comb* or *rattle-grass* (Rhinanthus); *eye-bright* (Euphrasia); *snap-dragon* (Antirrhinum); *figwort* (Scrophularia); *foxglove* (Digitalis); *trumpet-flower* (Bignonia); *monkey-flower* (Mimulus); and *honey-flower* (Melianthus).

You are not to expect that all the plants in this class have ringent corollas, for you will find some to depart very much from that form, being salver-shaped, as in Browallia; rotate, as in Celsia; funnel-formed, as in Barleria; campanulate, as in Digitalis and Linnæa; very long, with the border trifid, as in Ovieda, &c.: and you will here find a number of examples of the *resupinate* or *reversed corolla* (corolla resupinata), which has the appearance of being turned upside down, as in *lavender, basil,* and *figwort.* In drying the plants belonging to this class, for your herbarium, you will find that many of them turn quite black. Those in the first order are mostly aromatic, and all are said to be innocent; but in the second order, Digitalis is poisonous, and perhaps a few others.·

CLASS XV.

TETRADYNAMIA. *Six* stamens, *four* long, and *two* short; flowers *cruciform.*

ORDERS two.

1. *Siliculosa,* fruit a *silicle.*

You have examples of this Order in *sea-kale* (Crambe *maritima*), *woad* (Isatis *tinctoria*), the common weed, *shepherd's-purse* (Thlaspi *bursa pastoris*), *candy-tuft* (Iberis), and *honesty* (Lunaria), &c.

2. *Siliquosa,* fruit a *silique.*

The *cuckoo-flower,* or *ladies' smock* (Cardamine *pratensis*), abundant in every moist meadow in the early spring, affords a pretty example of this order. It is mentioned under the above name by Shakspeare, in Love's Labour's Lost.

> When daisies pied, and violets blue,
>   And *lady-smocks* all silver-white,
> And cuckoo-buds of yellow hue,
>   Do paint the meadows with delight.

In the Cheiranthus genus you may find two very familiar plants almost all the year round, the Cheiranthus *Cheiri*, and Cheiranthus *incanus*.

> The yellow wall-flower stain'd with iron-brown;
> And lavish stock, that scents the garden round.

Here also are the *rocket*, Hesperis; *cabbage*, Brassica; *mustard*, Sinapis; and *radish*, Raphanus, &c. Some of the plants in this class are shrubby, but none assume the appearance of a tree. They are not abundant in America, and in China are so scarce, that Osbeck did not, when in that empire, observe one uncultivated species. Humboldt, indeed, remarks, that "in the equinoctial regions of both continents, where the mean temperature of the air rises above twenty-two degrees, the cruciform plants are scarcely ever to be seen."*

CLASS XVI.

MONADELPHIA.   Filaments united at bottom into a tube.

ORDERS eight, *formed from the number of the stamens.*

* Pers. Nar. vol. i. p. 272.

1. *Triandria.* Here is the genus Tamarindus, consisting of only one species,

> —————— the spreading tamarind, that shakes,
> Fann'd by the breeze, its fever-cooling fruit.

Ferraria, whose fugitive flowers scarcely last one forenoon, and Galaxia, whose beauty is almost as transient. In this Order also is the pretty genus Sisyrinchium, and the Aphyteia, which grows on the roots of the *Barbary spurge*, and has neither stem, leaves, nor root.

2. *Pentandria* contains about nine genera, among which is the extensive genus Passiflora (*Passion-flower*), but this, according to Sir J. E. Smith, "belongs most unquestionably to *Pentandria Trigynia*, and by no means to this Class."

3. *Heptandria* contains only Pelargonium.

4. *Octandria*, Pistia, and Aitonia.

5. *Decandria*, Geranium, and some others.

6. *Endecandria.* Brownea, *Rosa del Monte*, belonging to this Order, has a stem about sixty feet high, and its heads of purple flowers consist of five or six hundred each.

7. *Dodecandria ;* twelve to twenty stamens. Acia, Monsonia, Plagianthus, &c. &c.

8. *Polyandria.* This Order contains a much greater number of genera than any of the others in the Class. Among these is the Adansonia, or *sour gourd*, of Senegal, whose immense trunk has been before noticed. Bombax, *silk cotton-tree ;* the very copious genus Sida ; Althæa, *marsh-*

mallow; Malva, *mallow;* Lavatera; Gossypium, cotton-tree; Hibiscus; Gordonia, *Loblolly bay;* Camellia, *Japan-rose;* the beautiful Barringtonia, &c. The latter fine tree is thus mentioned by Forster: " We crossed One-tree-hill, and descended into one of the first valleys of O-Parre, where we were gratified with the sight of one of the most beautiful trees in the world, which we called the Barringtonia. It had a great abundance of flowers, larger than lilies, and perfectly white, excepting the tips of their numerous chives, which were of a bright crimson. Such a quantity of these flowers were already dropped off, that the ground underneath the tree was entirely strewed with them." *

CLASS XVII.

DIADELPHIA. When the filaments are joined as in the last Class, provided that the corolla is *papilionaceous,* or else, that instead of being in *one* set, so as to form a perfect tube, they are in *two.*

ORDERS four.

1. *Pentandria.* Monnieria, a plant of Guiana, having two filaments, the upper with two anthers, the lower with three.

2. *Hexandria.*
Saraca, which has three stamens on each side of

* Forster's Cooke's Voyage, vol. i. p. 347.

the throat of the corolla; and Fumaria, *fumitory* (of which some British species are very common), having two membranaceous filaments, each with three anthers.

3. *Octandria.*

The extensive genus Polygala, and a very few others, — the Polygala *vulgaris* is a common, but very beautiful little plant.

4. *Decandria.*

This is a copious Order, and the species belonging to a number of its genera are very numerous. I shall mention only a few plants belonging to it. Pterocarpus: the Pterocarpus *Draco*, a tree of the West Indies, thirty feet high, is one of those whose resinous exudations form the *dragon's blood* of the shops, as is also the Pterocarpus *santalinus*, or *red saunders-tree* of India. Dipterix: the *Tonca bean*, whose fragrance is well known, is the seed of the Dipterix *odorata*, a tree sixty feet high, which grows in Guiana. Abrus *precatorius, Jamaica wild liquorice*, whose scarlet seeds, marked with jet black at the end, are formed into necklaces. Erythrina, *coral-tree ;* Piscidia, *Jamaica dogwood ;* the Piscidia *Erythrina* is used, like the Galega *piscatorum*, the Jacquinia, and a number of other plants, for poisoning fish; Spartium, *broom ;* Genista; Ononis, *rest-harrow;* Anthyllis, *kidney-vetch;* Lupinus, *lupin ;* Phaseolus, *kidney-bean ;* Dolichos ; the setæ, or hairs of the Dolichos *pruriens*, and Dolichos *urens*, especially those of the legumes,

P

cause an intolerable itching pain when applied to
the skin, and, when taken internally, are among the
most powerful vermifuges known; Pisum, *pea ;*
Orobus, *bitter-vetch ;* Lathyrus, Vicia, *vetch ;*
Ervum, *tare ;* Cicer, *chick-pea ;* the Cicer *Lens*
is the celebrated *lentil ;* Cytisus, of which the
laburnum (Cytisus *Laburnum*) is a familiar example;
Robinia, *false acacia ;* Colutea, *bladder-senna ;*
Glycyrrhiza, the roots of the Glycyrrhiza *glabra* are
the liquorice-root of the shops; Coronilla; Orni-
thopus, *bird's foot ;* Hippocrepis, *horse-shoe vetch ;*
Scorpiurus, called *caterpillar*, because its legumes
resemble that kind of larva; Hedysarum, one
species of which, Hedysarum *gyrans*, the *sensitive
hedysarum*, or *moving plant*, is much celebrated on
account of the spontaneous motions of its leaves;
Indigofera, *indigo-plant ;* Galega, *goat's rue ;*
Astragalus, *milk-vetch ;* the Astragalus *Tragacantha*
affords the gum tragacanth; Trifolium, *trefoil ;*
Lotus, *bird's foot trefoil ;* Medicago, some species
of which have their legumes crescent-shaped, and
are thence named *Moon trefoil ;* and others having
them spirally twisted, are named *medick.* I should
have sooner mentioned the " blossomed furze un-
profitably gay " (Ulex *europæus*), whose frequency
alone makes it little valued, for scarcely any plant
is more brilliant than it when in full blow. It
cannot stand the cold of winter in Sweden; and
when Linnæus first saw it flowering in England,
he is said to have fallen on his knees and offered

up a prayer of thanksgiving to the great Author of nature. The odour exhaled from furze-blossoms is very delightful, though peculiar, and it is amusing on a hot summer-day, as we explore

—— the path with tangling furze o'er-run,
When bursting seed-bells crackle in the sun,

to listen to the snapping noise of its ripe legumes opening to disperse their contents.*

The plants belonging to this Class are, generally speaking, so wholesome, that even Linnæus supposed that it contained no deleterious species. The seeds of *laburnum*, however, are said to be violently emetic, and some others have a little virtue as medicines, but on the whole his assertion is pretty correct. No plant has hitherto been discovered, I believe, with corollas entirely black; we have indeed what are called black roses, &c., but on closely examining these, you will perceive that they are of a very dark brown or purple colour. The corolla of the *bean* (Vicia *Faba*), which is in this order, exhibits a large spot in its corolla, purely black, which is the most remarkable instance of this colour in any flower with which I am acquainted.

* Vide Smith's Intr.

CLASS XVIII.

POLYADELPHIA.

In this Class the stamens are united by their filaments into *three* or *more* bundles or parcels, but
their line of union at the base is sometimes so very
narrow, that unless your examination be minute,
you will perhaps overlook their junction.

ORDERS four.

1. *Decandria* contains only the Theobroma of
South America, whose kernels furnish the *cocoa*
and *chocolate* of our breakfast-table.

2. *Dodecandria.* Bubroma, *Bastard cedar* of
Jamaica; Abroma of the East Indies.

3. *Icosandria.* Citrus: Citrus *medica* is the lemon;
of which the *lime* is merely a variety; Citrus *au-
rantium*, the *orange;* Citrus *decumana*, the *shaddock.*

4. *Polyandria.* Among a few others in this Order
is the Hypericum, *St. John's wort;* a number of
species of which are British.   In times more unen-
lightened than the present a number of superstitious
ceremonies were practised on midsummer eve, and
on the following morning, or St.John's Day. They
bore some resemblance to those of Hallow-eve in
Scotland, being thought to prognosticate the good or
bad fortune of young men and maidens as to their
obtaining partners for life.   Some of these are still
practised on the Continent; and in Lower Saxony,
the young girls gather sprigs of St. John's wort on
midsummer-night, fasten them to the walls of their
bedchamber, and by the state of the sprig on the

ensuing morning, anticipate whether or not their
state shall soon be changed from one of " single
blessedness." If the plant remain fresh, (which
will entirely depend on the dampness or dryness of
the wall,) a suitor may be expected; if it droop
and wither, the willow-garland must be their fate
for the ensuing year. This superstition has given
origin to the following beautiful and affecting lines
from the German: —

The young maid stole through the cottage-door,
And blush'd as she sought the plant of power;—
"Thou silver glow-worm, O lend me thy light!
I must gather the mystic St. John's wort to-night,
The wonderful herb whose leaf will decide
If the coming year shall make me a bride."

   And the glow-worm came,
   With its silvery flame,
   And sparkled and shone
   Through the night of St. John,
And soon has the young maid her love-knot tied.
   With noiseless tread
   To her chamber she sped,
Where the spectral moon her white beams shed:—
" Bloom here, bloom here, thou plant of power,
To deck the young maid in her bridal hour!"
But it droop'd its head, that plant of power,
And died the mute death of the voiceless flower;
And a withered wreath on the ground it lay,
More meet for a burial than bridal day.

And when a year was pass'd away,
All pale on her bier the young maid lay,
   And the glow-worm came,
   With its silvery flame,
   And sparkled and shone
   Through the night of St. John,
As they closed the cold grave o'er the maid's cold clay.*

---

* Blackwood's Magazine, Jan. 1821.

CLASS XIX.

SYNGENESIA.

Anthers *united* so as to form a tube around the style; flowers *compound*.

I have until now delayed giving you any account of *compound* flowers; and, in describing them, I shall use the words of Rousseau, for it would not be in my power to give any description either so clear or interesting as his. " Take one of those little flowers which cover all the pastures, and which every body knows by the name of *Daisy.* Look at it well; for by its appearance, I am sure you will be surprised when I tell you that this flower, which is so small and delicate, is really composed of between two and three hundred other flowers*, all of them perfect; that is, having each its corolla, germ, pistil, stamens, and seed; in a word, as perfect in its species as a flower of the hyacinth or lily. Every one of those leaves which are white above and red underneath, and form a kind of crown round the flower, appearing to be nothing more than little petals, are in reality so many true flowers; and every one of those tiny yellow things also which you see in the centre, and which at first you have perhaps taken for nothing but stamens, are real flowers.— Pull out one of the white leaves from the flower: you will think at first that it is flat from

* This is rather exaggerated; the whole number is about one hundred and seventy. — J. L. D.

one end to the other ; but look carefully to the end
by which it was fastened to the flower, and you will
see that it is not flat, but round and hollow, in form
of a tube, and that a little thread, ending in two
horns, issues from the tube; this thread is the forked
style of the flower, which, as you now see, is flat
only at top.

" Now look at those little yellow things in the
middle of the flower, and which, as I have told
you, are all so many flowers; if the flower be sufficiently advanced, you will see several of them open
in the middle, and even cut into several parts.

" These are monopetalous corollas, which expand; and a glass will easily discover in them the
pistil, and even the anthers with which it is surrounded. Commonly the yellow florets towards
the centre are still rounded and closed. These,
however, are flowers like the others, but not yet
open ; for they expand successively from the edge
inwards. This is enough to show you by the eye
the possibility that all these small affairs, both
white and yellow, may be so many distinct flowers ;
and this is a constant fact. You perceive, never-
theless, that all these little flowers are pressed and
enclosed in a calyx, which is common to them all,
and which is that of the daisy. In considering,
then, the whole daisy as one flower, we give it a
very significant name, when we call it a compound
flower.—You have observed two sorts of florets
in the daisy: the yellow ones, which occupy the

middle or disk of the flower, and the little white tongues or straps which surround them.

" The former are something like the flowers of the lily of the valley, or hyacinth in miniature : and the latter bear some resemblance to those of the honeysuckle. We shall leave to the first the name of *florets ;* and to distinguish the second, we shall call them *semi-florets ;* * for in reality they have a little the air of monopetalous flowers, gnawed off on one side, and having scarcely half the corolla remaining.

" These two sorts of florets are combined in the compound flowers in such a manner as to divide the whole tribe into three sections, very distinct from each other.

" The first section consists of those which are entirely composed of semi-florets both in the middle and circumference ; these are called *semi-flosculous flowers*, and the whole is always of one colour, which is generally yellow. Such is the common dandelion, the lettuce, and sow-thistle; the succory and endive, which have blue flowers; the scorzonera, salsafy, &c.

" The second section comprehends the *flosculous flowers*, or such as are composed of florets [tubular florets only] : these are also commonly of one colour ; as immortal flowers, burdock, wormwood, mugwort, thistles, and artichoke, which is nearly

---

* Also called *ligulate* florets (*ligula*, a strap, *Lat.*) The florets are now all distinguished into *ligulate* and *tubular*, the term *semi-floret* seldom being used. — J. L. D.

allied to them: it is the calyx of this that we suck, and the receptacle that we eat, whilst it is yet young, before the flower opens, or is even formed. The choke which we take out of the middle is an assemblage of florets which are beginning to be formed, and are separated from each other by long hairs fixed in the receptacle.

" The third section is of flowers composed of both these. They are always so arranged that the [tubular] florets occupy the centre of the flower, and the semi-florets [ligulate florets] the circumference, as you have seen in the daisy. The flowers of this section are called *radiate*. Botanists have given the name of *ray* to the set of semi-florets which compose the circumference; and of *disk* to the area or centre of the flower occupied by the florets. In the radiate flowers the disk is often of one colour, and the ray of another; there are, however, genera and species in which both are alike.

" Let us endeavour now to fix in your mind an idea of a *compound flower*. The common clover is in blow at this season; the flower is purple: if you should take one in hand, seeing so many little flowers assembled, you might be tempted to take the whole for a compound flower. You would, however, be mistaken. In what? say you. Why, in supposing that an assemblage of many little flowers is sufficient to constitute a compound flower; whereas, besides this, one or two parts

of the fructification must be common to them all;
so that every one must have a part in it, and no
one have its own separately; these two parts in
common, are the calyx and receptacle. The flower
of the clover, indeed, or rather the group of
flowers, which has the appearance of being but
one flower, seems at first to be placed upon a sort
of calyx; but remove this pretended calyx a little,
and you will perceive that it does not belong to
the flower, but that it is fastened below it to the
pedicle that bears it. This then is a calyx only in
appearance; but in reality it belongs to the foliage,
not to the flower: and this supposed compound
flower is only an assemblage of very small legu-
minous or papilionaceous flowers, each of which
has its distinct calyx, and they have nothing common to them but their being fastened to the same
pedicle. Vulgarly, all this is taken for one flower:
it is a false idea, however; or, if we must look
upon it as such, we must at least not call it a
compound, but an *aggregate* or *capitate* flower, or
a *head* of flowers; and these terms are sometimes
so applied by botanical writers." *

If, in addition to these observations, you recollect the junction of the anthers into a tube, you
will have no farther difficulty in recognising a compound flower, but it would be well also for you to
read what Rousseau says farther on the subject.

The SYNGENESIA Class contains five ORDERS.

* Rousseau's Letters on the Elements of Botany, by
Professor Martyn.

1. *Polygamia æqualis.* This Order is characterised by the florets being all furnished with a pistil
and stamens, and each in consequence perfecting
its own seed. The Order is divided into three
sections, which we may head with the letters A.B.C.

A. *Florets all ligulate;* as examples of which
you may examine Tragopogon, *goat's beard;*
Sonchus, *saw-thistle;* Lactuca, *lettuce;* Leontodon,
dandelion; Hieracium, *hawk-weed;* Cichorium,
succory, &c.

B. *Flowers in heads.* Examples, Arctium, *burdock;* Carduus, *thistle;* Cynara, *artichoke,* &c.

C. *Florets tubular, forming a disk-like congeries,
without any ray;* as in Bidens, *bur-marigold;* Chry-
socoma, *goldy locks;* Tarchonanthus, *African flea-
bane;* Santolina, *lavender-cotton.*

2. *Polygamia Superflua.* Florets of the *disk* furnished with both stamens and pistils; those of the
margin or *ray* with pistils only. They are all fertile, but plants of this Order would continue and
increase independent of the marginal florets, those
of the disk being perfect. In this point of view,
therefore, the margin or ray is unnecessary, and
hence the term *Superflua,* superfluous.

Examples. Tanacetum, *tansy;* Artemisia, *worm-
wood;* Gnaphalium, *everlasting;* Conyza, *flea-bane;*
Tussilago, *colt's foot;* Senecio, *groundsel,* or *rag-
wort;* Aster, *aster, starwort,* or *Michaelmas daisy;*
Solidago, *golden rod;* Doronicum, *leopard's bane;*
Bellis, *daisy;* Chrysanthemum, *ox-eye;* Pyrethrum,

feverfew; Anthemis, *chamomile;* Achillea, *yarrow;* and many others.

3. *Polygamia frustranea.* Florets of the *disk* having both stamens and pistils, those of the *ray* neither. The radiate florets therefore cannot produce seeds, and hence the term *frustranea,* which means vain or ineffectual.

Examples. Helianthus, *sunflower;* Rudbeckia; Coreopsis; Gorteria; Centaurea, *knapweed,* &c. &c.

4. *Polygamia necessaria.* In this order the florets of the *disk* have stamens, but no pistils, and those of the *ray* have pistils but no stamens; and hence the term *necessaria,* as they are necessary to each other.

Examples. Milleria; Silphium; Polymnia; Calendula, " *The marigold* that shutteth with the light;" Arctotis; Othonna, *African rag-wort;* Parthenium, *bastard feverfew;* Filago, *cotton weed,* &c.

5. *Polygamia segregata.* "When in a compound flower, besides the common perianth, each floret is furnished with its own particular calyx." Sometimes, however, each partial calyx contains more than one floret.

Examples. Elephantopus, *elephant's foot,* in this the calycles are four-flowered; Jungia, calycles three or four-flowered; Sphœranthus, calycle eight-flowered; Echinops, *globe-thistle,* &c. &c.

This Class contained a sixth Order named *Monogamia,* which is abolished. It comprehended *simple* flowers, whose anthers were united into a tube, as Seriphium; Corymbium; Jasione; Lobelia; Viola; and Impatiens.

CLASS XX.

GYNANDRIA.

Stamens placed upon the pistil or germen.

1. *Monandria.* Orchis, Satyrium, Ophrys, Dendrobium, Cymbidium, Epidendrum, &c.

2. *Diandria,* Cypripedium, *ladies' slipper.*

3. *Hexandria,* Aristolochia, *birth-wort.*

4. *Octandria.* Cytinus.

CLASS XXI.

MONŒCIA.

The plants belonging to this Class do not bear perfect flowers, for those which are furnished with stamens have no pistils, and those furnished with pistils have no stamens, but both are on the same individual plant.

ORDERS eight.

1. *Monandria.* Artocarpus, *bread-fruit-tree ;* Casuarina.

2. *Diandria.* Anguria.

3. *Triandria.* Typha, *cat's tail ;* Sparganium, *bur-reed ;* Zea, *Indian corn ;* Coix, *Job's tears ;* Carex, *seg* or *sedge-grass ;* Hernandia, *jack in a box ;* Cucumis, *cucumber ;* Momordica, *balsam-*

apple ; Cucurbita, *gourd;* Trichosanthes, *snake gourd.* *

4. *Tetrandria.* Urtica, *nettle;* Morus, *mulberry;* Buxus, *box-tree;* Betula, *birch;* Betula *alba* is the scientific name of the common birch, the term *alba* being given to it on account of the white paper-like epidermis of its trunk and larger branches, which Swift compares to a fine doublet of white satin. The generic term is derived from *batuo,* to beat, because from time immemorial the twigs of the birch have been employed as an instrument of terror and punishment in the hand of the magistrate, and the teacher of youth. " Its twigs," says Threlkeld, " are used for beesoms and rods; the one for the cleanly housewife to sweep down the cobwebs, and the other for the magisterial pedagogue to drive the colt out of the man." In reference to its latter use there are some fine lines in Shenstone's School Mistress.

> In every village mark'd with little spire
> Embower'd in trees, and hardly known to fame,
> There dwells in lowly shed, and mean attire,
> A matron old, whom we school-mistress name ;
> Who boasts unruly brats with birch to tame;
> They grieven sore, in piteous durance pent,
> Awed by the power of this relentless dame ;
> And oft times on vagaries idly bent,
> For unkempt hair, or task unconn'd are sorely shent.
> And all in sight doth rise a birchen tree
> Which learning near her little dome did stowe ;

---

* I follow Turton's edition of the System of Nature. In the Hortus Kewensis and some other works, the cucumber, gourd, &c. are arranged in the *Monadelphia* Order.

Whilom a twig of small regard to see,
Though now so wide its waving branches flow,
And work the simple vassals mickle woe;
For not a wind might curl the leaves that blow,
But their limbs shudder'd and their pulse beat low,
And as they look'd they found their horror grew,
And shaped it into rods, and tingled at the view.

The system of corporal punishment in schools
is now much relaxed. It can never, indeed, be entirely dispensed with, but the practice of constant
flogging has the worst effects both on the progress
of the child's learning, and on his dispositions. It
makes him abject and slavish, depresses the spirit
of emulation, and excites a disgust towards those
acquirements which should lay the foundation of
his future happiness, and raise him to eminence in
society. In the address delivered by the late Dr.
Drennan, at the opening of the Belfast Academical
Institution, in 1814, in the part of it directed to the
teachers of the school-department is this apposite
passage: — " We [the managers] would, in general, express our desire that the system of school-
government were made as much remunerative, and
as little penal as possible; that it should act by
motives on the mind, rather than by pains inflicted
on the body; that example should teach, emulation
should quicken, glory should exalt, a sentiment of
honour should be cultivated, rather than to recur,
oftener than is absolutely necessary, to manual correction, or corporal punishment. The correction
of the master's hand is sometimes the unhappy consequence of the carelessness of his eye and a sort

of compensation for the suspension of his vigilance; and we must be allowed to express our serious doubts on the efficacy of a *principal* corporal punishment, either on the object of it, or in the example; although it may have been defended by the stern authority of Dr. Johnson, and of that Dionysius, who was once a tyrant at Syracuse, and afterwards became a schoolmaster at Corinth. A chaplet of *laurel* is, in our minds, worth a cart-load of *birch;* and we think there is a magisterial *authority* to be attained, sufficient for its ends, without recurring to frequent manifestations of power."

The uses of the birch are too numerous to mention here; it is indeed almost absolutely necessary to the existence of the inhabitants of Lapland and some other northern nations; and even its leaves are not unimportant, being employed by the Finland women in forming a soft elastic couch for the cradle of infancy. Acerbi has given a specimen of a wild lullaby song in which this is alluded to; and which seems to have been copied in these lines of Leyden:

Sweet bird of the meadow, oh, soft be thy rest!
Thy mother will wake thee at morn from thy nest;
She has made a soft nest, little red-breast, for thee,
Of the leaves of the birch and the moss of the tree.

5. *Pentandria.* Xanthium, *small burdock;* Amaranthus, *amaranth;* Bryonia, *bryony.*

6. *Hexandria.* Zizania, *Canada rice;* Cocos, *cocoa-nut-tree.*

7. *Polyandria.* Begonia; Myriophyllum, *water millfoil;* Ceratophyllum, *horn-wort;* Poterium, *burnet;* Sagittaria, *arrow-head;* Arum, *cuckoo-pint;* Fagus: Fagus *Castanea* is the *Spanish chesnut,* and Fagus *sylvatica* the *common beech;* Quercus, *oak;* Juglans, *walnut;* Corylus, *hazel;* Platanus, *plane-tree;* Caryota; Areca.

8. *Monadelphia.* Pinus, *pine;* Cupressus, *cypress;* Siphonia, *elastic gum-tree;* Ricinus, *castor-oil plant;* Hippomane, *manchineel;* &c. &c.

CLASS XXII.

Diœcia.

Flowers *staminiferous* only, or *pistilliferous* only, as in the last Class, but *on different individual plants.*

ORDERS fourteen.

1. *Monandria.* Pandanus, *screw-pine,* &c. &c.

2. *Diandria.* Cecropia, *trumpet-tree;* Salix, *willow;* &c. &c.

3. *Triandria.* Empetrum, *crake-berry;* Ruscus, *butchers' broom;* Myristica, *nutmeg-tree;* Phœnix, *date-palm;* &c. &c.

4. *Tetrandria.* Viscum, *miseltoe;* Hippophae, *buck-thorn;* Myrica, *candle-berry myrtle;* &c. &c.

5. *Pentandria.* Pistacia, *pistachia-tree;* Xanthoxylum, *tooth-ache-tree;* Securinega, *Otaheite myrtle;* Spinacia, *spinage;* Acnida, *Virginian hemp;* Cannabis, *common hemp;* Humulus, *hop;* &c. &c.

6. *Hexandria.* Tamus, *black bryony;* Dioscorea, *yam;* Elais, *oily palm-tree;* Borassus, *fan-palm;* &c.

7. *Octandria.* Populus, *poplar*; Rhodiola, *rose-root*.

8. *Enneandria.* Mercurialis, *herb-mercury;* Hydrocharis, *frog-bit.*

9. *Decandria.* Coriaria, *sumach;* Schinus, *Peruvian, mastick-tree.*

10. *Dodecandria.* Datisca, *bastard-hemp;* Menispermum, *moon-seed;* Stratiotes, *water-soldier.*

11. *Icosandria.* Xylosma, &c.

12. *Polyandria.* Cycas, *cycas palm;* Zamia.

13. *Monadelphia.* Juniperus, *juniper;* Taxus, *yew-tree;* Ephedra, *shrubby horse-tail;* Cissampelos; Nepenthes.

14. *Gynandria.* Cluytia.

CLASS XXIII.

POLYGAMIA,

Includes such plants as produce three different kinds of flowers, namely, some with *pistils* only, some only with *stamens*, and others with *both*, either on the *same* individual, or on *two* or *three* different plants.

ORDERS three.

1. *Monœcia.* Musa, *plantain-tree;* Veratrum, *while hellebore;* Holcus, *soft grass;* Œgilops, *hard grass;* Valantia, *cross-wort;* Parietaria, *pellitory;* Atriplex, *orach;* Brabejum, *African almond;* Feronia, *Indian elephant apple;* Clusia, *balsam tree;* Acer, *maple;* Celtis, *nettle-tree;* Gouania, *chaw-stick;* Mimosa; &c.

2. *Diœcia.* Gleditschia, *honey-locust;* Diospyros, *date-plum;* Nyssa, *tupelo;* Carica, *papaw-tree;* Panax, *ginseng;* Chamærops, *palmetto;* &c.

3. *Triœcia.* Ceratonia, *carob-tree;* Ficus, *fig.*

CLASS XXIV.

CRYPTOGAMIA.

In several of the Classes last mentioned, I have merely given the names of some of the genera they contain, lest, by doing more, the work should become too large for popular use. Where the materials, indeed, are so extremely copious, it is difficult to keep within moderate bounds, and I have often, in writing the preceding pages, done violence to my wishes by suppressing many curious and interesting histories of plants. The present Class I cannot pass over so unceremoniously, though, when its vast extent is considered, my observations must still be comparatively very limited.

It consists of five ORDERS.

1. FILICES. *Ferns.*

2. MUSCI. *Mosses.*

3. HEPATICÆ. *Liverworts.*

4. ALGÆ. *Flags,* including Lichens, Sea-weeds, &c.

5. FUNGI. *Mushrooms.*

The essential organs of fructification (the stamens and pistils) have been discovered by the aid of the microscope in some of these orders, but that circumstance must not employ our attention here, and it is of less importance as each order forms a natural family by itself.

In the Cryptogamic class are found the smallest tribes of vegetables, and I may observe of every department of nature that its minute parts almost invariably afford the greatest pleasure in their study. Hence it is, that when the botanist comes to be engaged in the investigation of the minuter Cryptogamics, his enthusiasm, in almost every instance, goes much beyond what it had previously been. The beauty, indeed, in form and structure, of these minor productions of the vegetable world, is sufficient to excite a high degree of admiration. Another circumstance, too, is the novelty accompanying our first investigations in this class. We seem as if introduced to a new creation, and find that we can scarcely take a walk without observing many vegetables of high importance in the great economy of nature, but of whose very existence we before had no conception. We learn that almost every situation abounds in specimens, which, though not recognised by the inattentive or ignorant, exhibit, when magnified, the most exquisite beauty, and, in form, the greatest singularity. The study of Cryptogamic plants, too, leads the botanist more frequently into wild and secluded scenes; it draws him from the parterre and the field, to converse with nature in her native garb, on heath and mountain, by the banks of untrodden streams and lakes,

and along the sands and shores of the ocean. How
delightful is it to explore with botanic eye some
wild and remote glen in the course of a mountain-
stream, when the silence and solitude around are
only disturbed by the gurgling of the passing
waters, the chirp of some flitting bird, or the hum
of insects sporting in the noontide air !

Cryptogamic plants, however, are not always
minute, since I have already mentioned one whose
great length has procured to it the epithet gigantic*;
and some ferns aspire to a height of from twenty
even to eighty feet; though others of the same
beautiful family are not more than a few lines long.

1. FILICES. *Ferns.*

Linnæus established the characters of his genera
of ferns on the situation and shape of the fructifications. When, for instance, the latter occupied
the *entire* back of the leaf or frond, such species
belonged to the genus Acrostichum; when they
formed distinct roundish spots on the back of the
frond, the Polypodium or polypody genus was
denoted, *Fig.* 81. (*a*), and their distribution in
straight separate lines in the same situation formed
the Asplenium genus, *Fig.* 81. (*b*). The genus
Blechnum was characterised by the fructifications
forming lines in contact with and parallel to the
ribs of the leaflets of the frond, *Fig.* 81. (*c*); Pteris
or *brake*, by their forming lines at the *edge* of the
leaf, *Fig.* 81. (*d*); and so on.

* Fucus giganteus, p. 150.

Fig. 81.

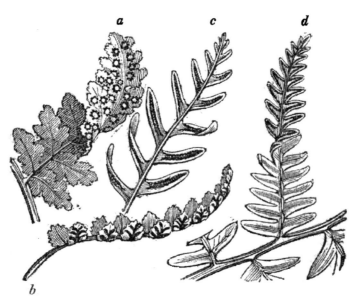

Besides attending only to the situation and shape of the masses of fructification, Sir J. E. Smith first pointed out the utility of considering, also, their involucrum or enveloping membrane, as to its presence or absence, and to the manner of its opening or bursting to let the seeds escape. His observations on this subject formed a very important improvement in the science, and led him to establish the genera of ferns on a better and surer basis than they had previously been.

The number of known ferns amounts to between six and seven hundred, but there can be little doubt that very many more remain to be discovered. In Great Britain there are about fifty species, but so much more copious are they in intertropical

countries,.especially islands, that Plumier collected
one hundred and sixty different species in Mar-
tinique and St. Domingo alone; and the native
ferns of Jamaica, already known, amount to above
two hundred.

Ferns, in general, prefer moist shady situations,
though some grow on walls and rocks, and some
on arid heaths. A considerable number, too, prefer the trunks and branches of old mossy trees.
Their aspect is very various, but in general the
frond is pinnated, the pinnæ gradually diminishing
to the top, giving a beautiful feathery appearance.
Sometimes, as in the *hart's tongue fern* (Scolo-
pendrium) it is undivided, and sometimes the whole
plant assumes the appearance of a palm, as in the
arborescent polypody or *tree cup-fern*, which rises to
the height of twenty-five feet, and whose foliage is
of the finest green and most elegant form.

In general, the root of ferns is very large, and
sends off innumerable fibres, or cords, which are
often of a perfectly black colour. The upper part
of the root is covered with chaffy scales, which are
sometimes so fine, and thickly set, as to resemble
wool or down. The Polypodium *Barometz* is a
memorable example of this. Its tubers are covered
on all sides with such scales, of a gold colour, very
fine, soft, and downy, whence, in India, it is named
golden moss, and is used for stopping hæmorrhage
in wounds. The tubers of this species sometimes
rise out of the ground supported on their rootlets,

and the plant has been described in old books, as being a vegetable sheep growing on a stem, and devouring every other species within its reach. Its thick matted roots probably prevent other plants from growing near it, and, with a little assistance from art, it assumes a tolerably striking resemblance to a little sheep. It is a native of Eastern Chinese Tartary, and hence has been called the Tartarian Lamb. Darwin thus speaks of it: —

> Cradled in snow, and fann'd by arctic air,
> Shines, gentle Barometz! thy golden hair;
> Rooted in earth each cloven hoof descends,
> And round and round her flexile neck she bends;
> Crops the grey coral moss, and hoary thyme,
> Or laps, with rosy tongue, the melting rime;
> Eyes with meek tenderness her distant dam,
> Or seems to bleat, a vegetable lamb.

In a number of other species, as the golden polypody (Polypodium *aureum*) of the West Indies, and the hare's foot fern (Davallia *canariensis*) of the Canary islands, the tubers protrude above the surface of the ground, but not in so remarkable a manner as the Barometz. It is not a little curious, too, that some, as the Asplenium *bulbiferum*, multiply their species by throwing out tubers from the stem and fronds, and that others, as the rooting-leaved Woodwardia (Woodwardia *radicans*) of Madeira, and the rooting spleenwort (Asplenium *rhizophyllum*) of North America, protrude rootlets from the tops of their fronds, which penetrate the ground.

In some of the lofty or arborescent ferns, the stem grows to a considerable thickness, that of the prickly-stemmed brake (Pteris *aculeata*) equalling the diameter of a man. The surface varies much, being in different species rough, smooth, chaffy, prickly, or downy; and I have before mentioned, that some American ferns are always covered with dust of a metallic appearance.

The experiments of modern times have proved that these vegetables may be raised from their seeds; but, as they bear no flower, in the common acceptation of the word, many of the older botanists thought that they multiplied by the root only. So numerous, however, are the seeds in reality, that it is supposed one hundred millions may be produced by a single frond of some species. While the herbalists were denying the existence of seeds in ferns, a belief in them was very general with the people at large, especially amongst the lower classes; but it was imagined that they could only be seen on St. John's night at the hour when the Baptist was born, and that whoever became possessed of them was thereby rendered invisible. In Henry the Fourth, Gadshill says to the Chamberlain, " We steal as in a castle, cock-sure; we have the receipt of fern-seed, we walk invisible." " Nay, by my faith (says the Chamberlain), I think you are more beholden to the night, than to fern-seed, for your walking invisible." The fern-seed, gathered at the propitious hour, was thought to pos-

Q

sess many magical properties, and the supposed possession of it was turned to a profitable account by pretenders to sorcery. It was believed, too, that the gathering it was not a little hazardous; since sometimes the collector had a battle with the enemy of mankind, or rather he got a severe drubbing from hands which he could very sensibly feel, but could not see. This is alluded to by Leyden in the following lines, which, however, are not written in his happiest manner: —

> But on St. John's mysterious night,
>   Sacred to many a wizard spell,
> The time when first to human right
>   Confest the mystic fern-seed fell;
> Beside the sloe's black knotted thorn,
> That hour the Baptist stern was born —
> That hour when heaven's breath is still, —
> I'll seek the shaggy fern-clad hill,
> Where time has delved a dreary dell,
> Befitting best a hermit's cell;
> And watch 'mid murmurs muttering stern,
> The seed departing from the fern,
> Ere wakeful demons can convey
> The wonder-working charm away,
> And tempt the blows from arm unseen
> Should thoughts unholy intervene.

The twenty-fourth of June is Midsummer, or St. John's day, and in many parts of Europe is held in a manner analogous to Allhallows eve in Scotland. In Ireland, some innocent freets, as they are called, such as dreaming on the leaves of the mountain ash, or confining a slug or naked snail under a bowl all night, to ascertain what letter its track may form, as the initials of the name of the fated lover,

are still practised on Midsummer eve; but I am
not aware that the superstition of the fern-seed ever
had a place in that country. I believe it is common in some parts of England, where

> The village maids mysterious tales relate
> Of bright midsummer's sleepless nights; the fern
> That time sheds secret seeds; and they prepare
> Untold-of rites, predictive of their fate:
> Virgins in silent expectation watch
> Exact at twelve's propitious hour to view
> The future lover o'er the threshold pass.*

I have already, when mentioning Hypericum,
in the Polyadelphia class, adverted to the supersti-
tions of St. John's day in Saxony. In some parts
of Spain they are not less interesting. In the
seventh volume of Blackwood's Magazine is a ver-
sion of the ballad, " which has been for many centuries sung by the maidens on the banks of the
Guadalquiver when they go forth to gather flowers
on the morning" of that day. A wether is enclosed
in a hut of heath, and if it remain quiet while the
girl sings, all is right; but should it grow restless
and break through the door or wall of that frail
habitation, she will then be forsaken by her lover.
This beautiful song is as follows : —

> Come forth, come forth, my maidens, 'tis the day of good St.
>   John,
> It is the Baptist's morning that breaks the hills upon,
> And let us all go forth together, while the blessed day is new,
> To dress with flowers the snow-white wether, ere the sun has
>   dried the dew.

---

* Bidlake.

Come forth, come forth, my maidens, the hedgerows all are
    green,
And the little birds are singing the opening leaves between,
And let us all go forth together, to gather trefoil by the
    stream,
Ere the face of Guadalquiver glows beneath the strengthening
    beam.

Come forth, come forth, my maidens, and slumber not away
The blessed, blessed morning of John the Baptist's day;
There's trefoil on the meadow, and lilies on the lea,
And hawthorn blossoms on the bush, which you must pluck
    with me.

Come forth, come forth, my maidens, the air is calm and cool,
And the violet blue, far down you'll view, reflected in the
    pool;
The violets and the roses, and the jasmines all together,
We'll bind in garlands on the brow of the strong and lovely
    wether.

Come forth, come forth, my maidens, we'll gather myrtle
    boughs,
And we all shall learn from the dews of the fern, if our lads
    will keep their vows.
If the weather be still, as we dance on the hill, and the dew
    hangs sweet on the flowers,
Then we'll kiss off the dew, for our lovers are true, and the
    Baptist's blessing is ours.

Come forth, come forth, my maidens, 'tis the day of good
    St. John,
It is the Baptist's morning that breaks the hills upon,
And let us all go forth together, while the blessed day is new,
To dress with flowers the snow-white wether, ere the sun has
    dried the dew.

We often find, that parts attached to seeds, or
their capsules, have a hygrometrical property, which
is of service in their dissemination. Hence the animated oat is so named, because when its arista, or
awn, is slightly moistened, it makes, by its contor-
tions, the whole seed move about like an animal.

A more remarkable example occurs in the Equisetum, or horse-tail fern, each seed of which has four
(sometimes three or five) pellucid threads, clavate
or club-shaped at their extremities, proceeding
from it. These curl and twist about in a very curious manner, and move the seed along with them
in various directions. If a spike of the Equisetum,
when ripe in spring, be shaken over a piece of white
paper, the seeds will fall out in form of a fine brown
powder; and if they be damped a little by gently
breathing on them, and be then examined with a
magnifier, they will be seen crawling about on the
paper, like so many little spiders.

The economical uses of the ferns are neither extensive nor important. The root of the common
brake (Pteris *aquilina*) is, indeed, when ground to
powder, and mixed with a little barley-meal, used
as food by the people of Palma and Gomera; but
this, as Humboldt justly observes, is only a proof
of the extreme penury of the lower classes in the
Canary islands. The brake, or bracken, and some
other species, afford a considerable quantity of alkali by burning, and in some places their ashes are
made into balls, and used as a substitute for soap.
They are sold by the name of *ash-balls*. The common brake is used also for heating ovens and lime-
kilns, and the heat it produces is said to be intense.
It is also employed as horse-litter, and for thatching; which purposes it fulfils extremely well. The
rough horse-tail fern (Equisetum *hyemale*) has, for a

long period, been imported from Holland under the name of Dutch rushes. It is used by cabinet-makers and other artists for polishing wood, &c.; its surface being hard and rough, from an impregnation of silicious earth.

Fig. 82. exhibits the beautiful Tunbridge fern, or goldilocks (Trichomanes *Tunbridgense*), of its natural size.

Fig. 82.

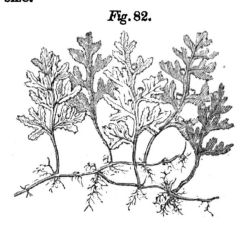

2. Musci. *Mosses.*

When you examine a moss in fructification, you may remark a number of urn or vase shaped bodies standing on peduncles which arise from among the green foliage. These vase-like bodies are the fruit, and all mosses produce their seeds in capsules of this description. In many species you will also observe that the peduncle supporting the capsule is surrounded at its base by a sheath of scaly leaves. This, before the peduncle grew up, served as a kind of calyx to protect the embryo fruit, and is named the *perichætium* or *sheath.*

Fig. 83.

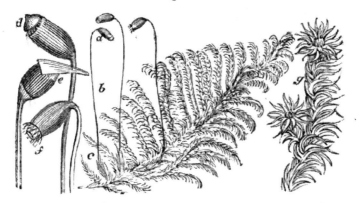

Fig. 83. (*a*) capsule; (*b*) pedicle; (*c*) sheath. But, before the capsule is ripe and has burst, there are two other parts connected with it, the *Operculum* or lid which closes its mouth, and the *Calyptra* or veil, which covers both lid and capsule over like a conical roof: (*d*) operculum; (*e*) calyptra. When the capsule is so ripe that these latter parts have been cast off, its mouth will, with a few exceptions, be seen surrounded by a row of teeth, and often, in addition to this, an internal jagged or lacerated membrane. This ring or edge of the mouth of the capsule is named the Fringe or Peristome, Peristomium. (*f*)

The mosses are almost all diœcious, and the staminiferous stems have a rosaceous or star-like appearance at the top (*g*). Their foliage is extremely beautiful, and forms a lovely object in the microscope. The leaves are never petiolated, often they are serrated, and often ribbed, but never divided nor branched. They are always very thin, pellucid, and reticulated. The root is always fibrous, and very often the stems and branches protrude fine radicles whenever they lie in contact with the ground, or body which supports them. Some species are so minute that a glass is necessary to recognise them; yet even in these there may be a stem; for very few mosses are destitute of that part, though in some it is extremely short. Some species have an arborescent habitude, and present the appearance of a beautiful tree in miniature. In general they are from one to three inches in height, though the great hair-moss (Polytrichum *commune*) which flourishes in marshy grounds, and some species of bog-moss (Sphagnum) which grow demersed, acquire a stature of above two feet.

The calyptra is generally, I believe, thought to be a corolla. Perhaps an attentive investigation of the office which nature intends the conical covering or calyptra of the young flowers in Eucalyptus to perform, might throw some light on the subject, which, whatever may be individual opinion, is certainly very obscure. It sometimes falls off very soon, but no moss wants it altogether. In the Polytrichum genus it is hairy. The Operculum seems not to be just so essential a part; since in one genus, Phascum (earth-moss), it is wanting.

In the investigation of cryptogamic plants the student will require a microscope, at least if he intend to study them very attentively: and he should use one with simple lenses; since these magnify enough for every botanical purpose, and show objects much clearer than the compound microscope. Ellis's Aquatic Microscope is in every respect the best. It is only occasionally however that this is required, and therefore a common magnifying-glass (such as may be bought for a few shillings) will be more frequently necessary. The student will, by a little practice, learn to use the latter; and simple as the means may appear, he will find it to open up to him a new world of wonder, entertainment, and instruction. Insects, flowers, leaves, mosses, lichens, the time-stained bricks and stones of old walls, the bark of aged trees, and indeed almost every natural object which comes in his way, he may examine with pleasure and advantage.

Ireland has been emphatically called a paradise of mosses, and there can be no doubt that the humidity of that country is very favourable to their growth. Most of these vegetables, indeed, prefer moist and shady situations: and some of them not only grow entirely immersed in water; but the Fontinalis *antipyretica* delights in the neighbourhood of cataracts, and flourishes most where the stream is most turbulent. In tropical countries, mosses prefer the shade of rocks and woods, but, still more, mountainous and alpine situations, where the heat and dryness of the climate are moderated by the elevation.

The mosses, however, like many other cryptogamics, are extremely tenacious of life; and, though rendered as dry as chaff, will, when again moistened, resume their functions and freshness of appearance as before. Hence there is scarcely any situation where air and light have a free access, in which some species may not be found, and we may observe on old walls, &c. exposed to the hot summer's sun, the tufts of moss and patches of lichen which cover them, burnt up, and, as it were, parched to dust, resume, after a heavy or continued shower of rain, their pristine vivacity and picturesque beauty. I have remarked, however, that when some mosses are attacked by drought at the time their capsules are ripening, but not yet come to maturity, the latter are instructed with the property of succulent plants, and absorb, but do not exhale moisture; so that the ripening of the seeds goes on unchecked, though the heaven denies it rain, and the earth is as iron. Still, however, mosses in general affect temperate and cold climates, and with the lichens they form the last trace of vegetation towards the limits of perpetual snow, whether on the tops of mountains or at the regions of the poles.

In the economy of nature, mosses are, perhaps, of more consequence than is yet ascertained. Still, we know that they protect innumerable young plants and seeds from the summer's heat, and the winter's cold. They form a retreat for insects and other animals, and serve as a soft bed for the young of birds. In cold countries they may protect trees from the cutting north-wind; for it is observed that they and other cryptogamics grow chiefly on the northern side of the trunk and branches, and this forms one of the marks by which the Canadian savage traces his way through the pathless forests.

The economical uses of the mosses are not numerous. The bog-moss (Sphagnum), from its property of retaining moisture, and at the same time being little liable to decay, is of considerable use in packing up young trees for sending to a distance. In Lapland this moss is employed as a soft bed for infants, and the Polytrichum *commune* serves a similar purpose for the adult.

3. HEPATICÆ. *Liverworts.*

Herb a frond, capsules not opening with a lid.

If the mosses be beautiful objects in the microscope, yet we must admit that in this respect they are surpassed by some plants of the present Order; in proof of which let me refer you to Dr. Hooker's splendid work on the British Jungermanniæ, the exquisite figures of which will, I hope, strike you with astonishment at the workmanship which nature exhibits in the formation of most of these humble vegetables. Until after some experience you will probably confound several of the Jungermanniæ with the real mosses: but should the specimens you collect be in fruit, you will observe that, as in Jungermannia *complanata* (flat jungermannia), *Fig.* 84, the capsule, instead of being covered by an operculum, and opening by a peristome, splits into four parts or valves. This species is common on trees in moist situations, and may be found in fruit from January to April.

Fig. 84.

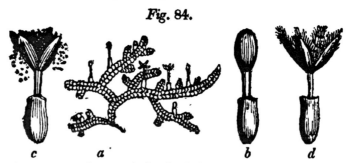

c　　　a　　　　　　　b　　d

(*a*) A plant of natural size in fruit.
(*b*) The fruit magnified, showing the perichætium or sheath, the peduncle rising from it, and the capsule at top not yet burst.
(*c*) The capsule splitting and discharging the seeds.
(*d*) The capsule empty showing its four valves.

There are several other genera in this Order which we cannot attend to.

4. ALGÆ. *Flags.*

Herb, a frond, having the seeds either imbedded in its substance or in that of some kind of receptacle attached to it.

You have observed the picturesque stains, and variety of colours assumed by rocks, old trees, and walls. These in general are produced by plants called Lichens, which belong to the present Order.

The fruit of the genus Lichen consists of tubercles, or of saucer-like bodies, in which the seeds are imbedded. The first time you take a walk, examine some of the bright yellow patches which you can scarcely fail to observe on old branches of trees, old tiles, wooden pales, &c. They will most probably be occasioned by the Lichen *parietinus*, and towards the centre of each specimen the saucer-like bodies to which I allude will be seen, as at (*a*) *Fig.* 85.

Fig. 85.

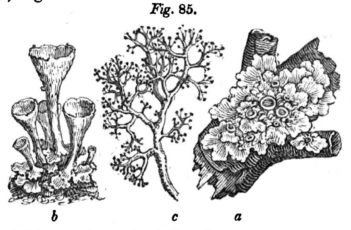

b   c   a

This species is leaf-like, but many are mere crusts resembling stains of colour. Some species, again, are of considerable size and branched, some resemble coral, some are like stags' horns, others filamentous like hair, and the fructifications of some, as the Lichen *pyxidatus* (*b*), resemble drinking glasses; but by examining the fourth volume of Withering, you may learn a great deal on this subject, and if you are lucky enough to have access to the " English Botany" of Sir J. E. Smith, you will find coloured figures of, I believe, about three hundred and fifty British species.

In an economical point of view, the Lichens are of more general importance than any other family in the Cryptogamic class. The very existence, indeed, of the Laplanders depends on the Lichen *rangiferinus*, or rein-deer moss, *Fig.* 83. (*c*), which forms almost the sole provender of that useful animal. This Lichen is very common on elevated or mountain heaths; but with us it seldom exceeds two or three inches in height, whereas in Lapland its length is above a foot. The rein-deer shows great sagacity in digging it up when covered over with several feet of snow. As this species is very abundant in many parts of Great Britain and Ireland, it might perhaps be found useful in times of scarcity, since a decoction of it in water is said to be very nutritive. Kalm was informed from several sources, that the French who pursue the fur trade in North America, drink its decoction when their provisions run short, during long journeys through the woods. The Iceland moss (Lichen *icelandicus*) also possesses nutritive properties, as do many others, perhaps, which have not yet been submitted to the test of experiment.

The Lichens, however, are chiefly useful as dye-stuffs. Litmus is prepared from the Lichen *Perellus;* and the celebrated Orchal, or Dyer's Lichen (Lichen *Roccella*), which is used for giving a crimson colour to wool, or silk, is of so much consequence, that it is said to have been sold when little of it was in the market, for one thousand pounds per ton. The Lichen *tartareus* forms the purple dying-powder, called Cudbear, corrupted from Cuthbert, the name of its inventor. The

Lichen *Omphalodes* (named *Corcar* in Ireland) is used by the country people there, and in Scotland, for dying wool of a dull crimson or purple colour. In the Archipelago a lake is prepared from Lichen *hispidus;* and many other species are used, especially by the inhabitants of mountainous and rocky districts, for colouring various kinds of wearing apparel.

We shall now attend a little to the sea-weeds, especially the Fuci. Let me suppose that you are rambling on the sea-shore, the tide is at ebb; the waves are murmuring around the rocky points and breakers which stretch from the land, but all is quiet in the little pools, among the rugged ledges, and loose stones at your feet. You observe various sea-weeds left dry by the recess of the mighty waters, and others waving their tufts of green and crimson in the translucent brine, whose light swell alternately sweeps them to and from the beach. The perriwinkle and dog-whelk are gliding with an almost imperceptible motion over the wave-worn stones; the limpet has formed her vacuum, and adheres strongly to her rocky couch; and the strand-nerite and the top-shell variegate the sands with studs of grey and saffron. You observe several rocks in the sea at some distance beyond the verge of low water, rising above the surface, and clothed with dark, coarse-looking sea-weeds, as are also many of the stones upon the shore, which have been left dry by the ebbing tide.

To these common and unattractive species we shall now in the first place attend.

I have before mentioned the Sargasso, or gulf-weed, and the circumstance of its being found floating in immense fields on the surface of the ocean. It is rendered thus buoyant by air vesicles of the size of small pease, which grow in great numbers on its stem, and which were described as berries by the earlier voyagers. Many other Fuci are furnished with air-bladders, though not intended by nature to float entirely detached, like the Sargasso, and you will find that some of the common species which grow along our shores are of this description. An apparatus of air-bladders is not, however, entirely confined to sea-plants, since some which grow in fresh water have a similar provision. Of this, the Jussiæa *tenella*, found in the rivers of Amboyna, is a remarkable example. Along its stalk are many large oval tubercles, full of air, and each of these is compounded of many others, so that the injury which the plant might sustain from foreign bodies striking against it, and breaking the bladders, is obviated.* In the frog-bit (Hydrocharis *Morsus-ranæ*), and a few other British aquatics, something similar may be observed, though, in general, floating leaves preserve their situation by the breadth of their under surface, and the antipathy which their upper has to water, by which the moisture is repelled and thrown off,

* Vide Labillardière's Voyages, vol. i. p. 334.

just as you have seen the drops of rain running like quicksilver over a cabbage-leaf.

The first sea-weed to which we shall attend, is the Fucus *nodosus* (knobbed fucus), which may be recognised by its compressed forked fronds, and its solitary turgid air-bladders, not supported on pedicles, but in its very substance. See *Fig.* 86. (*a*). For a minute description, you must consult Turner's Synopsis of the British Fuci, or the fourth volume of Withering's Arrangement.

The air-bladders in this species are very large, being sometimes, in old plants, even four inches long. They are thick, very tough, and, when dried, . become as black as ebony; and are sometimes polished and strung into necklaces. The boys, in Scotland, select the largest of these air-bladders, and, cutting them transversely at the end, transform them into whistles; on which account the plant is there named " Sea-whistles." The Fucus *nodosus* is often six or more feet long, and as its air-bladders are not only large, but very numerous, it will be obvious, that, at high water, the strain upon the plant, produced by its buoyancy, and the action of the waves, must be very great. It appears that this, and some other fuci, have no dependence on their root for nourishment; and therefore, instead of being ramified, it is merely a disc or button, by the adhesion of which, assisted perhaps by atmospheric pressure, the weed keeps an uncommonly firm hold of the rock to which it is attached. Mr.

Turner, in his description of this species, observes, that in some fresh specimens lying before him, the diameter of the base "is hardly more than the eighth part of an inch, so that the power they possess of sustaining, by the mere adhesion of so small a surface, a plant so large against the fury of the waves, is almost beyond the power of human imagination to conceive." It often happens too, that this species has more than its own burthen to support, being frequently covered over with deep brown or black tufts of the beautiful Conferva *polymorpha*. The latter species I have never seen in any other situation. It is described as growing on other fuci; but though I have been pretty conversant with the sea-shore, I have never seen it do so.

Another, even more common, sea-weed is the Fucus *vesiculosus*, bladder-fucus, or sea-ware, formerly named *Quercus marina*, or sea-oak. In this the bladders are axillary, and at the sides of the midrib. The plant is generally about one or two feet long, sometimes four, but scarcely any species assumes so many varieties in size and figure. Its root, like that of the Fucus *nodosus*, is a small expanded disc.

This species, like many other fuci, forms an excellent manure, and affords a considerable quantity of mucilage, on which account it is used in Gothland, when boiled with meal, for feeding hogs. In some of the Scottish isles the cattle go regularly down to the shore at ebb tide, and feed on various sea-weeds; and it is observed that they know their time exactly, even when far from the sea, and not within view of it. The Fucus *vesiculosus* affords, by burning, a large quantity of mineral alkali or soda. Great quantities of this useful article are now produced on all the rocky shores of Ireland and Scotland, from the larger sea-weeds indiscriminately, though the present species, the Fucus *nodosus*, and the Fucus *serratus* are, I believe, the most productive. The plants are cut from the rocks, or collected from the rejectamenta of the sea, and dried in the open air. An excavation, like a grave, is made in the ground, and lined with large stones, and in this, which is named a kelp kiln, the dried weeds are burned; the fire being kept up by constantly throwing them on the flames. The melted alkali, mixed with many impurities, accumulates in the bottom of the kiln, and when cold, forms a hard bluish mass which is named *kelp*, and is a substance of great importance in bleaching, and in the manufacture of soap and glass. Almost the entire rent of the island of Rathlin, on the northern coast of Ireland, is thus paid from the produce of its sea-weeds; and from this source alone, the rents of one highland chief have of late years, it is said, increased two thousand pounds per annum.

The smoke rising from the kelp-kilns on a fine calm day, has a very picturesque effect, and during the night they suggest the idea of so many altars employed in nocturnal sacrifice.

What clouds of smoke in azure curls aspire,
From many an altar's dark and smouldering fire?
What shadowy forms dim gleam upon the sight,
Now hid in fume — now clear with sudden light?
Do Greece's priests revive in Erin's sky,
Or dread weird sisters rites unholy try?
Ah no! a race inured to toil severe,
Of manners simple, and of heart sincere,
Sons of the rock and nurslings of the surge,
Around the kiln their daily labours urge,
O'er the dried weed the smoky volume coils,
And deep beneath the precious kali boils.*

Fucus *serratus* is another common species having the same habitats, and resembling in general appearance the two mentioned, though it is destitute of air-bladders. Its frond is beautifully serrated, and its fructifications occupy the ends of the branches in form of tubercles, each opening at the top and discharging oblong bodies, supposed to be the seeds. And here I may observe that the Fuci, with a few exceptions, do not inhabit very deep water; since, like other vegetables, they require light, and many of them, also, the occasional contact of air. A great part, therefore, of the seeds they produce, being conveyed by currents, tides, and the reflux of the waves into the bosom of the deep, cannot germinate, and being never again brought to shore, perish. We should here expect that nature would compensate for such destruction by ordering the formation of seeds in these plants to be very copious, and that such is the case, one

* From the Giant's Causeway; a Poem, by Wm. H. Drummond, D.D. &c.

observation will prove. Mr. Turner was led from curiosity to make a rough estimate of the number of seeds produced by a specimen of Fucus *nodosus*. The specimen was small, being little more than a foot long, and its fructifications were by no means numerous, yet on the most moderate computation the number of its seeds amounted to one hundred and ninety-two thousand.

The three fuci I have now spoken of are little attractive in their appearance; and have, with some other species, been stigmatised as the most vile and worthless productions of nature; but at the present day we judge more wisely and justly than to estimate the value of objects solely by their outward appearance.

The smaller fuci are in general extremely beautiful, and some of the most attractive in this respect are common on most of our rocky shores; as instances of which I may mention the pectinated crimson fucus (Fucus *coccineus*), the feathery fucus (Fucus *plumosus*), the winged fucus (Fucus *alatus*), and some of the species whose fronds are broad, as the jagged fucus (Fucus *laciniatus*), the dotted (Fucus *punctatus*), which in some places is abundant, and the oak-leaved fucus (Fucus *sinuosus*), one of the most frequent. The dock-leaved fucus (Fucus *sanguineus*), is perhaps the most beautiful of the whole tribe; its midribs have the semitransparency of wax, and the whole frond is of the most brilliant pink colour inclining to crimson.

Some of the fuci are esculent, of which the most

generally known species is the Fucus *palmatus*, named dulse or dillisch. When dried (but not too much so) it has the flavour of violets, and is very pleasant in the mouth, but is seldom swallowed. The Fucus *esculentus* is common on the N. E. coast of Ireland, where the leaflets forming the wings at its base are eaten under the name of *murlins*. These are pleasant, but when chewed in any considerable quantity leave a tenacious crust on the roof of the mouth, which, while it remains, is very disagreeable. The Fucus *pinnatifidus* has a pungent taste, on which account it is in Scotland called pepper dulse. The fucus *edulis* is also reported as being esculent, and without doubt it is very grateful to the taste of some marine animals, since it is almost constantly gnawed into holes; but were I to judge from self-experience, it is very ungrateful to the human palate. We are as yet, however, little acquainted with the culinary uses to which the Fuci may be converted; for it appears that, in China, various species are formed into jellies which are held in estimation; and in Kamtskatcha the natives ferment the Fucus *saccharinus*, which contains a considerable quantity of sugar, into an exhilarating beverage.

Under the general appellation of Sea-weeds, there are included many plants belonging to the genera of Conferva and Ulva; and it is not unusual for the young botanist to confound the beautiful tribe of Corallines, which abound on some sandy shores, with sea-plants, though they are really of animal origin. The confervæ in general are jointed, and many of them to the naked eye, but all in the microscope, are singularly beautiful. The Fuci are all marine; but in every pool, rivulet, lake, and indeed wherever there is water, salt or fresh, confervæ are to be found. The species belonging to the Ulva or *Laver* genus are much less numerous. The umbilicated laver (Ulva *umbilicalis*) is well known under the name of Sloke.

With respect to the Fuci, I may further state that some of them, when wounded, throw out new fronds or leaves from the injured part. Hence, if the Fucus *vesiculosus* be perforated, a new leaf soon protrudes from each side of the puncture; and I have often been pleased in finding specimens of it, in situations where at low water it had been trampled on, sending out many tufts of new leaves from its bruised extremities. Some trees exhibit an analo-

Fig. 86.

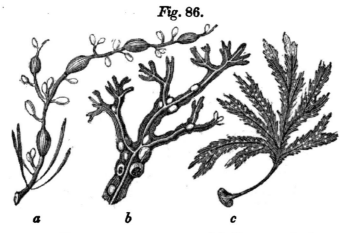

a   b   c

(a) Fucus nodosus.   (b) Fucus vesiculosus.
(c) Fucus serratus.

gous proliferous tendency; and Brown says of the Papaw-tree (Carica *Papaya*), that it " never shoots into branches, unless it be broken while young."[*]

5. FUNGI.

On the under surface of the *cap* or *pileus* of a mushroom (Agaricus *campestris*) are seen a great many perpendicular flesh-coloured laminæ or gills running from the stipe to the circumference, *Fig.* 87. (*a*). This presence of gills forms the essential character of the *agaric* genus (*Agaricus*), which is so numerous that even above three hundred *British* species are at present known. In the young state of the mushroom these gills are hidden from sight; for the pileus is then globular or button-like, and a thin membrane extends from its edge to the stipe, embracing the latter all round. *Fig.* 87. (*b*). The gills are the parts which produce the seeds, and the membrane alluded to protects them, when in the young state, from the contact of earth and other

Fig. 87.

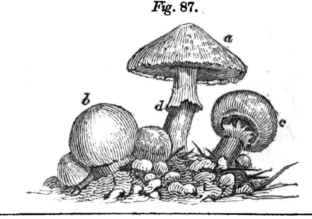

[*] Brown's Jamaica, p. 360.

foreign bodies. Linnæus called it the *Volva* or curtain, and considered it, very properly I presume, as a species of *calyx*. When the mushroom is more advanced, we find that in consequence of the expansion, this volva cracks and gives way all round the circumference of the pileus, so that then the gills become exposed (*c*); and when the plant is full grown the edge of the pileus or hat has a ragged appearance, caused by the remains of the volva, while the portion of the latter originally attached to the stipe continues there in form of a ring, and hence gets the name *Annulus, Fig.* 87. (*d*)

The volva, however, is not in every case attached to the pileus, for sometimes it entirely encloses the latter like a case, and then the plant in growing bursts through, and leaves it at the *bottom* of the stipe, as in Agaricus *volvaceus, Fig.* 88., in which (*a*)

Fig. 88.

shows a young plant bursting through the volva, and (*b*) a mature one with the lacerated remains of the latter placed round its base. This form of.

volva is called the *wrapper*, and in some species of the Lycoperdon genus it assumes a rather puzzling appearance, splitting into a number of acuminate elastic segments, which, as the plant expands, curve back like so many claws, and the volva being thus turned inside out, supports the fungus on its inverted centre, either on a number of pillars, as in Lycoperdon *coliforme*, Fig. 88. (*c*), or sessile, as in Lycoperdon *recolligens*, Fig. 89. (*a*), and Lycoperdon *stellatum*, Fig. 89. (*b*). In the turret puff-ball (Ly-

Fig. 89.

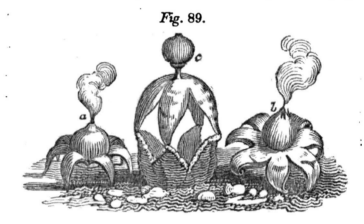

coperdon *fornicatum*) a still more singular appearance is presented. In it there are *two* wrappers, one within the other, and these show very different dispositions, the nature of the outer leading it to split passively like the volva of the Agaricus *volvaceus*, but that of the inner to rebound upwards, as in the Lycoperdon *stellatum*. They each, however, in bursting, split into four corresponding divisions, and the points of these divisions remain in contact, so that this puff-ball, when mature, is " a globe supported upon four arched rays, the four points of the arches resting upon the four points of the outer wrapper which form an inverted arch."* *Fig.* 89. (*c*).

There are many other genera of FUNGI besides those now mentioned, which cannot be attended to here, but the excellent plates and descriptions in Sowerby's BRITISH FUNGI will afford the student a very large fund of information on the subject; and there is every reason to expect that the attention of philosophers' will be much attracted to the study of these interesting vegetables, by the able work now publishing at Edinburgh, by Mr. Greville.

Some of these vegetables are of large size, but, as in the other orders of the twenty-fourth class, a great number are very minute, and only to be examined clearly by the magnifying glass. They chiefly attack decaying animal and vegetable substances, especially the latter, and their seeds being extremely minute, are carried by the air, and hence FUNGI are to be found in almost every situation. An acute botanist might possibly even in a London cellar, or above the dome of St. Paul's, discover some rare or new species of these vegetables.†

Some FUNGI are eatable, but many poisonous,

* Withering.
† Mr. Sowerby, speaking of the Trichia *polymorpha*, says, " I first found this in the outside gallery above the dome of St. Paul's Cathedral, London, April 5th, 1794, on a cindery substance." — *Sowerby's English Fungi*, vol. ii. pl. 180.

and hence their use has often proved fatal. The rapidity of their growth is proverbial, and in many is astonishingly rapid, though some species of the Boletus genus are slow in coming to perfection, and continue for years before they perish; many have an offensive smell, but some are as fragrant as newly-mown hay. Some live at the bottom of mines and other places excluded from the light, and the *truffle* only grows under ground, where it is discovered by the aid of dogs and pigs, which have been taught to trace it by the smell.

When Linnæus published his immortal system, the Palms were little known, and as he could not refer them to their respective classes, he added them as an appendix. Most of them have now taken their regular places in the System, and therefore the necessity for attaching them to it in an appendix is no longer necessary. I shall, notwithstanding, however, attempt to give some idea of the great importance of these noble vegetables, by stating a few particulars respecting the cocoa-nut-tree (Cocos *nucifera*). You know that the kernel or white fleshy lining of the shell of the nut is esculent, and very rich and palatable, but this forms a small part of the uses of the cocoa-palm. The trunk of the tree is used for beams and rafters of houses, and the fronds make an excellent thatch. These are used also as fans, and are woven into beautiful mats. The nut-shell forms bowls and cups, and from the kernel, when dried, a very sweet oil is expressed, while the refuse serves for feeding cattle and poultry. The husk of the shell is fibrous, and is manufactured into cables, twine, and cordage of every description, which is more durable than that made from hemp. " In the Nicobar islands, the natives build their vessels, make the sails and cordage, supply them with provisions and necessaries, and provide a cargo of arrack, vinegar, oil, jagree or coarse sugar, cocoa-nuts, coir, cordage, black paint, and several inferior articles for foreign markets, *entirely from this tree.* Gibbon, the historian, writing of the palm-tree, adds, that the Asiatics celebrated, either in verse or prose, the three hundred and sixty uses to which the trunk, the branches, the leaves, the juice, and the fruit, were skilfully applied." *

* Forbes's Oriental Memoirs, vol. i. p. 23.

CONCLUSION.

I HAVE now, reader, introduced you to a slight acquaintance with the Linnæan System of Botany. My aim has not been to give all the information I could, but, to stimulate to exertions on your own part in acquiring a deeper knowledge of the subject. And having now led you a certain way into the garden of Flora, I leave you to explore her flowery paths and verdant mazes, by your own efforts; recommending such guides as Withering, Willdenow, and Smith; by whose aid you may scrutinize with increasing instruction and delight,

> —— each lane, and every alley green,
> Dingle, or bushy dell ——
> And every bosky bourn from side to side.

Yet, before parting, let me say a few words on two subjects, which are intimately connected with botanical pursuits; I mean the diversity of the seasons and the variety of the earth's surface. The researches of the botanist usually commence in spring, that period of the year which has in all ages

formed a theme of song and gratitude. The harsh-
ness of winter has then fled; the winding-sheet of
snow, which had enshrouded all nature, has dissolved before the breath of the west wind; and
every bud is prepared to burst the cradle in which
it lay safe through the cold and storms of the
preceding months. The snowdrop, that raised
her apparently delicate form in defiance of the
wintry blast, now shrinks, as if afraid of the embraces of a warmer sun. The golden crocus glows
with the lustre of the richest vegetables of the
Tropics, and the modest primrose expands her
pale cheek, gemming the green moss of bank and
brae; the little celandine opens her varnished petals
on the brink of the rivulet; the catkins of the hazel,
and the birch, wave in the passing breeze; the
daffodils,

> That come before the swallow dares, and take
> The winds of March with beauty,

sparkle upon the lawn; the anemone, " child of the
wind," adorns the wood and plantation; and
several other flowers lend their aid to form the
garland of the young spring, and ensure to us a
fulfilment of the important promise, that, *while
the earth remaineth, seed-time and harvest, and cold
and heat, and summer and winter, and day and night,
shall not cease.*

Still, however, the hours vibrate as if doubtful

R 4

whether to submit to the dominion of frost, or yield to the blandishments of spring.

> As yet the trembling year is unconfirm'd,
> And Winter oft at eve resumes the breeze,
> Chills the pale morn, and bids his driving sleets
> Deform the day delightless.

In a few weeks, however, this struggle comes to an end; the sun predominates; the vapours disappear, and the blue concave of heaven shines out refulgent and serene; the groves echo to the warble of birds; the lambkins bound upon the lea; the butterfly bursts the cerements and flutters in the gale; the hum of its bee falls on the traveller's ear, and the bosom of earth is spread with herbs profusely wild,

> —— beyond the power
> Of botanist to number up their tribes :
> Whether he steals along the lonely dale,
> In silent search; or through the forest, rank
> With what the dull incurious weeds account,
> Bursts his blind way, or climbs the mountain rock,
> Fired by the nodding verdure of its brow.

Still, as the year revolves, *new* buds and blooms are produced; for the Great Parent of seasons has ordained, that as one race dies, another shall succeed smiling in youth and beauty. The violet, therefore, and other spring flowers, having bloomed their allotted period, and withered away, are followed by others born of the voluptuous winds of

June and July—the rose and carnation blush in the sunbeam; the mignonette perfumes the garden, and the meadow-sweet the field. Then comes August spreading her golden light upon the grain, and dyeing the fruit of shrub and tree in the brightest hues.

> ———— The mealy *plum*
> Hangs purpling, or displays an amber hue;
> The luscious *fig*, the tempting *pear*, the *vine*
> Perchance, that in the noontide eye of light
> Basks glad in rich festoons. The downy *peach*
> Blushing like youthful cheeks; the *nectarine* full
> Of lavish juice.

The year declines still farther, and Autumn,

> " Crown'd with the sickle and the wheaten sheaf,"

declares the reign of Summer at an end; the herbage becomes embrowned over the landscape, and the leaf withers on the tree. The season still advances, forming at length a narrow boundary between the charms of Summer which are just departed, and the glooms of Winter that are on the eve of approach. This is generally considered as a period of melancholy, but it is a melancholy which is pensive and pleasing; and we should never forget, that one great blessing possessed by these happy islands consists in the constant changes which the face of nature assumes; and that if the Spring delight by its opening buds, and all the promise of the coming year; if Summer unfold, in their full extent, the glories of the vegetable world, yet, that

even the Winter wants not *its* charms, while the
russet Autumn is perhaps the most delightful of
the revolving seasons.

When Autumn and her fruits have passed away,
and Winter has succeeded

> —————— to rule the varied year,
> Sullen and sad, with all his rising train ;
> Vapours, and clouds, and storms,

the vegetable creation seems abandoned to desola-
tion and death. Yet the pursuits of the botanist
are not even then necessarily suspended, since many
cryptogamic plants, especially the mosses, put on
their best attire, and to the inquiring eye exhibit a
structure more beautiful than is to be perceived in
the noblest trees of the forest. At this season, too,
the fuci and other sea-weeds furnish an abundant
harvest : and Nature, ever benignant, retains some
of the natives of the bright Summer, and furnishes
her admirers with a few sweet specimens to compensate in some degree the loss of the more numerous, and gaudy progeny of the sunny days that
are gone by. As one example, let me mention the
daisy, that " crimson-tipped flower," so sweetly
sung by the lamented Burns. It is one of the most
beautiful with which we are acquainted, though its
familiarity may render us little sensible to its humble charms. It blooms almost throughout the year,
glowing in profusion on the lap of Summer, and
bestowing also its gems on the scanty chaplet that

enwreathes the brow of Winter. Its "silver crest and golden eye" expand on moor and mountain, on height and hollow, by rock and stream, braving the storm on the precipice, and playing with the sunbeam in the valley.

> There is a flower, a little flower,
> With silver crest and golden eye,
> That welcomes every changing hour,
> And weathers every sky.
>
> The prouder beauties of the field
> In gay but quick succession shine,
> Race after race their honours yield,
> They flourish and decline.
>
> But this small flower, to Nature dear,
> While moons and stars their courses run,
> Wreathes the whole circle of the year,
> Companion of the sun.
>
> It smiles upon the lap of May,
> To sultry August spreads its charms,
> Lights pale October on his way,
> And twines December's arms.
>
> The purple heath and golden broom,
> On moory mountains catch the gale,
> O'er lawns the lily sheds perfume,
> The violet in the vale.
>
> But this bold floweret climbs the hill,
> Hides in the forest, haunts the glen,
> Plays on the margin of the rill,
> Peeps round the fox's den.
>
> Within the garden's cultured round
> It shares the sweet carnation's bed;
> And blooms on consecrated ground
> In honour of the dead.

R 6

The lambkin crops its crimson gem,
The wild-bee murmurs on its breast,
The blue-fly bends its pensile stem,
Light o'er the sky-lark's nest.

'Tis Flora's page: —— in every place,
In every season fresh and fair,
It opens with perennial grace,
And blossoms every where.

On waste and woodland, rock and plain,
Its humble buds unheeded rise;
The rose has but a summer-reign,
The daisy never dies. *

Thus, at all times there is much for the botanist to investigate and admire, and he in a peculiar degree ought to be grateful for the revolution of the seasons. This indeed is of importance to all, whether naturalists or not, for the human mind cannot be satisfied without change; and hence, a perpetual summer would prove extremely tiresome, and were there no winter we should have little idea of the delights of spring.

If the vicissitudes of the seasons be favourable to the pursuits of the botanist, the variety of the globe's surface is not less so. It is not a continued plain, but is diversified with every imaginable form and combination of hill and dale, mountain and valley, here sinking into abysses, and there towering to the skies. Hence, even under the warmest sun, may be found the various temperatures that characterize the several seasons with us, for, as the

* Montgomery.

heat decreases in proportion to the height from the level of the sea, there may be experienced every variation of climate, from the glow of the hottest summer to the chill of the coldest winter, even in a day's journey up a lofty mountain, such as the majestic Etna,

> Whose head in wintry grandeur towers,
>   And whitens with eternal sleet,
> While summer in a vale of flowers,
>   Is sleeping rosy at his feet. *

Mountains, again, give origin to rivers, and thus the most sultry countries are supplied with unceasing stores of water; and numerous plants are nourished which otherwise could not exist. Rivers in *their* course form lakes and cataracts. Within the spray of the latter are found vegetables not seen in other situations, and in the former are many species that would not grow in the river's current.

In the damp and obscurity of caverns, ravines and quarries, the scientific botanist finds many curious though minute and microscopic plants peculiar to such situations. The various fossils, too, and soils, which compose the crust of the globe, are favourable to the production of a variety of plants, for the number of the latter would be much limited, were the surface of the earth formed every where of the same material, since many

* Lalla Rookh.

vegetables are confined to one kind of soil, or rock, and will grow on no other.

It is owing perhaps to the artificial combination of various materials that many vegetables grow on and around ruined fortifications and castles, among whose relics the botanist finds frequent objects of interest: the campanula nods on the battlement, and the wall-flower gives her odours to the breeze as it sighs round the lonely pile which had once echoed only to the voice of cheerfulness or revelry. The works of man are ever going to decay; those of nature are in perpetual renovation.

> The weed is green when grey the wall;
> And blossoms rise where turrets fall.

But perhaps no scene, nor situation, is so intensely gratifying to the naturalist as the shore of the ocean. The productions of the latter element are innumerable, and the majesty of the mighty waters lends an interest unknown to an inland landscape. The loneliness, too, of the sea-shore is much cheered by the constant changes arising from the ebb and flow of the tide, and the undulations of the water's surface, sometimes rolling like mountains, and again scarcely murmuring on the beach. As you there gather

> Each flower of the rock, and each gem of the billow,

you may feel, with the poet, that there are joys in solitude, and that pleasures are to be found in the investigation of nature, of the most powerful and pleasing influence.

> There is a pleasure in the pathless woods,
> There is a rapture on the lonely shore,
> There is society where none intrudes,
> By the deep sea, and music in its roar. *

But nothing can be more beautiful than a view of the bottom of the ocean, during a calm, even around our own shores, but particularly in tropical climates, especially when it consists alternately of beds of sand and masses of rock. The water is frequently so clear and undisturbed, that at great depths the minutest objects are visible; groves of coral are seen expanding their variously-coloured clumps; some rigid and immovable, and others waving gracefully their flexile branches. Shells of every form and hue glide slowly along the stones, or cling to the coral boughs like fruit; crabs and other marine animals pursue their prey in the crannies of the rocks, and sea-plants spread their limber fronds in gay and gaudy irregularity, while the most beautiful fishes are on every side sporting around.

> The floor is of sand, like the mountain-drift,
>   And the pearl-shells spangle the flinty-snow;
> From coral rocks the sea-plants lift
>   Their boughs where the tides and billows flow:
> The water is calm and still below,
>   For the winds and waves are absent there,

---

* Byron.

And the sands are bright as the stars, that glow
  In the motionless fields of upper air;
There with its waving blade of green,
  The sea-flag streams through the silent water,
And the crimson leaf of the dulse is seen
  To blush like a banner bathed in slaughter;
There, with a light and easy motion,
  The fan-coral sweeps through the clear deep sea;
And the yellow and scarlet tufts of ocean
  Are bending like corn on the upland lea;
And life, in rare and beautiful forms,
  Is sporting amid those bowers of stone,
And is safe, when the wrathful spirit of storms
  Has made the top of the wave his own:
And when the ship from his fury flies,
  Where the myriad voices of ocean roar;
When the wind-god frowns in the murky skies,
  And demons are waiting the wreck on shore;
Then far below, in the peaceful sea,
  The purple mullet and gold-fish rove,
Where the waters murmur tranquilly,
  Through the bending twigs in the coral grove.*

It would be easy to advance many more instances, in which the modifications of the masses of matter composing the surface of the earth favour the production of plants, but it is unnecessary, and we may rest satisfied that the present constitution of our globe is better suited to its inhabitants at large, whether animal or vegetable, than it could be by any change which the most ingenious mind could suggest; and we should never lose sight of the gratitude we owe to that Great Being who formed all the tremendous, the awful, and the

---

* These beautiful lines are from an American poet.

beautiful scenes which surround us in the heavens above, and in the earth beneath.

The radiant sun ; the moon's nocturnal lamp,
The mountains and the streams : the ample stores
Of earth, of heaven, of nature. From the first,
On that full scene his love divine he fix'd,
His admiration ; till, in time complete,
What he admired and loved his vital power
Unfolded into being. Hence the breath
Of life informing each organic frame :
Hence the green earth, and wild resounding waves :
Hence light and shade, alternate ; warmth and cold ;
And bright autumnal skies, and vernal showers,
And all the fair variety of things.

INDEX.

S

Under-shrub, 42.
Undulatum, 134.
Unguis, 204.
Unilocular, 222.
Universal involucrum, 194.
.... umbel, 194.
Upright stem, 56.
Urens, 99.

V.

Vaccinium, 277.
Valeriana rubra, 238.
Vallisneria, 229.
Vanilla, 162.
Varnish-tree, 267.
Vegetable-camel, 34.
Veined, 116.
Venosum, 116.
Venus's fly-trap, 91.
Verbascum, 94.
Verbena, 240.
Verticillated, 128.
Verticillus, 128. 197.
Verrucosus, 89.
Vexillum, 205.
Viburnum opulus, 284.
.... tinus, 267.
Violet, 170. 180. 259.
Virginian creeper, 156.
.... dogwood, 247.
Virgin's-bower, 305.
Viscid, 89.
Vitis Labrusca, 138.
Voluble stem, 66.
Volva, 361.

W.

Wabret, 246.
Water-crowfoot, 141.
.... houseleek, 32.
.... lily, 303.
.... melon, 138.
.... star-grass, 30.
.... withe, 138.
Waved, 134.
Wedge-shaped, 125.
White cedar, 37.
.... lily of Jamaica, 270.
.... saxifrage, 283.
Whorl, 128. 197.
Whortle-berry, 278.
Wild-pine, 138.
...... squash, 70.
Winged petiole, 109.
.... seeds, 213.
.... stem, 56.
Wings, 205.
Winter's-bark, 303.
Woodroof, 244.
Wood-sorrel, 285.
Woody stem, 43.
Wrapper, 361.
Wrinkled, 135.

Y.

Yucca gloriosa, 102.

Z.

Zig-zag-stem, 72.

THE END.

s 4

LONDON :
Printed by A. & R. Spottiswoode,
New-Street-Square.

CPSIA information can be obtained at www.ICGtesting.com
Printed in the USA
BVOW082320190412

288141BV00003B/21/P